The Last Resort

Nevada Studies in History and Political Science

Eleanore Bushnell and Don W. Driggs, *The Nevada Constitution: Origin and Growth* (6th ed., 1984)

Ralph J. Roske, *His Own Counsel: The Life and Times of Lyman Trumbull* (1979)

Mary Ellen Glass, *Nevada's Turbulent '50s: Decade of Political and Economic Change* (1981)

Joseph A. Fry, *Henry S. Sanford: Diplomacy and Business in Nineteenth-Century America* (1982)

Jerome E. Edwards, *Pat McCarran: Political Boss of Nevada* (1982)

Russell R. Elliott, *Servant of Power: A Political Biography of Senator William M. Stewart* (1983)

Donald R. Abbe, *Austin and the Reese River Mining District: Nevada's Forgotten Frontier* (1985)

Anne B. Howard, *The Long Campaign: A Biography of Anne Martin* (1985)

Sally Zanjani and Guy Louis Rocha, *The Ignoble Conspiracy: Radicalism on Trial in Nevada* (1986)

James W. Hulse, *Forty Years in the Wilderness: Impressions of Nevada, 1940–1980* (1986)

Jacqueline Baker Barnhart, *The Fair but Frail: Prostitution in San Francisco1849–1900* (1986)

Marion Merriman and Warren Lerude, *American Commander in Spain: Robert Hale Merriman and the Abraham Lincoln Brigade* (1986)

A. Costandina Titus, *Bombs in the Backyard: Atomic Testing and American Politics* (1986)

Wilbur S. Shepperson, ed., *East of Eden, West of Zion: Essays on Nevada* (1989)

John Dombrink and William N. Thompson, *The Last Resort: Success and Failure in Campaigns for Casinos* (1990)

Kevin J. Mullen, *Let Justice Be Done: Crime and Politics in Early San Francisco* (1989)

Eugene P. Moehring, *Resort City in the Sunbelt: Las Vegas, 1930–1970* (1989)

Nevada Studies in History and Political Science

The Last Resort

Success and Failure in Campaigns for Casinos

John Dombrink *and*
William N. Thompson

University of Nevada Press
Reno and Las Vegas

Nevada Studies in History and Political Science No. 27

Studies Editor Wilbur S. Shepperson

Library of Congress Cataloging-in-Publication Data
Dombrink, John.
 The last resort: success and failure in campaigns for casinos/
John Dombrink and William N. Thompson.
   p. cm.—(Nevada studies in history and political science:
 no. 27)
  Bibliography: p.
  Includes index.
  ISBN 0–87417–140–7 (Alk. paper)
 1/ Casinos—Government policy—United States. 2. Casinos—
Political aspects—United States. I. Thompson, William Norman.
II. Title. III. Series.
HV6711.D66 1990
  363,4'2'0973—dc20   89–14821
                      CIP

The paper used in this book meets the minimum requirements of American
National Standard for Information Sciences—Permanence of Paper for Printed
Library Materials, ANSI Z39.48–1984. Binding materials were chosen for
strength and durability.

University of Nevada Press, Reno, Nevada 89557 USA
Designed by Dave Comstock
Printed in the United States of America

9 8 7 6 5 4 3 2 1

In memory of Henry Dombrink, Jr.
and Mary Brosnan Dombrink.

In honor and memory of Hubert Thompson,
Marion Bauschard Thompson, and
Ruth Kempf Thompson.

Contents

Acknowledgments

During the course of researching and writing this book we were very fortunate to have enjoyed the cooperation of many people who provided us with valuable information and insight.

For the past ten years, we have conducted more than a hundred interviews with interested parties in the various efforts to legalize casinos in several states, with representatives of the casino gaming industry, and with stock analysts and other experts in the areas of legal gaming and gaming control. During this period we have benefited from structured informant interviews with these insiders and have supplemented that source of data with the collection of government hearings, analyses by government agencies or other interested organizations, and hundreds of newspaper stories from the states we have focused on. We would like to single out the following people for their assistance. In Nevada, we benefited from the learned observations of B. Mahlon Brown III, former United States attorney for Nevada, and the late Gabriel Vogliotti. Susan Jarvis made available to us the outstanding holdings of the Special Collections Library of the University of Nevada, Las Vegas. Howard Schwartz of the Gamblers Book Club in Las Vegas provided us with access to extensive newspaper clipping files. In New Jersey, Martin Waldron, Trenton bureau chief of the *New York Times*, opened doors and gave direction in the early stages of research there. Dennis Gomes offered perspective on both Nevada and New Jersey events. Later, Professor Alan Arcuri of Stockton State College commented on drafts of some of the chapters. In Florida, Jim Krog, advisor to former governor Reubin Askew, and Rich Morin, a reporter with the *Miami Herald*, were generous with their time and assistance in recounting the story of the 1978 casino referendum. In New York, President Gerald Lynch and John J. Collins, of the John Jay College of Criminal Justice, provided us with a wealth of interview subjects and background materials on the discussion of casino legalization there. Robert Webb of the Legislative Research Bureau of the Commonwealth of

Massachusetts was a valuable resource and guide to consideration of casinos in that state. John Verna, of Pueblo, Colorado, provided information, contacts, and hospitality during our research there, and Tim Atkinson of Governor Richard Lamm's office was very helpful as well. Our research in Michigan was aided by Leo Kennedy of the Legislative Reference Service in Lansing and state representative Mary Brown. Information on Iowa was provided by attorney John Thompson of Tama, Iowa.

Several generous colleagues read drafts of chapters and assisted in formulation of our analysis. Foremost among these was Jerome Skolnick at the Boalt Hall School of Law, University of California, Berkeley. Many of our accomplishments and none of our inaccuracies are due to his supervision and support of Dombrink's graduate work. David Matza and Troy Duster provided valuable critiques of Dombrink's dissertation at Berkeley. Gilbert Geis of the University of California, Irvine, was a demanding editor and an encouraging colleague. Henry Pontell and Mark Baldassare, both at Irvine, offered important advice on publishing matters. David Hansen of the Business Research Center at Duquesne University was helpful with his comments in chapter drafts, as was Professor David Houghton of Western Michigan University. We also thank Professors William Eadington of the University of Nevada, Reno, James Frey of the University of Nevada, Las Vegas, and I. Nelson Rose of the Whittier College School of Law for their collegial advice.

The research for this book was made possible through grants from the Graduate Research Fellowship Program of the National Institute of Justice, United States Department of Justice, the Faculty Research Fund and Barrick Fund of the University of Nevada, Las Vegas, the Faculty Research Fund of the University of California, Irvine, and the generosity of the Center for the Study of Law and Society at the University of California, Berkeley.

Drafts of the manuscript were expertly prepared by Ingrid Barclay and Christina Miller at Berkeley's Center for the Study of Law and Society under Rod Watanabe's direction; by Susan Salter of the Marketing Department at the University of Nevada, Las Vegas; and by Carol Wyatt, Jill Vidas, Fran Renner, and Diane Siu at the Program in Social Ecology, University of California, Irvine.

Nicholas Cady, acting director of the University of Nevada Press, supported this project through its many revisions. The outside reviewers were very helpful in providing contructive suggestions. Kathy Lewis, along with Cindy Wood and Cam Sutherland from the press, comprised the stalwart editorial and production staff.

Finally, Maya Dunne and Kay Thompson were very supportive spouses, and Laura, Steve, and Tim Thompson were understanding children during the creation of this book.

1 ~ Las Vegas in the American Eye

Legal casinos had been operating in Atlantic City for three years when the nation's governors met there for their annual conference in August 1981. The New Jersey coastal town, which had been a prominent resort for over a hundred years before encountering its most recent decline in the 1960s in at least the tourist sector, had been rejuvenated by the opening of several casinos between 1978 and 1981. As the only state except Nevada with legal casino gaming, New Jersey was initiating its experiment with casinos on a large scale. In 1980, gross gaming revenues had reached $642 million for the Atlantic City casinos and would later approach Nevada levels for gaming receipts. The casinos held out promise of economic revitalization for Atlantic City and tax relief for the rest of New Jersey, a welcome prospect for the industrial northeastern state.

Like many of its neighbors, New Jersey had experienced a downturn in the state economy and had raised state income taxes in 1975, a year before casinos were approved. The population of Atlantic City had declined 20% between 1960 and 1970. Available hotel rooms had dropped by 40%. The levels of real estate, local luxury-tax collection, and convention delegates had all receded during this period. Between 1965 and 1975, Atlantic City lost 4,500 jobs, as unemployment and welfare rolls grew (Economics Research Associates 1976). The enabling legislation that established the regulations for controlling an industry with its roots in organized crime had explicitly referred to the economic development potential of casinos. Atlantic City was rising, phoenixlike, out of the ashes, and many associated with its resurgence predicted that all New Jersey residents would benefit greatly from casinos in Atlantic City. Assessed valuation of real property had risen nearly 200% between 1977 and 1980; 30,000 jobs had been created; and tourists were returning to Atlantic City by car, airplane, and bus.

Not everyone who examined Atlantic City's success was sanguine about it. According to some critics, displacement of the elderly and the poor, jobs primarily for suburbanites, and increased public safety costs left most of Atlantic City an economic wasteland, much as it was before the casinos.

Still, the National Governors' Association, a bipartisan group representing the country's fifty state executives, was still learning about the costs and benefits of legal casinos. Many had probably read the *Business Week* cover story on the projected boom in legalized gambling in June 1978. Casinos had been touted as a unique economic revitalization tool for those states with an established tourist industry or located near a significant population base. As a source of tax revenues, casinos were being promoted as a form of "painless prosperity." Many of the governors had no doubt witnessed, as had Wall Street and stock market investors nationally, the wild climb in gambling stock prices between 1978 and 1981. For several months, gambling was the glamour stock on Wall Street.

In 1981, however, several of the governors whose states had introduced legislation to permit a vote on casinos were also concerned about the possible social and economic costs created by casinos. Many of these governors represented states like New York, Massachusetts, and Michigan, with sizable low-income and urban populations. By contrast, Nevada is a sparsely populated desert state, and Atlantic City a fairly remote resort area. Both are removed by a few hours' drive from the large populations of poor people who might be tempted to gamble improvidently in legal casinos.

Governors like Hugh Carey of New York and Edward King of Massachusetts had been publicly neutral toward the idea of legal casinos in their states before the Atlantic City conference. New York legislators had been prompted by Catskills hotel owners and Niagara Falls lobbyists to propose a package of legalization bills for the state. Some of the bills allowed for casino gambling in various boroughs of New York City, a scenario that frightened even neutral observers. However, the votes of New York City legislators would be necessary for the passage of any bill legalizing casinos. Consequently, those legislators who desired a share of the action for New York City kept it alive as a possible location for casinos. In Massachusetts, the competition from Atlantic City for tourist dollars was not as pronounced as in New York. Massachusetts casino proponents were considering two locales for legal casinos. Pennsylvania, Michigan, and Washington policymakers, among others, were contemplating casino legalization. The nation's governors were not in Atlantic City to discuss gambling, but to assess the impact of the Reagan administration's "New Federalism" on their jurisdictions. Nonetheless, legal gambling presented one alternative to raising taxes to cope with any revenue shortfalls and was an implicit agenda item for the 1981 conference.

Aside from King and Carey, the rest of the Northeast was represented by governors William O'Neill of Connecticut, Hugh Gallen of New Hampshire, J. Joseph Garrahy of Rhode Island, and Richard Thornburgh of Pennsylvania. Along with William Milliken of Michigan and James Thompson of Illinois, these governors represented the Frostbelt states considering casinos between 1978 and 1985. From the West and Sunbelt came governors Robert Graham of Florida, Richard Lamm of Colorado, and William Clements of Texas. Arkansas was represented by Frank White, Washington by John Spellman, Louisiana by David Treen, and Arizona by Bruce Babbitt. Some, like Milliken, Babbitt, and Thornburgh, either were adamantly opposed to casinos or were staunch crime fighters. Others were neutral, and none really approached the enthusiasm that Brendan Byrne had shown for casinos while he was New Jersey's chief executive.

In New Jersey, the governors were able to view the success of the Atlantic City casinos, while at the same time they heard from critics of the economic revitalization experience there. One group of demonstrators in August 1981 expressed unhappiness with the results of the rebuilding efforts tied to the casinos. A representative of a civic organization of building trade professionals and service and supply jobholders in Atlantic City spoke to that point, saying: "We supported the referendum, but it has not accomplished what it promised. For example, in the first three years of the industry, minorities got less than 1 percent, or less than $1.5 million" (*New York Times*, August 16, 1981).

Surrounded by signs of success and possible unkept promises, the nation's governors left Atlantic City and returned to states where casinos were being considered. All of them were no doubt aware of the increased interest in all forms of legal gambling as sources of tax revenue, but casinos remained untested beyond the cases of Nevada and Atlantic City. In 1981, the third wave of legalized gambling in America was still cresting, and casino gambling's place in that phenomenon was still unsettled.

The Powerful Imagery of Las Vegas

In many ways, the campaigns to bring casinos to any of almost twenty states in the past decade have been referenda on Las Vegas. Gambling and Nevada have been synonymous for more than a century. The earliest gold and silver miners who were attracted to the Comstock Lode and other nineteenth-century mineral strikes came without the social support of family and formed ephemeral communities that relied upon gambling, drinking, and the company of prostitutes to offset the drudgery, danger, and loneliness of the miner's life (Twain 1962; Goldman 1981). Gambling flourished in the Nevada saloons, as it did in other frontier settlements. When the first modern Las Vegas casinos were constructed soon after World War II, they were built in the context of decades of wide-open gambling, whether legal or illegal (Skolnick 1978).

The history of casino gambling in this country, at least in its legal forms and its recent embodiment, has been so intertwined with the history of Nevada that it remains difficult to assess which attributes were a result of the nature of the games and the institution of the casino itself and which were the result of the unique form of ownership and control of the Las Vegas casinos. Proponents of casino expansion cite the economic generative effect of casinos and point to the growing acceptance of gambling in American society. Las Vegas is used as one example of the powerful development capability of casinos as a form of economic revitalization. Opponents of casino legalization point to the harmful influence of casinos and to revelations of organized crime involvement and political corruption scandals like the ABSCAM affair, which tarred the New Jersey casino situation.

The corporatization of casino gambling in Las Vegas was over a decade old by the time the states discussed here came to consider allowing casinos in their jurisdiction. Respectable leisure corporation entities such as Hilton, Hyatt, and Ramada Inn had brought needed stability to an industry and a state that had reeled from intense pressure brought by federal officials on allegedly mob-controlled hotel-casinos, and later by the sizable ownership presence of Howard Hughes. To those who lived in Las Vegas, many of whom were directly or indirectly connected to the casino economy, the "horrible" industry was in fact a fairly routine business, serving tourists and selling release, excitement, or simply gambling. Las Vegas is in many ways a company town, and the citizens, city officials, and local businesspeople accommodated themselves to the city's prominent industry. Even the Mormon church found ways for members to live alongside the often notorious casino owners and operators (Gottlieb and Wiley 1982).

For twenty-five years, Las Vegas casinos have been a financial marvel. The virtually recession-proof legal casino industry regularly showed 15% annual increases in revenues throughout the 1960s and 1970s. Only when Atlantic City casinos opened in 1978 did the revenue outlook in Las Vegas dim for a few years. The success of the casinos in Las Vegas has been based on their appeal to a wide range of playing customers, even to those who gamble little but enjoy the many shows and forms of recreation available in the desert resort town. For the "high-roller," or high-stakes gambler, the extravagance of several of the Strip hotel-casinos is a key attraction. Luxurious two-story suites with oversize beds, sunken tubs, and spectacular views catered to the fantasies of the highest-paying customers. These players may be wagering thousands of dollars on a blackjack hand or roll of the dice and earn their right to cushion such a financial risk with the best rooms available. For middle-class visitors, whether conventioneers or annual vacationers, many of the upscale hotels offer room rates and travel packages that are well within the budgets of average Americans. This second class of players may gamble at identical casinos at moderate levels of $5 to $25 per blackjack hand or roll of the dice within yards of the high-rollers, but they do so within the confines of a more restrained budget.

Several aspects of the games and the constellation of the gambling opportunities provided in Las Vegas are unique. For example, the nature of the Las Vegas experience is in essence to remove oneself from society, to travel across a stretch of desert that requires a five-hour automobile drive from the nearest large city, or to travel by air in a preplanned manner. This aspect supported those, like the marketing director of the Las Vegas Convention and Visitors Authority, who argued that the money gambled in Las Vegas was the discretionary income of essentially middle-class gamblers who could plan and save for an occasional trip with a predetermined acceptable loss limit (Ralenkotter 1976). Moreover, Las Vegas could offer other activities on a trip otherwise marred by the overly quick loss of gambling funds. For those who really came along on the trip for the nongambling attractions, the spectacular shows and the 24-hour action—including all-night bars and discos—nicely supplemented the daytime pleasures of tennis, golf, swimming, boating, and shopping.

Many have written about the timelessness of the casino environment (Wolfe 1965; Puzo 1977). It is a fact that there are no clocks in the gambling areas, indeed in the hotels themselves. The notion that oxygen is piped in to give an energy boost to those gamblers whose spirits and stamina might be sagging is less certain. But these features are but a part of the central defining feature of the hotel-casino: its self-contained nature. Some who travel to their favorite Las Vegas casino rarely venture outside. Others may keep within the confines of a few places, while many are frequenters of several casinos, perhaps even competing to see how many they can visit during a brief trip. With the total environment geared toward removing a person from normal surroundings—indeed, the trappings and anxieties and inhibitions of everyday life—casinos have a different meaning than the corner convenience store that sells lottery tickets or the off-track betting office. The resort nature of the hotel-casino is paramount. In many ways, even without offering gambling, some of the premier hotel-casinos have many of the features of the more successful and exclusive resort hotels in the country.

While the Boca Raton or Coronado might be a suitable counterpart for the Las Vegas resort hotel, of late there is a decidedly middle-class bent to the Las Vegas resorts. At prices under $100 for a very pleasant room, they can appeal to many who would be closed out of the upper end of the scale at the resort hotels. Indeed, the Las Vegas dream of recent years has been essentially a middle-class phenomenon, combining the vacation spot with the release from everyday routine and worries, including changes in the hour of rising and retiring. By comparison, this type of gambling, if made available to a more heterogeneous population in a large urban center, such as New York City, would certainly generate more inquiries into the amount of compulsive gambling associated with its revenues. This was one of the key issues in the debate over which parts of the varied state of New York would be included in any compromise legislation to offer casinos in both the New York City area and the resort counties upstate.

At the lower end of the hotel-casino scale are the frequenters of the low-stakes casinos, or "grind joints," whose revenues depend upon a high volume of business. The blue-collar gambler may venture occasionally into the upscale world of Caesars Palace or the Desert Inn, but only as a tourist and occasional show attendee, not as a player. The blue-collar gambler tends to spend time at comfortable downtown gambling houses like Binion's Horseshoe—where the chili is authentic and free photographs of customers in front of a well-laminated $1 million in cash are available—or the Union Plaza or the Showboat (which had the best profits-to-revenues ratio in the early 1980s of all publicly traded casino corporations, which cater to the $1 to $10 per wager bettor). Ironically, the same atmosphere that makes cowboys in dusty boots comfortable at the Horseshoe also creates a wide-open attitude toward table limits. The Binions operate a craps game with no financial limit, and on at least two occasions they have allowed a player to wager over $700,000 on one roll of the dice. The first time, the gambler won. The second time, he lost $1 million and soon after killed himself, reportedly as the result of an unsuccessful love affair.

Once the almost exclusive province of males, especially males who had gambling experience, contemporary casinos are now in large part patronized by those who have not participated in illegal gambling and do not gamble much outside their trips to Las Vegas. Unlike European casinos, where roulette prospers, Las Vegas casinos thrive on three games: blackjack, craps, and slot machines. Poker adds some variety, bingo appeals to an older female crowd, baccarat occupies a few well-heeled players, and sports books capitalize on a surge of sports betting in the country—but blackjack, craps, and slots dominate. In 1965, before the corporate entities began to alter the contours of the basic Las Vegas casino, revenues were slanted toward the two table games. Slot machines always ran a distant third and were considered the province of women, who occupied themselves while their husbands or male companions played more "serious" games of blackjack and craps. That has changed. The demographics of slot playing are apparent to anyone who watches the play in a contemporary Las Vegas casino. The relative shares have shifted to a point where slot machines account for 55% of Nevada casinos' annual gambling revenues, as opposed to 34% ten years ago (Curtis 1986). When recessions began to affect the previously recession-proof casino industry in the late 1970s, the blue-collar gambling houses fared better than their more elegant Strip counterparts. One theory held that this was because they depended in large part on the business of resident gamblers, or "locals," who didn't need to advance the often sizable investment in airfare, room, and food to gamble in Las Vegas.

The relative share of revenues between casino and hotel operations had also changed substantially in the twenty years since corporate ownership of casinos was allowed in Las Vegas. In the days before corporate giants like Hilton, Ramada, and Holiday Inn began investing in Nevada casinos, the generosity of casino managers was legendary. The power to issue "comps"—complimentary room, food, beverage, or airfare—had been widespread and often utilized by casino executives. Numerous 49-cent breakfasts and inexpensive steak dinners and lavish buffets were used as "loss leaders" to attract customers into the casinos, where they would eventually support the resort through their gambling losses. The restaurant portion of a casino was not intended to be a revenue-generator—nor were the lounges where comedians like Don Rickles and musicians like B. B. King and Fats Domino performed, often for only a one-drink admission charge.

After the corporations entered Nevada gambling, however, more normal cost accounting methods began to be introduced, as the hotel and leisure industry decision makers sought to regularize the informal world of the casino executives (Schreck 1976; Gomes 1979). While casino operators, possibly as a throwback to the business's illegal roots, had traditionally relied upon unwritten recordkeeping, they were now to be introduced to the rigorous accountability mechanisms of standard corporate life. The state itself encouraged such behavior, passing at about the same time stricter accounting controls to allay the fears of federal authorities that much of the profit of Las Vegas casinos was siphoned off in the form of "skimmed" proceeds from the casino counting rooms. With the advent of corporate gaming, costs accounting eventually led to demands for profit making—or at least breaking even—in all of a casino's cost centers such as food and beverage, rooms, and gambling. No longer would the first two centers be used in support of the third. Longtime Las Vegas observers longed for the "good old days," when the older operators were generous in their handling of valued customers. It was all part of the changing face of Las Vegas, the maturing of the dream born in a small, dusty town, being realized in 1989 in a congested metropolis of more than half a million residents.

Las Vegas was not the only beneficiary of gambling's growing legitimacy. Various games in different forms had become popular in the 1960s and 1970s. As a social reform, gambling legalization was not new to the American landscape.

The Third Wave of Legalized Gambling

America is now in the midst of what has been termed the "third wave" of legalized gambling to sweep the nation (Rose 1980). Between 1964 and 1989, thirty-two states and the District of Columbia joined New Hampshire and initiated public lotteries. Many of these jurisdictions also run legal numbers games as well. Most states now allow legal bingo games. Forty-two states permit either horse race betting or dog race betting. Jai alai betting is legitimate in four states, card betting rooms in nine states, and off-track betting in three states (*Gaming & Wagering Business,* July 5, 1988). The first wave of legal gambling lasted from the colonial era through the Civil War. The second wave ranged from the Civil War through a period of being banned in the early twentieth century and the relatively quiet decades of the mid-twentieth century. The third wave began in 1963, with the passage of the New Hampshire lottery law.

The lottery, private as well as public, punctuated the first wave. As early as 1612, the Virginia Company sponsored a lottery to offset expenses of colonization (Chafetz 1960:20). As America was colonized, the popularity of the lottery grew. The lottery was integral to the development of the colonies as a supplementary finance mechanism for government and as a fund-raising tool for projects too large for local governments to handle or for private concerns to finance alone. Harvard, Princeton, and Columbia, among other institutions of higher learning, were financed in part by lottery proceeds. The Virginia Company of London, in order to further its colonization of North America, benefited from a lottery chartered by the king of England expressly for its purposes (Ezell 1960:41). One report estimates that between 1790 and 1860, twenty-four of thirty-three states financed internal improvements by lotteries, with total revenues of $32 million, benefiting 47 colleges, 300 lower schools, and 200 church groups (Asbury 1938:77–78). McMaster, writing about widespread utilization of the lottery to raise money for public works projects, describes the scope of these lotteries: "Whenever a clumsy bridge was to be thrown across a little stream, a public building enlarged, a school house built, a street paved, a road repaired, a manufacturing company to be aided, a church assisted, or a college treasury replenished, a lottery bill was passed by the legislature" (McMaster 1914:587–588).

The lotteries were respectable operations: small, locally managed, and sponsored by public-minded citizens. The authorized lottery was really not considered a form of gambling and thereby escaped the common objections raised against games of chance. The most common rationalization for lotteries was that they were simply an efficient method of voluntary contribution to worthwhile causes: "Lotteries organized for public projects . . . were not regarded at all as a kind of gambling; the most reputable citizens were engaged in these lotteries, either as selected managers or liberal subscribers. It was looked upon as a kind of voluntary tax for paving the streets, erecting wharves, buildings, etc., with a contingent profitable return for such subscribers as held the lucky numbers" (Cornell Law Project 1977:75).

While some economists such as Adam Smith denounced the lottery as an inherently losing venture for the participants, few raised strenuous objections to the odds as long as the lottery was portrayed as a form of voluntary taxation. This state of encouragement of one form of gambling was an early indication that certain elements of American society were willing to make crucial distinctions among the various forms of gambling and endorse, if only tacitly, the notion of limited gambling as a revenue-raising mechanism (Ezell 1960.)

Another development reinforced this official ambivalence, a pattern that appeared at first in the South but that describes gambling's treatment generally in the country. Those forms of gambling that had the potential to cause a public nuisance were prohibited; otherwise, the state remained neutral, and the legislature gave certain forms—especially horse racing—its blessing, considering them more a sport than a game of chance. Distinctions, in large part class-based, began to be drawn among the various forms of gambling. For instance, "civilized" poker games played by gentlemen planters were to be distinguished from casino games enjoyed by the masses in taverns and other public places. While these noisier forms of gambling were considered harmful, other forms were left untouched as important parts of southern culture. In South Carolina, a blanket ban on casino-type gambling was adopted in 1802, outlawing all gaming in taverns and other public places and criminalizing the use of gaming tables in public and private. At the same time, however, this act did not threaten the pastimes of the gentlemen planters—poker and horse racing. The forms that were prohibited deserved sanction because of the antisocial consequences they tended to produce among the lower classes—drunkenness, idleness, and the inevitable loss of money by those least able to afford such setbacks (Cornell Law Project 1977:236–267).

Taken together, the state sanction of lotteries to raise revenues for public work projects amidst strong religious opposition to other forms of gambling and the differentiation between upper-class "gentlemanly" games and lower-class "tavern" games suggest that official ambivalence toward gambling has existed throughout this country's history. Moreover, it appears that gambling generated condemnation mainly among the middle class—which adhered to the values of ascetic Protestantism and subscribed to a work ethic that frowned upon gains acquired through any other means but honest, hard work—while various forms of gambling drew customers from the lower and upper classes.

By 1831, eight states ran 420 lotteries, selling over $66 million in tickets, which was five times as great as the federal budget that year. Scandals and swindles became prevalent and, coupled with a wave of morality that swept the nation, soon led to abolition of lotteries. In 1833, Pennsylvania, Massachusetts, and New York all abolished their lotteries. By the time of the Civil War, all but three states had declared the drawings to be illegal, and the first wave had receded (Blanche 1950:72; Berger and Bruning 1979:136–137).

Following the Civil War, a second wave of legalized gambling saw the lottery revived and other forms of gambling thrive as well. This comeback was most prevalent in the states of the Reconstructed South as they sought mechanisms to cope with extreme financial difficulties. Gambling also thrived in open areas and frontier cities of the West and gained popularity in major urban areas. The professional gambler developed as a recognizable entrepreneur, and gamblers organized in the face of attacks by moralists and suppression by police.

During this same period, the Gold Rush and silver strikes in California and Nevada caused an influx of miners and speculators to those territories in the 1840s and 1850s. Gambling became an integral part of the boomtown atmosphere of the Mother Lode area and of Nevada mining towns like Virginia City. The combination saloon/bordello/gambling hall became the main center for recreation for the thousands of miners and cowboys, who were mostly on their own, without families or wives. Gambling also thrived in Kansas City, Denver, and San Francisco, which all gained notoriety as gambling capitals during the 1850s. Those antigambling laws that were passed proved to be ineffective and served only to drive the games underground, where they were allowed to exist partly through the actions of law enforcement officials who either disagreed with state prohibition attempts or merely seized the opportunity to extract payoffs from the gambling operators. A licensing-by-fines system existed to regulate illicit gambling.

In the East, an important development took place during the middle decades of the nineteenth century: gambling shifted from a profession populated by talented individuals to an activity run on business principles (Johnson 1977:18). Between 1840 and 1877, Johnson writes, "gamblers created complex and subtle connections among themselves, their customers, politicians and the police which redefined the context in which law enforcement occurred" (1977:18). By creating conditions that severely restricted the ability of the police to suppress them, gamblers not only were able to assure their own profit, but at the same time laid the foundations for modern versions of American organized crime. Haller agrees:

> The years from the 1880s to about 1905 may, indeed, have been the period when activities that are often called "organized crime" had their greatest impact upon American society. During this period, gamblers and vice entrepreneurs generally exercised an influence on local politics and law enforcement that has seldom been equalled since that time. In many neighborhoods, it was not so much that gambling syndicates influenced local political organization; rather, gambling syndicates were local political organizations, and had, in addition, a broad impact upon other aspects of urban life. . . . To some extent, then, politics and gambling were tied together by common ethnic bonds, as well as common organizational structures. . . . Long before national prohibition and the development of bootlegging, then, there had already been close ties among gambling syndicates, vice activities, politics, sports, and entertainment. (1979:88)

The gaming houses that thrived in New York, Chicago, and other urban areas—particularly the houses frequented by members of the upper class—had a subsidiary economic impact on the neighborhoods surrounding them. The gambling houses also received public support because they were major employers.

However, the second wave of legal gambling activity did not persist. Only a Louisiana lottery remained after 1878. This notorious lottery, which was authorized by the state legislature, promoted by bribery, and run by a New York syndicate, became the subject of a federal campaign to abolish all lotteries. With its position as a public monopoly, the lottery enjoyed great success through its sale of tickets throughout the nation. Federal pressures were exerted through the Post Office Department. In 1890, Congress gave the postmaster general authority to refuse delivery of mail to lottery agents; in 1895, a bill was passed prohibiting the use of all forms of interstate commerce by lottery companies. This effectively cut Louisiana off from its market and spelled its doom (Berger and Bruning 1979:136–137). In the same period, other forms of legalized gambling were also abolished. By 1900, only three states—Maryland, Kentucky, and New York—permitted betting on horse races. New York outlawed gambling in 1910. When Nevada banned casinos in the same year, the nation became virtually free of legalized gaming (Curtis 1981:19).

The 1930s saw the return of casinos to Nevada and the return of horse race betting to twenty-one states. A trend of expanding such track wagering continued through the 1940s. Other states permitted charity bingo games in the 1950s, and Florida permitted bets to be placed on jai alai games. Lotteries, however, were not to enjoy a legalized status again until New Hampshire passed a sweepstakes law in 1963. According to Rose (1980), the initiation of the lottery in the Green Mountain State in 1964 ushered in the third wave of legalized gambling in America.

While the social considerations of gambling's value shifted during American history, displaying a deep-seated societal ambivalence toward this popular vice, debates also focused on the intrinsic nature of gambling—was it addictive, merely pleasurable, or possibly functional? In many ways, the societal ambivalence toward the proper use of governmental power in controlling gambling was derived from attitudes toward gambling's intrinsic nature, as well as the question of the advisability of government pursuing unattainable goals in criminalizing an essentially uncontrollable vice.

The Social Value of Gambling

Sociological and psychological explanations of gambling behavior can be categorized according to the emphasis placed on the purpose of gambling activity. Analyses of the act of gambling as action (Goffman 1967), proof of status (Geertz 1973; Udell 1974), compulsion (Freud 1953), anality (Bergler 1957), or work (Zola 1963; Herman 1967; Kaplan 1979) differ primarily on what exactly the gambler derives from gambling. While some sociological analyses emphasize the irrationality of the gambling enterprise—particularly in the reliance upon chance—others consider the central characteristics to be related to skill and deliberation. Encouragement of idleness, reliance upon luck, and exhibition of irrational behavior could all be factors that would contribute to a negative assessment of the social functions of gambling. However, exhibition of character-building skills or establishment of status would be the opposite—acts that would help, rather than harm, the social fabric. These ambivalent interpretations of the nature of the gambling act possibly explain the most striking feature of gambling behavior: its ability to thrive, across cultures and over time, despite its prohibition, and its ability to maintain some sort of protected status as a tolerated vice.

Of all the vices, gambling has encouraged the least vociferous opposition, in part because its harmful effects are not easily specified and are not biological in nature, but also because it serves certain functions for individuals (Geis 1972). For instance, it may provide an arena for the discovery and display of decision-making skills and coolness under pressure. Gambling can also serve social functions—as a social safety valve or a means of diverting the frustration of the working class. The ambivalence of gambling in American society can be stated as follows: while gambling supports some important precepts of the Protestant ethic and capitalist accumulative imperatives—primarily those accentuating risk—it challenges basic values of thrift and industry. This intrinsic ambivalence is central to any consideration of gambling. As mentioned earlier, it is especially important because it led to the development of an illegitimate but tolerated gambling industry. The ambivalence toward gambling was magnified by the lack of consensus supporting attempts at criminalization or at least strict enforcement of existing law.

As Geis (1972) states, gambling in America has been the quintessential organized criminal activity. It is profitable and "victimless." Whatever harm is caused is not physical; addiction apparently afflicts only a small percentage of those who engage in the activity; "victims" enter it willingly; and respectable citizens participate in it. Given the intrinsic ambivalence of gambling behavior, and state sanctioning of some forms of gambling operations, illegal gambling operators had the basis for establishing a situation of nonenforcement by police officials. With that protection, and with the broad organizational forms that could later develop, illegal gambling became a large-scale, politically connected, and essentially respectable enterprise by the late 1800s. The professionalization of organized crime provided for its integration into legitimate circles, which in turn supported further professionalization (Johnson 1977; Haller 1979).

The state's attempts to control gambling activity have proven to be ineffective, with little hope for reversing this situation. Criminologists propose several reasons for this (Rubinstein 1974; Duncan 1976). Police departments give it low priority: it is difficult to close down gambling operations because fines are imposed instead of jail sentences—the cost of fines can easily be absorbed and new operations can be opened elsewhere. In short, the costs of the sanctions are not sufficient to deter participants. In addition, those prosecuted are generally resourceful. This situation generates corruption, since law enforcement agents who are positioned to enforce gambling fines selectively are not necessarily inclined toward strict enforcement anyway and can be made less so through acceptance of a bribe. The inevitability of gambling and the proven ineffectiveness of the state—for a number of structural reasons—give support to those who argue for legalization as a prudent societal response, a pragmatic reassessment of current criminal justice policies, or a last resort in the fight against organized crime.

From an analysis of the casino gambling legalization campaigns, and the results of public opinion poll data, the argument most frequently proposed for the legalization of gambling is to resolve the fiscal crisis. This is in contrast to the most frequent arguments for the relaxation of laws regulating other vices. Consequently, the proposed benefits of gambling legalization are such that they reduce attention that might otherwise be focused on the participant as addict or deviant.

Aside from the regressivity issue, the most important variable in the continued criminalization of gambling has been its status as a major source of revenues for organized crime (Kefauver 1975; Peterson 1951; Reid and Demaris 1964; King 1969; National Advisory Committee, 1976). This is both a concern of law enforcement agencies and policymakers and a generalized concern of the public—based on the historic involvement of organized crime in illegal and legal gambling settings. Public opinion polls taken during the period of this study have shown that, where all other sources of opposition disappear, the threat of organized criminal involvement remains. For those who support decriminalization as a policy prescription, the role of organized crime would clearly diminish when it could not compete with legal forms of gambling. Clearly, however, many citizens—rightly or wrongly— fear organized criminal involvement in legal casino gaming.

Rationality and Social Functions of Gambling Behavior

Why do people gamble? Is it a form of punishment, a celebration of risk, an irrational impulse, a desperate act of the poor, an unproductive indulgence of the rich? Psychological and sociological explanations range from those that consider it a compulsive activity and a form of self-punishment to those that interpret it as an act that reveals crucial skills of decision making and autonomy.

Many of the opponents of legal gambling present their opposition in terms of the harmful effects legal gambling would have on the working class (Commission on the Review 1976:66; Suits 1977; Kaplan 1979:34). These perspectives emphasize that gambling has no social benefits and undermines capitalist ethics of thrift and industry. To theorists holding this position, the fatalistic value system of gambling is in conflict with the underpinnings of capitalism: rationality, disciplined work habits, prudence, thrift, methodical adherence to routine, and the assured correlation of effort, ethical merit, and reward. Gambling blurs the distinction between well-earned and "ill-gotten" gains. It is debased speculation, a lust for sudden wealth that is not connected with the process of making society more productive. Government support of gambling, whether through legalization or direct state operation, gives an imprimatur to the pursuit of wealth without work and breeds a politically irresistible demand for other forms (Starkey 1964; Moody 1965; Coggins 1966; Kristol 1973; Will 1976; McWilliams 1979).

In addition, gambling is portrayed as an addictive activity that preys upon the weakness of the gambler, especially those working-class gamblers who are most anxious to strike it rich and least able to bear the burden of gambling losses (Kusyszyn 1972; Martinez 1972). Gambling is therefore strongly associated with improvidence. Legal gambling, inasmuch as it depends upon working-class wagers, is a regressive tax. Legalization, it follows, might have the detrimental effect of encouraging proliferation of gambling, creating new gamblers, and breeding a politically irresistible demand for other forms (Commission on the Review 1976). Many articulate theorists have examined the various properties of gambling behavior, differentiating between compulsive or pathological gambling and "conventional" or functioning gambling (Kusyszyn 1972; Fuller 1974; Abt et al. 1985). While acknowledging the possibility of the proliferation of problem gambling, this study accepts the contention of those scholars who consider pathological gambling to be a relatively infrequent occurrence compared to professional gambling or leisure activity.

If the propositions regarding the pathological nature of gambling were true, then a society that legalized gambling, for whatever reasons—even those as acceptable as generating revenue without raising taxes, reducing law enforcement costs, and spurring economic development—would do so in the face of possibly serious consequences for those persons who do gamble. While it might be suggested, cynically or in support of libertarian ideas, that society might as well accept individuals' right to choose to participate in such activities, however harmful to themselves, and then tax the sickness so that the state can at least derive some benefit from it, many studies challenge the idea that gambling is actually a harmful activity, for society or for individuals. Those sociological and psychological explanations of gambling behavior that refute the charges of irrationality and unproductivity in turn emphasize the ways in which gambling is either not harmful or actually productive.

Gambling as Play Activity and Entertainment

Caillois (1962) argues that gambling is a subtype of play activity (alea) that consists of games of chance. In the isolation from real life, gambling allows the participant an escape from work and disciplined labor. As an entertainment activity, gambling provides an outlet, an escape from the routine and boredom characteristic of much of modern life. Taking a chance, whether by small or large wager, destroys routine and therefore is pleasurable. Gambling introduces an element of anticipatory hope into what otherwise are often drab existences. This is particularly true of games of chance, where the outcome of the gamble is independent of the player's skills. To Caillois, it is the very capriciousness of chance that constitutes the unique appeal.

Gambling as Substitute Social System

Other explanations of gambling behavior consider gambling an activity found in all individuals and all societies. People need to participate in games of chance as a response to the perceived uncertainty of the social environment. In modern social systems, Caillois (1962) argues, gambling serves the function of providing a substitute world in which natural and individual differences are abolished. Zola (1963) interprets the interaction of lower-class gamblers in the betting shop as the effort to establish a primary group in a self-contained refuge from the often hostile or indifferent outside world.

Gambling as a Display of Character

To understand this element of gambling's appeal, one must appreciate the value of risk taking. To the outside observer, some actions may seem unnecessarily risky, with little or no gain for the participant, and a loss of money, threat of injury, or waste of time. Some students of gambling behavior argue that risk taking is essential to the development of character and is also conducive to material advancement (Ginsburg et al. 1976; Knowles 1976). Gambling is a means of satisfying this drive when more legitimate, professional, or socially sanctioned enterprises are foreclosed. In games of skill, the act of gambling forces the player to rely upon himself or herself. Games of skill demand that contestants utilize their ability to surmount obstacles—to make critical decisions under pressure—and thereby maximize critical or analytical skills. Through decision making under stressful conditions, the gambler exhibits subterranean values—toughness, excitement, and disdain for routine work. In this view, it is not so much the monetary value of the wager that is at stake, but one's character that is being placed on the line. The "action" of the gamble is a celebration of self-determination, through the revelation of character under stress, and the rewards—for the winner *or* the loser—can be many: courage, gameness, integrity, gallantry, composure, and presence of mind. Newman describes the functional social attributes of the gambling situation: "the bettor, in the company of his comrades and peers, is offered the opportunity of displaying characteristics of steadfastness, valour, and coolness; where he is able to exhibit the qualities of modesty in his moments of triumph and imperturbability in times of despair; where norms are evolved and internalized, where roles are rehearsed and refined, and where collective consciousness is constantly refined and redefined" (1972:6). Moreover, as Goffman proposes, the immediacy of the reward for success—which contributes substantially to the sense of "action" in the gamble, the uninterrupted nature of the risk sequence giving the various games their intensity—is in stark contrast with everyday life: "The distinctive property of games and contests is that once the bet has been made, the outcome is determined and payoff awarded all in the same breadth of experience" (1967:156).

Herman (1967), Newman (1972), and Zola (1963) argue that these properties of display of character and exhibition of skill are especially attractive to

lower-class men, for whom gambling contains essential elements of es-
teemed entrepreneurial roles absent in real-life occupational, familial, and
recreational roles. Given the uncertainty of lower-class life, gambling provides the illusion of control over the environment, an attractive feature to
lower-class men, who are often frustrated in their everyday work and family
experience.

While this may explain lower-class gambling behavior, it does not explain
gambling by those whose productive drives are not frustrated by class-based
stratification. Tec (1964), for instance, found the propensity to gamble highest among the upper lower class of Swedish society, among those who most
experience status frustration. Devereux (1949) attributes the apparent propensity to gamble among both the lower class and the upper class to a lack of
internalization of the Protestant ethic and the attendant religious beliefs
concerning the capitalistic means of financial acquisition.

Gambling as Rational Pursuit of Economic Gain

This perspective disputes the irrationality argument: the most obvious
reason to wager is to win. Various forms of gambling—particularly those like
the lottery or the numbers game—allow a person to win phenomenal
amounts of money while wagering little. The gamblers observed by Zola,
Goffman, and Herman in their studies are realistically aware of the prospects of winning: they weigh the odds, conserve their resources, and are
thrilled by the action. Herman (1967) was struck by the evidence of careful
deliberation, sustained concentration, and disciplined composure of race
course attenders, closely resembling the socially most highly valued aspects
of the typical middle-class work situation. Newman (1972) observes a similarity between the cultural objects found in gambling and those in conventional entrepreneurial roles—systematic study, attention to fluctuation of
market conditions, estimation of probabilities, and, finally, the backing of
personal judgment with real cash.

Whether the gambler is receiving the direct and immediate source of
satisfaction from the thrill of gambling or from the reward of winning, the
portrait of the gambler offered by Zola, Newman, Goffman, Herman, and
Devereux is one of a rational, socially adaptive, problem solver. Newman
concludes:

> To scrimp and save to lay by a few pounds to see these eroded by
> inflation, wiped out and exposed in their foolish inadequacy in a sud-
> den family emergency or, worst of all, to leave your few accumulated
> possessions to be fought over when you die—no other single cause, by
> all accounts, exerts comparable power as a detonator of family unity—
> is poor sense. To use this money in the hope of a big strike—who

knows, you might even win enough to put down a deposit on a house—is surely superior rationality. (1972:228)

Gambling as a Realization of Work Values

Contrary to the hypotheses of those who feel that gambling detracts from a worker's attention to his or her task, gambling may satisfy needs that are going unrealized in the workplace. Tec (1964) found that gambling behavior was correlated with the gambler's dissatisfaction with work. This finding concurs with those (Bloch 1962; Downes et al. 1976) who emphasize gambling's role as a response to the routine and boredom of modern industrial life. Interpreting the causality of the correlation as a product of gambling—in other words, implying that the lure of the games softens the worker's ability to produce while at work—would lead one to the conclusion that gambling was dysfunctional for society. The interpretation of Tec (1964), Kaplan (1979), Herman (1967), and Weinstein and Deitch (1974) reads the correlation in the opposite way—gambling is seen as a source of satisfaction of work needs given the degradation of work, rather than as a disruption of work pattern. "Gambling," Kaplan explains, "rather than the cause of dissatisfaction, may be a symptom of and a source of relief from the frustration of work in a highly automated, industrial society. The triumph for the skillful gambler—the thrill of victory, the status awarded by one's colleagues when one has made a correct assessment of a sporting contest—can become a substitute for the achievement, recognition, and self-actualization lacking in the work setting" (1979:30). Therefore, in addition to the monetary inducements to gamble, one can see the tangibles involved. "In a work world which offers little opportunity for creativity and independence," Kaplan argues, "where work pace, routine, and decisions filter down from the wages and salaries eroded by inflation, people turn to gambling in search of the challenge and opportunities absent in their jobs and to divert their thought from the frustration and boredom which daily confront them" (1979:30).

Gambling as Social Safety Valve

A British bus conductor/gambler told one student of gambling behavior:

You must realize that a working-class chap is an under-dog and feels like one. He is not satisfied with present conditions, so he often escapes into a world of dreams. This world he finds in religion, socialism, or gambling. Socialism is a dream for himself personally. He can't hope to save enough to get out of his dreary existence. He can't work himself up, that is open only to a very few of the best men. The only way out of the mines, or cotton mills, or foundry work or navvy work on the road, is to win in a big way. Only in that way can he gain his real freedom. (Fuller 1974:35)

Zola argues that gambling, while it may appear unproductive, is not necessarily dysfunctional: "Gambling may be a way of harnessing or channeling otherwise destructive frustration" (1963:360). "Instead of lashing out at society [working-class] gamblers lash out at 'the system.' In this sense, gambling may be an activity which helps reinforce and preserve some of the major values of the larger social system."

Fuller supports this point, writing that gambling, rather than exhibiting neurotic tendencies, is a wholly rational pursuit that serves a hegemonizing function: "Gambling is a safety valve in the capitalists' system. By offering apparent potential wealth to a tiny minority, it seduces the mass of the people, and deadens inclinations which they might have toward organized, revolutionary activity. As long as a worker believes that he, individually, has a chance of freeing himself from the oppression of capital, however remote that chance, he will be less likely to feel class solidarity, or to engage in political activity" (1974:37).

The studies cited in the previous sections, taken together, offer a theory that challenges the definition of gambling as unproductive and irrational behavior. They suggest that there is a basis for legalization arguments in the nature of the gambling behavior itself.

Organized Crime and Casino Gambling

"Casino gaming expansion to other states was stalled for almost three decades because of the public and political perceptions of the problems associated with controlling it and with the history in Nevada of criminal influences in the industry."
—Public Gaming Research Institute, 1980

More than the nature of gambling sets Las Vegas apart. To a great degree, the distinctiveness of Las Vegas has been in the heritage of the ownership of the legal casinos. While mobsters may be reviled in public, they have also often been considered romantic in some private quarters, part of America's fascination with and ambivalence toward the gangster. Nevada's long history with transplanted illegal gamblers has historically caused the state a number of problems with its image. If casino development on such a scale had happened in Michigan or California or Massachusetts, the unique industry might have had more ability to integrate, or at least to reduce its visibility alongside the more mainstream automobile, electronics, or aerospace industries.

While Nevada officials have taken great care over the past thirty years to remedy this image problem and to create a structure that would ensure careful monitoring of any deleterious behavior or presence in the gambling industry, the image looms large. It matters not that reputable CPAs, attorneys, managers, and fiscal agents have devoted many years, on both the state regulation side and the industry side, to implement successful systems for the more careful management and more regular accountability of the casinos—nor that gambling stocks rose to an all-time high on Wall Street as the glamour stock of the late 1970s and early 1980s, finally achieving a measure of respectability.

To those outside Las Vegas, the new respectability of the gambling industry is as yet unproven. The gaming business magazines that chronicle the regularization of the gambling industries, in many forms, across many regions of the country, have not reached the consciousness of average people in the states where casinos have been voted upon, and voted down, since Atlantic City gambling was authorized by New Jersey voters in 1976. The residual ambiguity of the basis of the Las Vegas success story remains a lively issue, ready to be explored by those opposed to casino gambling in their town.

The ABSCAM scandal in the late 1970s indicated to many that political corruption can thrive in any state that ventures into the casino industry. It was a point made eloquently by Miami attorney William Colson, an advisor to former governor Reubin Askew and a member of one of the key committees devoted to the defeat of the 1978 Miami Beach casino referendum, which had been patterned after the Atlantic City success. It was an issue that led New York attorney general Robert Abrams to come out firmly against casinos, thereby tipping the balance in favor of its rejection.

The previous sections developed the theme that gambling has been treated ambivalently by state authorities throughout American history—prohibited in some forms, condoned in others, and used as a revenue-raising mechanism in still others. This ambivalence gave rise to a powerful underground economy of vice and a gambling industry that, while illegal, was nonetheless politically integrated. It also gave rise to a legal gambling industry that took many forms.

Since Prohibition, illegal gambling has been a major source of revenue for American organized criminal groups. After the repeal of the Volstead Act, and the onset of the Great Depression, cash-rich organized criminal entrepreneurs turned to gambling as one of a number of activities designed to diversify and secure their illegal holdings. Illegal gambling was not a new enterprise for organized criminal syndicates. Since it had begun to proliferate in eastern cities of the United States in the mid-1800s, illegal gambling had flourished, contributed to the growth of the urban political machine, and survived because of the necessary protection arrangements it made with police departments and politicians. As a place of recreation and socialization, the gambling establishment provided a locale for the meeting of wealthy gamblers and powerful politicians (Hammer 1975; D. Johnson 1977).

With the legalization of certain forms of gambling, especially casino gambling, organized criminal capital found its way in the post–World War II years, directly and covertly, through a number of hidden investment and control schemes, into legal gambling operations. Bugsy Siegel, who oversaw the construction of the Flamingo Hotel and Casino in 1947 with organized crime's backing, is often referred to as the "father" of modern Las Vegas. An associate of organized criminal mastermind Meyer Lansky gave this account of 1950s Las Vegas to Lansky's biographers:

> differences were ironed out peaceably in those early days in Vegas. For instance, when they were building the Stardust Hotel, which was the largest one then, Dalitz complained that it would give too much competition to this Desert Inn. The man behind the Stardust was Antonio Stralla, or as we called him Tony Cornero, an old bootlegging friend. It looked like an old-fashioned war might break out, but Meyer suggested a meeting and we all flew in for it. I was there with Dalitz, and his right-hand man, Kleinman, was there, and Longie Zwillman, and so forth. We worked out a deal that gave each group an interlocking interest in each other's hotels, and our lawyers set it up so that nobody could really tell who owned what out there. (Eisenberg et al. 1978:266–267)

While the nature and extent of this type of organized criminal involvement in the legal casino industry have been subject to interpretation and conjecture, the presence of some measure of investment by marginal financiers in legal casino gambling has been accepted since 1950 as a necessary outcome of the legalization of a vice whose primary purveyors had been organized criminal entrepreneurs (Skolnick 1978).

From the time of the Kefauver hearings, Nevada's legal casino industry was considered by federal law enforcement authorities to be infiltrated by— if not totally controlled by—organized criminals (Kefauver 1951). Following Siegel at the Flamingo, organized criminal interests from Cleveland, Chicago, and Detroit invested in new hotel-casino complexes. To Nevada authorities, who were compelled to live with a given number of formerly illegal operators in their state's dominant industry, this federal concern over organized crime was an encroachment upon Nevada's right as a sovereign state to set its own laws in licensing businesses (Glass 1981). From the governor down to the sheriff, Nevada authorities were concerned with the image of its gaming industry (Vogliotti 1975; Sawyer 1976). It didn't help that, when Frank Costello was shot in New York City in April 1957, the figures of that day's receipts at Las Vegas's Tropicana Hotel were found in his pocket. It was clear to federal authorities that organized criminals alone were responsible for the financing of the Las Vegas casino industry, and that belief was widespread throughout the financial community—with the effect that institutional leaders shied away from Nevada gaming, considering the industry an unsafe investment.

The tainted roots of Las Vegas gaming gave rise to the definition of the casinos there as a pariah industry, one that could not seek legitimate capital for necessary expansion in the 1960s (Skolnick 1978). Faced on one side with a lack of expansion capital and on another with the increasing vigilance of the federal government, Nevada's gaming operators were in need, by the 1960s, of a source of respectable capital (Eadington 1982). Howard Hughes, who sold his TWA stock in 1966 for $584 million, provided precisely the relief that the gaming industry sought. As an industry newsletter reported at the time:

> Back in 1966, Nevada had hit a new low. Its gambling was under unremitting attack from Washington, and Nevada was under ultimatum to straighten out, to get rid of certain hotel managements. This might have taken years except for the sudden appearance of Hughes who bought three in five months. . . . By getting into the gambling business he convinced millions that gambling can't be dirty or Hughes—genius of helicopters, space vehicles, electronics— wouldn't get into it. It was a public relations breakthrough for Nevada that could not have been delivered by Madison Avenue for $50 million. (*Nevada Report* 1969:2)

Later reports would show that Hughes had declined from a path-breaking economic entrepreneur to a seclusive and obsessive codeine addict between his purchase of the Desert Inn and his death in 1976. In 1966, however, he was a leading and respected businessman. His entry into Las Vegas and his purchase of several casinos was a watershed event in the transition of the Nevada gaming industry to respectability. Following Hughes's arrival, the Nevada legislature approved the Corporate Gaming Act, which provided for the ownership of casinos by publicly traded corporations. Within six years, Hilton, Hyatt, and Metro-Goldwyn-Mayer invested in Nevada and upgraded the image of the mob-controlled city.

Governor Paul Laxalt confirmed the "Hughes effect," when he reported to Nevadans in 1966: "Mr. Hughes' involvement here has absolutely done us wonders. I just returned from a trip to the East where I spoke to some industrialists in mid-town Manhattan and their questions no longer are concerned with the Mafia, the skimming, the underworld. . . . People come here now feeling they can come here in respectable, safe circumstances" (Davenport and Eddy 1976:155).

The attraction of "respectable capital" changed Las Vegas casinos' dependence upon local or disreputable sources of investment capital, whether questionable financiers or "pariah" lenders like the Teamsters Central States Pension Fund (Skolnick 1978). Some of the very same corporate entities who are the leaders in the nearly legitimized casino field are among those that have been designated by federal labor and law enforcement agencies as "connected" to organized crime. That the federal designation of their impropriety is described as "organized crime connected" or "associated" is an indication of the problems of assessing disreputable activity. Should one presume that organized criminal roots give an enterprise a tendency to continue unethical or illegal behavior? Or does the possibility exist that, after an initial stage of illegal development and transformation into legal forms, an organized criminal enterprise may "go legitimate"? Nevada officials have been forced gingerly to evaluate their corporate entities according to precisely such a subjective calculus.

One certain effect of this legitimation has been that it allows certain institutional actors—investors and lenders—to participate where they were previously wary. As a result, there is a ripple effect as the growing respectability discourages the imputation of deviance to the casino industry. Widespread investment diffuses the financial backing of what were formerly organized criminal holdings, and the interest in organized crime is reduced to those agencies specifically charged with organized crime control. When important financial institutions stopped resisting the gaming industry, it narrowed the base of those who might assign it a deviant identity. A vice-president of Merrill Lynch explained in 1978 that the ability to make damaging accusations is by necessity limited to those who have access to confidential information:

> we also maintain the view that the gaming industry, as it is called, has the potential to be one of the high growth segments of the economy during the next five years. . . . We believe that there are several well-regarded companies with good performance records in this industry, and that such companies represent a potential universe for long-term investment in casino gaming's growth. The last assertion does not, however, imply that the industry today is necessarily totally free of some undesirable participants . . . the historical facts all seem to indicate that early development interest and financing for some Las Vegas hotel-casinos were, if not dominated, at least partially influenced by some organized crime elements. All of this obviously poses a problem for fiduciaries and for the analysts who advise them. In essence, the problem boils down to the following: securities analysts have neither the expertise, the inclination, the resources, nor the time to conduct investigations in the law enforcement field, and it is thus only possible to make judgements and assumptions from a distance—based on interviews with, and on general reputations of, top management in each company. There can never be any guarantee that the industry has completely outgrown some of its tainted roots, but because of close scrutiny and regulation by various governmental agencies, and because of the need to rely on public capital for expansion, we believe that for

most of the major companies in the industry this concern is no longer a primary consideration. (Vogel 1978:3–4)

While evidence of continued organized crime involvement in legal casino gambling is provided in court-authorized wiretaps, as well as testimony by organized crime figures, the presence of organized crime as an active member in the legal casino industry has always been denied by the industry itself, particularly after it began to seek fiscal respectability with the entrance of nongambling corporations, especially hotel-leisure corporations, in Nevada after 1966. The legal casino gambling industry has always been stigmatized by its organized crime roots and anxious to dispel any intimations that organized criminals are continuing partners in certain "suspect" casinos. Still, it remains a nagging issue, the specter that haunts the industry.

In those states where the legalization of casino gambling has been promoted as a method of increasing tax revenues and offsetting impending fiscal crises and revenue shortfalls, the "organized crime issue" has loomed large, both in the consideration by political and economic elites and in the public campaigns surrounding specific ballot measures. No other single issue— including compulsive gambling and the regressivity of legalized gambling as a taxation device—poses as many problems for the legitimation of casino gambling as does the question of organized crime involvement.

In effect, those who have supported legal casinos as a form of economic development and those who have opposed them rely upon similar data in drawing their conclusions. Thus, the legitimacy and reputability of the organized crime–stigmatized legal casino industry, whether in fact it has been sanitized or merely carefully conceals continued involvement with organized criminal capital, depend upon the will of powerful political and economic actors. It is crucial how elites perceive the threat associated with the legal casino industry, which had its roots in organized crime and continues to be tainted by periodic revelations of organized criminal ownership, control, or association. In the early attempts at legalization of casinos in the 1970s, the threat of organized crime was a crucial issue. In Florida, important political and economic actors viewed the integration of the legal casino industry into their state as threatening to the existing economy, and legalization was blocked. In New Jersey, similar elites considered casino legalization a creditable economic development mechanism, and their support was crucial to the referendum's success. Several states since New Jersey have considered allowing legal casino gambling without a single state following New Jersey's lead in permitting casinos. To understand why these states failed to accept casino gambling, we must first consider whether the New Jersey and Florida examples are deviant cases.

2 ❧New Jersey, 1974 and 1976: Legalization as Economic Development

> In the day we sweat it out in the streets of a
> runaway American dream
> At night we ride through mansions of glory in
> suicide machines
> Sprung from cages on Highway 9
> Chrome wheeled, fuel injected
> And steppin' out over the line
> Baby this town rips the bones from your back
> It's a death trap, it's a suicide rap
> We gotta get out while we're young
> Cause tramps like us, baby we were born to run*

". . . legalized casino gambling has been approved by the citizens of New Jersey as a unique tool of urban redevelopment for Atlantic City . . . to attract new investment capital to New Jersey in general and Atlantic City in particular."

—Casino Control Act 1977

New Jersey has probably been as maligned as any state in the union, the butt of jokes by New Yorkers and other East Coast residents who look upon it at best as a second-rate power, a state that suffers all the ills of industrial life without reaping any of the cultural benefits. It has often been referred to as a burial place for the remnants of gangland slayings or as the void that exists beyond New York City—in short, a state with nothing to recommend

---

*—Bruce Springsteen, "Born to Run" (©1974 Bruce Springsteen, ASCAP), proposed for adoption in New Jersey State Assembly (Concurrent Resolution #121, April 17, 1980) as the unofficial theme of New Jersey's youth.

it. Ironically, this ninth largest of the United States, which calls itself the Garden State, exists as a colony of sorts in the Northeast. Northern New Jersey is home to people who work by day in New York City and commute home at night to the New Jersey suburbs, where single-family dwellings are more affordable. Although its industrial base is substantial, New Jersey cannot be described as a rich state, and it became no richer during the 1970s. Symbolic, perhaps, of the state's dependency on its surrounding neighbors is the fact that there are no national network television affiliate stations located in New Jersey—a state of over 7 million people (U.S. Bureau of the Census 1980). Instead, New Jerseyites are forced to rely upon New York and Philadelphia television stations for their news.

New Jersey's reputation as a breeding ground of organized criminal activity and political corruption is not the product of media exaggeration—the record of the past decade supports a federal prosecutor's charge that organized crime blatantly controls New Jersey politics (Dorman 1972). Mayor John Armellino of West New York, New Jersey, pleaded guilty in 1971 to conspiring with an organized crime boss to protect mob gambling activities. Mayor Thomas Whelan of Jersey City, along with seven other public officials, was convicted in 1971 of conspiring to extort money from companies doing business with the city and county governments. John B. Theurer, the Republican chairman of Hudson County, pleaded guilty to charges of conspiring to appoint a county prosecutor who would protect mob gambling interests. Assemblyman Peter Moraites, the former Speaker of the New Jersey Assembly, pleaded guilty in 1971 to accepting illegal fees for helping various companies obtain $2.4 million in "improvident" loans from a bank of which Moraites was a director. The indictment had been handed down by a grand jury investigating organized crime and official corruption. Moraites, a former aide to New York's Senator Jacob Javits, subsequently explained his resignation from the Assembly was "not because I did anything wrong, but because I cannot operate effectively from jail" (Dorman 1972:36–71). In the late 1970s, the mayor of Camden was ensnared in the ABSCAM net, as was one of New Jersey's United States senators.

Portions of New Jersey are lush and green, especially along the 127-mile-long Atlantic Ocean coast, where a string of small resort towns fill up during the summer months with city dwellers on vacation. Along this coastline, 134 miles from New York City and 60 miles from Philadelphia, sits Atlantic City, the "Queen of the Jersey Shore." Since the late nineteenth century, this resort town, which combined the natural beauty of an Atlantic Ocean beach town with the man-made attractions of resort hotels, had symbolized extravagance and fantasy.

By the 1970s, however, Atlantic City was in decline. Its resort hotels, once considered the epitome of glamour and elegance, were aging. The emergence of air travel as an affordable option for vacationers cut into Atlantic City's clientele. As people's vistas grew, Atlantic City began to pale in comparison to the beach resorts in the Bahamas and other Caribbean sites. Falling from a position of prominence, Atlantic City was quickly abandoned by tourists. One historian attributes this demise to altered forms of travel and leisure:

> changing modes of transportation practically destroyed the resort's ability to attract patronage across class lines, threatened the physical appearance of the city, and sapped the illusion-creating potential the city once so vigorously exploited. Atlantic City did not "fall"—it was abandoned—though a large part of its patronage continued to respond eagerly to what it offered, an important minority left it behind, to return no more. (Funnell 1975:151)

Atlantic City had run out of appeal and out of customers. It had degenerated into a "crowded, noisy, dirty, garish, and cheerfully vulgar resort" (Funnell 1975:157). The population of Atlantic City had decreased 20% between 1960 and 1970. Available hotel rooms had dropped by 40%. Real estate, local luxury-tax collection, and numbers of convention delegates had all declined during this period. Between 1965 and 1975, Atlantic City lost 4,500 jobs, as unemployment and welfare rolls grew (Economics Research Associates 1976). Some drastic measure would be required to catapult the city back to a position of respectability, even to a position where it could compete with other New Jersey resort towns.

That measure arrived in 1976, in the form of a referendum on the New Jersey ballot to permit legal casino gambling in Atlantic City, as a means of revitalizing the decaying resort town. And, while some observers were skeptical of the ability of Atlantic City to rebuild with enough flair to compete with Las Vegas for the gambling dollar, the events of recent years have proved otherwise. In 1976, Atlantic City counted 3 million visitors. By 1987, 30 million had visited the city (*Press*, July 24, 1988). Casino gamblers left nearly $2.5 billion behind in 1987. (Casino Control Commission 1988) and property values climbed, a change that was unthinkable only a few years earlier. One of the city's busiest real estate speculators, who bought 15 acres of land near the marina in 1975 for $37,000, later concluded an agreement to sell the property—zoned for casino development—for $20 million (*New York Times*, June 17, 1980). The new prosperity that has engulfed Atlantic City and enhanced New Jersey's tourist industry was not easily achieved. In fact, the success of the 1976 gambling referendum was somewhat of a surprise to political observers, who had witnessed the resounding defeat of a similar measure in 1974.

In November 1974, New Jersey voters had rejected, by a vote of 1.2 million to 800,000, a referendum that would have permitted casinos in New Jersey (New Jersey Election Commission 1977). While the indication was that such casinos would probably be restricted to resort areas such as Atlantic City, the initiative itself did not specify where casinos could operate. Consequently, casino proponents later admitted that a large number of voters apparently rejected the proposal primarily because they did not want to see casinos in their own community. Sanford Weiner, the political consultant who ran the successful 1976 campaign, reiterated this opinion when he said about the 1974 measure, "I wouldn't have gone near it . . . the voters weren't going to buy it the way it was written. They didn't go for the idea of casinos in their backyards" (Weiner 1978a).

The political wisdom about the 1974 vote was that many voters had feared the proliferation of casinos in the urban areas of New Jersey, and this fed an apprehension that gambling would prey upon those unprotected members of the working class who hoped to strike it rich, exactly the people who could not afford to squander even a small amount of a paycheck on games of chance. The Commission on the Review of the National Policy toward Gambling recommended, in its 1976 final report, *Gambling in America*, that "legalization of casino gambling be restricted by the state to relatively isolated areas where the impact on surrounding populations can be minimized" (Commission on the Review 1976:102). Only in rare circumstances, the report went on, should casino gambling be permitted in a major metropolitan area. Las Vegas, encircled as it is by the Mojave Desert, thrives in an enclave that sets the city off—gamblers have to decide to go there. In order for the issue of gambling preying upon the urban working class to fade, gambling legalization proponents realized in 1976 that they would have to emphasize the Atlantic City–only angle and stress the natural fit of casino gambling to a resort town like Atlantic City. Potential sites for casinos, following the Nevada model, should obviously be places like Atlantic City, Miami Beach, the Catskills, the Poconos—verifiable vacation spots, rather than the industrial metropolitan areas of New York City, Pittsburgh, Cleveland, or Baltimore. So already there was a sort of self-selection involved in the legalization process. Only those states that could approach voters with the notion of the renovation of an existing tourist area—particularly one that caters to the type of tourist and conventioneer that Las Vegas attracts—would prevail. The 1974 legalization referendum also allowed for state ownership and operation of the casinos, a provision that may have frightened away some potential supporters of privately owned casinos, who were unconvinced that the state of New Jersey should invest millions of dollars in a risky venture.

One of the most telling signs of the unattractiveness of casino gambling to voters in the 1974 campaign was the unequal spending figures for the campaign. The anticasino group No Dice spent only $30,000 in its successful opposition to the initiative, while casino proponents invested half a million dollars in their effort to convince voters (New Jersey Election Law Enforcement Commission 1977). To many political observers in 1976, it seemed clear that the New Jersey electorate had resoundingly rejected casino gambling in 1974 as a method of taxation and economic development; unless some superior strategy was developed to sell the idea to voters at some later date, the issue would remain dead.

The subsequent success of the 1976 initiative can probably be attributed to the powerful political and economic base of the casino supporters and to their success in improving the enabling legislation for the legalization of casinos. They specified that casinos would operate only in Atlantic City, that they would be privately owned, and that the gaming taxes would be placed in a special fund within the state treasury and earmarked for tax relief programs for the elderly and disabled. Atlantic City had been heralded in 1974 as one obvious site for casinos. In the 1976 referendum package it would be the *only* location for casinos. More importantly, the 1976 success can be attributed to the emergence of a powerful alliance involving Atlantic City real estate and development interests, Atlantic City legislators, the governor of New Jersey, and a major casino corporation with reputed organized crime ties and a history of influence-buying in the Bahamas.

Several factors that surfaced between 1974 and 1976 undoubtedly increased the appeal of some sort of tax relief measure for New Jersey voters. The effects of the 1974 recession had made New Jersey taxpayers interested in additional sources of support; the adoption of a state income tax in 1975 evidenced that need (New Jersey Statutes 1976). But perhaps the crucial difference was the role of the state. The 1976 campaign was not a private effort pushed by special interests and developers. The state of New Jersey— in the persons of the governor and influential Atlantic City legislators—gave its blessing to the referendum early and wholeheartedly. In January 1976, Governor Byrne threw his support behind a proposal that would permit casinos in New Jersey, given the three modifications mentioned earlier: Atlantic City only, private ownership, and tax relief for the elderly and the disabled. Byrne predicted that casino gambling's expansion to the East Coast was inevitable and appealed to New Jerseyites' sense of state pride: New Jersey should make the most of Atlantic City's potential and beat New York or Florida to the punch by legalizing casino gambling first. Byrne described the casino plan as an attempt to reverse Atlantic City's situation of decreasing revenues (*New York Times*, January 20, 1976). Large revenues—tax dollars, investment capital, convention spending—were all apparently waiting for the first eastern state that legalized casinos.

Easterners could be considered particularly hospitable to legalization appeals, since there were more gamblers in the general population there than in other regions of the country. A gambling commission poll reported that northeasterners tended to participate more heavily in gambling (80%) than the national average (61%), and they had shown a willingness as far back as 1951 to support legalization of gambling, at a time when no other region of the country was so inclined (Commission on the Review 1976:60).

Atlantic City officials and labor leaders were generally pleased with the governor's decision. Even Atlantic City police chief William Ten Brink stated at an early legislative hearing on the matter that gambling casinos were "absolutely necessary to attract the 'risk capital' needed to revitalize the coastal resort town" (*New York Times*, April 15, 1976), especially in light of reports that unemployment in Atlantic City had recently been as high as 25%. Labor support for the casino proposal was similarly strong. Charles Marchiante, the New Jersey president of the AFL-CIO, offered the strong backing of labor and called the casino concept "a valuable means of revitalizing New Jersey's $7 million tourist industry" (*New York Times*, April 15, 1976). Gambling, he felt, would act as a catalyst that would benefit the entire New Jersey tourist business. Casinos in Atlantic City would spur depressed construction, tourist, and support industries. A spokesman for the Central Labor Council of Atlantic City best illustrated the economic appeal of the crusade for gambling when he testified at a legislative hearing: "The purpose in having casinos in Atlantic City is to end hunger in Atlantic City and the surrounding area . . . to provide jobs for the jobless . . . to make Atlantic City a financial asset to the great State of New Jersey instead of a liability" (Levin 1976).

But, before that could happen and the casino proponents could take advantage of the support of the AFL-CIO, the serious flaws of the 1974 initiative would have to be worked out. This was the immediate concern of the legislators sponsoring casino legalization. Two Atlantic City legislators, Assemblyman Stephen Perskie and Senator Joseph McGahn, introduced a resolution in the New Jersey state legislature to place a referendum on the November 1976 ballot to legalize casino gambling in New Jersey (*New York Times*, May 2, 1976). The bill contained a private ownership provision that would remove the state from the actual operation of gambling, with several consequences. It took the state out of the risky position of investing millions of dollars directly in a business that had been proven successful in a legal form in only one state. A more important consideration was that the state, now removed from the actual ownership and operation of casinos, could concentrate on involvement in strict gaming control. New Jersey would not be torn between promoting its state-owned activity and adequately policing it to prevent organized crime from gaining a foothold, as had been done in every other locale where casinos were legal (Skolnick 1978).

The bills introduced by Perskie and McGahn contained another important political and economic clause: rather than entering the state's general fund, any money derived from the tax on casinos' gross gaming revenues would constitute a special fund to be used solely to reduce property taxes, utility taxes, and rent for the elderly and disabled. Gambling proponents estimated that $5 to $15 million annually would be earmarked for this special fund, at least in the first few years of operation of Atlantic City casinos. It was a clear appeal to a powerful bloc of voters. Perskie said of his bill: "This is a unique proposal. It proposes nothing less than the salvation of one of the major cities of New Jersey. We need help. We need assistance in a special form. We're not asking for money. We're not asking for a handout. We're not asking for state resources, state revenues to rebuild this community. We're asking for a vote to help ourselves" (*New York Times*, May 4, 1976).

Perskie's resolution passed the New Jersey State Assembly on May 3, 1976, on a fifty-two to twenty-three vote, four more than the necessary forty-eight votes (*New York Times*, May 4, 1976). Some opponents of the measure had predicted a "bureaucratic nightmare" if the state were forced to take on the role of gaming controller. But this and other concerns about the involvement of organized crime, and the deleterious secondary effects associated with gambling, were not enough to stop the bill, or the Senate bill passed on June 28, by a twenty-four to nine vote. Senator McGahn had assured his colleagues that the state of New Jersey would assume strict control over gambling and that the governor would veto any unreasonable number of licenses and suggest appropriate methods of police control.

The supporters of the gambling referendum, buoyed by the governor's support and the passage of the legislative resolutions, now turned their attention to the public campaign that needed to be waged if casinos were to be successfully legalized. The supporters remembered that procasino sentiment had been reversed in the late stages of the 1974 campaign and that a half-million-dollar effort had been unsuccessful—surprisingly so, considering the early prolegalization sentiment lead in public opinion polls. To protect against a reoccurrence of that reversal in 1976, the proponents recognized the need for a spirited campaign that would involve a wide spectrum of influential leaders. The naming of the support committee was the first indication of an evolving strategy: the Committee to Rebuild Atlantic City was the official procasino group. Moreover, to emphasize the "Atlantic City angle," and thereby to offset the antagonism of people who had voted against gambling in 1974 because they feared it might spread to their home districts, Mayor Joseph Lazarow of Atlantic City was named chairman of the committee (*New York Times*, July 18, 1976).

The proponents were less provincial in choosing a campaign manager. They went all the way to California to select a political consultant who had experience with referenda—a political process more developed in California than in New Jersey (Weiner 1978a). Sanford Weiner had earned a reputation as one of the country's most successful campaign managers. It was reported, upon Weiner's hiring by legalization proponents, that his firm had managed 172 political campaigns, 157 successfully (*Advertising Age* 1976). While there was some dispute over such figures, he was credited with having a long winning streak with such referenda.

Given the outcome of the 1974 legalization measure, Weiner approached the 1976 New Jersey campaign as one of his most difficult. He went in with the fear that the 1974 vote had established a track record of sorts for gambling initiatives. He sensed a geographic problem as well. Most of the voters in New Jersey live in the northern part of the state, adjacent to New York City, while the immediate impact and benefit from gambling would accrue to Atlantic City and surrounding areas in the south. Finally, there was the problem of gambling itself. In order to legalize gambling, Weiner felt, the campaign would have to overcome many strong and fixed opinions, some imbued within religious fervor. The campaign would have to withstand the fact that gambling itself, in Weiner's opinion, was "a bad word" (Weiner 1978a). The polls that Weiner took upon his arrival in New Jersey in the summer of 1976 revealed a split in New Jersey's electorate on the gambling question: roughly one-third supported legalization and one-third opposed it, with one-third undecided. The goal, for either side in the legalization campaign, was clearly to move that undecided third into their camp.

Casinos as Redevelopment: The Proponents' Campaign

> If we don't get it this time, you might as well put a fence around Atlantic City and put up a sign, 'Ghost Town.'
> —Atlantic City gas station owner
> (*New York Times*, July 18, 1976)

Since money would not be an object—with $1 million set as the budget— Weiner could afford to leave little to chance. He had to identify his potential supporters, the issues that troubled them, and the arguments that swayed them. Then his task would be to reach them in a convincing way. "Where opposition was known to exist," one New Jersey magazine reported, "sound trucks and canvassers were sent in to neutralize it. Where indecision was detected, media ads were increased to saturation levels and brochures distributed by the hundreds of thousands" (Douglas 1977:23). Weiner began his work with demographic surveys and polls of potential New Jersey voters: 34% of voters polled in an August survey favored casinos in Atlantic City; another 31% opposed it. Naturally, the final undecided 35% was the prize that both sides sought to capture. The most important finding of that early poll was that 78% of those surveyed believed that casinos could generate significant revenues for the state (Douglas 1977:23–24).

Surrounded on one side by the near fiscal collapse of New York City (Alcaly and Mermelstein 1977; Auletta 1980) and the enactment of New Jersey state income tax in 1975, New Jersey voters were primed for an appeal to their financial worries. In the summer of 1976, New Jersey casino gambling proponents were in the perfect position to present casino gambling as a revenue-raising mechanism that would soften the impact of an imminent fiscal crisis. The procasino campaign sought to take advantage of this, willing to gamble that a revenue-based appeal to voters would take hold of the consciousness of the electorates on the following points (Mahon 1980; Sternlieb and Hughes 1983; Abt et al. 1985; Lehne 1986).

First, gambling was not an evil, parasitical activity that wrecked homes, sent degenerate gamblers to the poor house, or depended upon the improvidence of the lower class for its profits. Rather, it was an increasingly middle-class—even family-oriented—leisure-time activity that relied upon the discretionary income of vacationing tourists, who had allotted a certain amount of their entertainment money for losses at the gambling tables.

Next, unlike alcohol or drug use, gambling did not exhibit any necessarily detrimental features. In fact, it would not be difficult to see the similarity between gambling and more socially acceptable forms of specialization and risk taking, the stock market being the most obvious example.

Third, gambling has been a pastime for centuries, and no governmental prohibition has ever been able to stamp it out effectively. The only result of such government action in twentieth-century America has been to drive gambling underground, where it thrives as one of the major revenue-producing activities of organized criminal syndicates. It would make sense as a policy imperative—especially given the contours of the fiscal crisis—to bring at least this one portion of the underground economic sector back into the mainstream economy. One consequence would be to take profits away from the organized crime syndicates that controlled illegal gambling and pump them into the "above-ground" economy. It was outmoded and over-moralistic to try to control individual gambling behavior by refusing to permit legal forms of an activity that people desired—indeed, would travel across the country to participate in.

Finally, there were worries about organized crime, but these fears would have to be allayed through the designing of the "strictest gaming controls in the world" (Committee to Rebuild 1976).

The prolegalization materials made these appeals explicit and graphic. "When you vote 'yes' for casinos in Atlantic City," Weiner's major campaign advertisement read, "and *only* Atlantic City—you'll be helping yourself. Because *every* resident of New Jersey will benefit directly" in the following ways. First, "new revenues will pour in, state-wide." The advertisement mentioned an estimated $58 million in annual tax revenue for the state within ten years. Business all over the state would be generated. Next, "we'll get dramatic help with unemployment, state-wide." By 1980, 19,000 jobs would be created, according to the supporters, and 33,000 by 1985. "That's year round work." Also, there would be "help for our senior citizens and disabled residents": a special fund would be established that would pour $30 million annually by 1984 *directly* into property tax, rent, and utility relief for these special populations. Finally, "the safeguards are built-in." Quiet, tasteful, European-style casinos were promised. Las Vegas—as an example of gambling running to excess—became an important campaign issue. Gambling would not run rampant in Atlantic City, the proponents promised, and a state gaming commission would license, regulate, and audit all casino operations (Committee to Rebuild 1976).

Gaming control was thus made a salient issue in the campaign. The state's ability to prevent organized crime infiltration of a legalized gambling industry was central to the debate between opponents and supporters of the referendum. If the proponents could convince the undecided that state control would be stringent and effective, then defeat would be foreclosed. For, while the 1974 successful opposition campaign had believed the "morality" issue to have triumphed, Weiner believed instead that the gambling advocates had lost because of their incompetence and lack of direction. Weiner's surveys revealed that at most 10–12% of the electorate opposed gambling on strictly moral grounds. An additional 10–20% opposed gambling because of the issues that would form the campaign debate: organized crime, economic benefits, and the propensity of gambling to run rampant once legalized.

The Opponents' Campaign

The opposition to casino gambling in 1974 had largely been centered around religious leaders, who had combined the position and constituencies of their office with a small amount of campaign funds to torpedo the gambling initiative. The group that formed in opposition to the 1974 measure reappeared in 1976, but did not recreate the organization that had successfully thwarted gambling. There were two sources of opposition in 1976: church groups brought up the inherent immorality of gambling and law enforcement officials expressed their concern over possible organized crime infiltration of the legalized casino industry.

The representative of the New Jersey Council of Churches presented the church opposition when he declared casino gambling to be a "paltry, piece-meal approach to a serious problem," namely, Atlantic City's economic depression. The legislature, the Reverend Layton Anderson stressed, would lose its credibility with the public if it put forth casino gambling as an economic solution (*New York Times*, April 15, 1976).

If the church position appealed to those who had strong moral opposition to gambling as an activity, the opposition of law enforcement officials was aimed at a potentially larger audience. If casinos were legalized, they argued, they would certainly be infiltrated and controlled by organized criminal interests. One state police official argued this position before the legislature, speculating that if casino gambling were to be legalized in New Jersey, "mobsters would undoubtedly be used to collect gaming debts" (*New York Times*, April 15, 1976). A casino cannot exist without allowing patrons to gamble on credit, he explained, and the New Jersey mob—which he alleged was active in the collection of gaming debts for Las Vegas casinos—would be used to collect debts generated in the Atlantic City casinos. The New Jersey state police, he continued, had evidence of organized crime connections to Nevada casinos, and there was no good reason for New Jersey legislators to believe that Atlantic City could escape the same fate.

Another law enforcement official who voiced the same objections, United States attorney Jonathan Goldstein, warned that legalization would attract criminals to Atlantic City and cause irreparable damage to the community, while only benefiting a few people. A growth of family and social problems would result, he felt, as well as the spread of crime and government corruption. "It makes no sense at all," Goldstein said, "to create in our state an environment that is certain to attract criminals of every type" (*New York Times*, September 28, 1976).

These two fronts—church representatives and law enforcement officials—comprised the heart of the opposition to gambling. The opponents of the measure attempted to have it removed from the ballot for alleged unconstitutionality. Under New Jersey law, a proposal, once defeated on a referendum vote, could not be brought back for a vote in substantially the same form until three elections had passed.

Assemblyman Perskie had earlier obtained an opinion from the state attorney general certifying the constitutionality of the referendum. In the opinion, William Hyland wrote that the 1976 measure was substantially different because of the three major changes: gambling in one locality only, private operation of the casinos, and proceeds to the elderly.

Horse racing interests, which had opposed the 1974 measure, indicated they would not do so in 1976. A state senator who was a prominent antigambling advocate in 1974 declined to take an active role. The attorney general, who had been an outspoken opponent in 1974, was less vociferous in 1976. The primary opposition came from the churches, which retained the name of the successful 1974 coalition—Casino: No Dice. Still, despite the imbalance in campaign financing—the churches knew they would be up against a million-dollar prolegalization effort—the general secretary of the Council of Churches believed that "no amount of money could match hundreds of sermons from church pulpits" (*New York Times*, October 26, 1976).

This absence of a powerful coalition in no way meant that the opposition lacked powerful supporters. The *New York Times* consistently sided with the gambling opponents, charging in one editorial, titled "Degrading Atlantic City," that with legalization New Jersey voters will "invite a cure worse than the disease: and "play directly into the hands of crooks, gamblers and speculators" (*New York Times*, July 4, 1976). Despite the power of the *New York Times* editorial—and presuming that New York–based editorials against New Jersey legalization would not be interpreted as interference in the politics of another state—the reality of the legalization opposition was its reliance upon the church base. This church-based opposition committed the antigambling group to an attack on the morality of gambling itself. In so doing, the opponents failed to mount an effective attack on the issues of organized crime, the limited extent of economic development promised by proponents, and the issue of the proliferation of gambling, once legalized.

With the themes of the two sides of the campaign established—and limited, as a result of their respective composition—the battle for the undecided vote began. The ability of either side to frame the legalization question in a way that would capitalize on the political sentiments of the New Jersey electorate would be crucial. When New Jersey voters made a decision on the legalization question in November, they would, as a *New York Times* article put it, "decide between the state's need for revenue and the moral objectives that have been raised" (*New York Times*, July 4, 1976). But they would decide within the contours of a debate framed by the revenue-conscious legalization advocates and the morality-minded, church-based opposition.

Campaign Financing and the Organized Crime Question

If the casino proponents expected to succeed where they failed in 1974— creating a united front that could withstand the attacks of the church-led opponents—they had to raise at least $1 million, spend it wisely, and attract a wide spectrum of support for the referendum. Toward this end, the casino proponents turned to big business, small businesspeople, doctors, lawyers, and hotel and motel operators for support. But the support for the referendum came primarily from Atlantic City interests. Nearly 60% of the contributions received on behalf of the referendum came from contributors listing Atlantic City addresses (New Jersey Election Law Enforcement Commission 1977). Another $200,000, or roughly 20% of the total, was given by Resorts International, a Miami-based casino gambling corporation, which operated a casino in the Bahamas and had long been suspected of ties to noted organized criminal figure Meyer Lansky. In addition, the second largest contributor, the Chalfonte–Haddon Hall Hotel in Atlantic City, was owned by a subsidiary of Resorts International (New Jersey Election Law Enforcement Commission 1977).

The disparity between the funds of the supporters and the opponents cannot be overemphasized. The committees supporting casino gambling spent $1,330,615, while the committees opposing it took in $23,230 and spent $21,250 (New Jersey Election Law Enforcement Commission 1977). In fact, there were four procasino contributors—Resorts International, the Chalfonte–Haddon Hall, the *Atlantic City Press* and *Sunday Press,* and Howard Johnson's—who *each* gave more money to the procasino side than the entire operating budget of the opposing committees.

The base for the referendum support among New Jersey corporate interests was strong when one considers the size of the contributions. Despite the emphasis that the legalization of casino gambling was meant to aid the unemployed of Atlantic City, the elderly and disabled, and those who were suffering from rising unemployment, in a poll taken by the Eagleton Institute of Rutgers University, two-thirds of the respondents felt uneasiness with the organized crime issue (*New York Times,* October 26, 1976).

There were several reasons why organized crime was defused as the vital issue in the campaign. Legalization opponents didn't seize upon the organized crime question, dwelling more on the morality of gambling; no state officials—Goldstein was a federal law enforcement official—came forward to portray a Resorts-backed campaign as a threat to New Jersey; gambling proponents were able to emphasize that the state of New Jersey, whose officials didn't address the possibility of organized crime infiltration of a legalized casino gambling industry—could devise, enact, and implement strict controls; those crucial state officials who might have rejected Resorts International as a partner in New Jersey's redevelopment instead invited the disreputable corporation to become an early investor in Atlantic City casino gambling.

Conclusion: The Selling of Casino Gambling

> You don't sell casino gambling. You sell the benefits of a thing
> called casino gambling. People don't care two cents who's standing
> around a roulette table. They care about what is going to put money in
> their pockets.
> —Sanford Weiner (Bearak 1978:8)

Speaking in 1978, one New Jersey state official who had figured prominently in state planning for gaming control gave his ideas on the success of
the 1976 casino gambling initiative: "They sold it to a lot of people in a lot
more sophisticated way, that's what it boiled down to" (Martinez 1978). To
that official, the success of the legalization drive was due to a combination of
factors: more money to spend, more effective campaign strategy, and the
change in significant parts of the 1974 measure. The political base was more
cohesive the second time, and the fiscal crisis more telling, but the funda-
mental turnaround was due to the ability of gambling proponents to sell
gambling to the voters.

The campaign Weiner directed was sophisticated, in both style and substance. Once the most salient arguments for legalization were set—economic development, tax revenues, and strict control—Weiner oversaw the
production of commercials and campaign literature highlighting these issues. One prolegalization counterappeal to the voters featured a New Jersey
county sheriff promising voters that controls would be imposed and that they
would work—organized crime would be kept out. Weiner considered this
his most effective ad (Weiner 1978a). A second television spot dramatized
the economic benefits of legalization; in yet another, labor officials talked
about New Jersey's unemployment rate—then the highest in the country—
and the jobs that gambling would create.

As the New Jersey Society of Architects, in endorsing the referendum,
expressed it, a large vote for casino gambling would be a vote for more work,
rather than one for gambling (*New York Times*, October 26, 1976). The
effect of this framing of the debate was to shift the discussion to the benefits
of legalization, which were economic, not social. Legalization was not meant
to undo the social ills of criminalization—to keep gamblers from being
designated as criminals, for example. It was meant, as the New Jersey legislature explicitly stated, to relieve the fiscal crisis of the state. With this type of
support, and within the framework established by the opponents' objections,
Weiner's campaign sold casino gambling to the voters from two angles. First,
it quieted fears, mainly through the effective wording of the Assembly bill
and the promise of strong controls. Indeed, Weiner felt that the Assembly
bill—promising strict controls—was especially important as a public docu-

ment during the campaign. Second, the campaign sold hope—for jobs, tax relief, and redevelopment for Atlantic City (Douglas 1977).

The progambling side ran a well-financed and well-developed campaign; the most generous assessment of the opposition effort is that it was over-matched financially and could not repeat the 1974 performance. There could be several reasons for this. For one, the gambling advocates were much more organized and ran a professional campaign. For another, the provisions of the new bill allayed the fears of the voters that gambling would spread into their community and that the state of New Jersey would, as the owner and operator, be taking a risk in operating casinos. (Unlike lotteries, states can lose at casinos: casinos do go out of business.) Once the state was not proposed to be an operator, it could more aggressively adopt the role of enforcer of the "strictest gaming control statutes in the world" (Committee to Rebuild 1976). While promoting casinos with one hand, the state could promise strictly to supervise casino operations with the other—a position that hypothetically was not nonsense, but had proved in the actual situation of Nevada to be improbable. Still, as long as Nevada was referred to as a negative model—and especially since it was the only state to permit casino gambling—this problem of political and economic dependence upon the casinos could be portrayed as a Nevada anomaly, one that the New Jersey enabling legislation could easily remedy.

Moreover, the restriction of casinos to Atlantic City was more than a limitation that excepted the other areas of the states; it also concentrated the campaign for casinos on the redevelopment of a once prosperous resort—in other words, a place that was dedicated to the exaltation of fun and play above all else and would otherwise continue to decay. Some casino opponents believed that casino gambling would only attract criminals and benefit only a few speculators—a position that has its basis in the history of Las Vegas as a gathering place and investment opportunity for American organized criminal families. However, the gambling advocates were able to emphasize the opposite: that gambling would attract many, especially out-of-state residents, who might otherwise spend their vacation and convention dollars elsewhere. Thereby, the residents of New Jersey—whether or not they ever expected to visit Atlantic City to gamble and no matter how they felt about the appropriateness of the state legalizing and taxing a vice—would benefit from legalization.

Still, the question of the opposition remains crucial. The lack of financing for a campaign against casinos was an important factor. So was the fragmentation of the 1974 coalition that had successfully defeated a much more expensive proponent campaign. The prominent opponents—state legislators, the attorney general, parimutuel interests—were not present in the same manner that they had been two years prior. Perhaps even the 1974 results had a deleterious effect upon the opponents.

Convinced that no amount of money could match the sermons from pulpits resounding an antigambling message, the opponents of casinos may have been complacent in fund raising and mobilization of those elites with like sentiments toward legalization of casino gambling. Most importantly, the active support of the governor of New Jersey for the referendum, as well as support from other powerful interests in the state—people who otherwise, in other states, or in the past, or under other circumstances, might be less willing to come forward and commit money and support—not only pushed the measure forward, but cut off the opponents from prominent and well-financed means of opposition.

Although the *New York Times* took an early and strong editorial stand against legalization, it could even be argued that such a posture only strengthened New Jersey voters in their decision to favor casinos. For instance, New York had to be seen as a competitor with neighboring New Jersey for future convention business and tourist trade resulting from casinos. It could be easy for New Jerseyites to construe the *Times* opposition as New York–based, in anticipation of the day when New York might adopt casinos and compete successfully with New Jersey. Indeed, indigenous New Jersey media supported the referendum. With the antigambling side cut off from any powerful base in the state, it was forced to rely upon the churches and their moral condemnation of gambling as the basis of opposition, not the most successful or sophisticated route to counter the professional, reasonable, and fiscally oriented messages of the supporters. This seems especially crucial when one considers one finding of Weiner's original poll—that only 10% of the New Jersey electorate was adamantly opposed, on moral grounds, to casino gambling.

Perhaps something more important historically had caused the change. Between 1974 and 1976, Communist forces in Vietnam had finally prevailed, bringing to an end America's twenty-year attempt to prop up an unpopular government. The president of the United States had been involved in one of the most massive scandals in the history of the presidency and had been forced to resign from office. Those in power in Washington had been revealed to be no less susceptible than neighborhood police to soliciting and accepting bribes, no more regulated by the laws of the land than petty thieves. Was it any wonder that, in the face of such a national trauma, a cynical attitude about the wisdom and effectiveness of legislating morality and prohibiting popular vice developed in a state like New Jersey, with its legacy of political corruption? It is clearly significant that 40% of the voters explained that they supported casino legalization even if it resulted in an increase in organized crime in their state.

If New Jersey chose legalization, one might think that other states would follow. Although Florida was geographically and socially far different from New Jersey, it might be expected to exhibit some of the same characteristics and attitudes toward the law as New Jersey did in the 1976 campaign. This certainly was the view of those Florida hotel owners who brought Sanford Weiner to Florida, hoping to reproduce his success in New Jersey. What they did not anticipate was that the rise of a powerful and wide-based opposition would attack casinos on precisely the grounds that the New Jersey opposition had chosen to ignore. Perhaps Florida, with its sizable Baptist population, did not provide the most conducive atmosphere for legalization. But Weiner did not think that when he went in. He thought, to the contrary, that Florida was more of a "natural" than New Jersey. Instead, there is a different story to be told in Florida, one of post-Watergate morality, of a reform-minded governor and a cohesive financial and business community. Together they opposed the introduction of questionable casino operators into their state's tourist industry. They rejected the notion of Miami, which saw itself as a burgeoning trade and financial capital for the western hemisphere, incorporating disreputable elements into its economy.

3 ∿ Florida, 1978:
"Painless Prosperity" Challenged

Some people say casino gambling is the best way to get new jobs. New industries and casino gambling simply do not go together. In the last few years, we have built up momentum in bringing new jobs to Florida, because we have beautiful weather, no personal income tax, and stable government. Casinos will severely damage these efforts to bring challenging, high paying jobs to our people throughout Florida. Casinos are a bad risk. Who needs casino gambling? We don't.
—Governor Reubin Askew (1978 anticasino television commercial)

On November 4, 1978, Florida voters overwhelmingly rejected a proposal to legalize casinos along the Gold Coast—and in Miami Beach in particular. By a lopsided seventy-three to twenty-seven margin, opponents of the casino legalization measure, led by two-term governor Reubin Askew, carried every county in Florida and beat back a referendum similar in style and substance to the successful 1976 New Jersey initiative.

There were many obvious differences between the two states, which might account for the disparity in the vote. Of these, two are particularly notable: Florida has a large Baptist population and is generally regarded as a politically conservative state and Florida's economy, including its tourism, was strong. This chapter considers those factors, but uses a more dynamic variable in explaining the anticasino vote in Florida. As late as August 1978, polls conducted for the casino opposition had concluded that, while the November gambling contest would be close, the momentum of the election appeared to be with the gambling proponents (Hamilton 1978a). In the few months between those polls and the November election, a spirited campaign against casinos led by influential south Florida commercial interests appeared and turned a once close contest into a one-sided race.

There were a few things that remained certain in the late 1970s in the

United States. The price of gasoline, once predictably stable, was no longer one of them. Nor was the integrity of the office of the presidency, which had been tarnished by the scandals surrounding Richard Nixon. Even the soap box derby was found to have been tampered with by a young contestant. Perhaps the one thing that a person could predict was that, almost every night, Walter Cronkite, said to be one of the most trusted men in America, would be at his desk on the CBS Evening News and would tell his fellow countrymen—who could no longer believe their president—what was happening in the world. While presidents and politicians slipped in their credibility, Walter Cronkite remained a symbol of integrity and security. Reubin Askew, the Democratic governor of Florida from 1971 to 1979, holds a distinct honor. According to political pollsters, Askew was the one public official who ranked higher than Walter Cronkite on the "trust index," a measure designed to gauge the trust respondents had for public figures (Krog 1979). While other things might not be taken for granted, Floridians could hold onto one thing: their governor, a strict, God-fearing Presbyterian with the easygoing charm of a southern gentleman, could be trusted.

So it was that the proponents of casino gambling along Miami's Gold Coast—the beachfront hotel resort area beginning at Miami Beach and extending north for twenty-one miles to South Hollywood—had to be worried when Askew decided to make the opposition to a casino gambling referendum on the November 1978 ballot the most important issue for the remaining months of his second term. Askew's decision to throw his considerable political influence behind the effort to defeat casinos in Florida was not made lightly; once it was made, it was not to be one man's moral crusade against gambling. It was a political and economic commitment by a popular politician, who then encouraged the support of the Florida power elite and business community, especially bankers and newspaper publishers. Until Askew's decision to dedicate himself to the campaign, Florida had been touted as a natural for the legalization of casino gambling as a means of revitalizing the declining Miami Beach area.

When it appeared, in late June 1978, that the procasino Let's Help Florida Committee would acquire the signatures necessary to place a referendum calling for the legalization of casinos along the Gold Coast on the November ballot, Governor Askew convened a breakfast meeting of some of his most influential supporters, at which he asked the business elite of Miami to pledge financial and political support to an anticasino campaign. Askew had indicated a month earlier his willingness to campaign against a casino gambling referendum, which he thought would be a tragic moral and economic mistake for the state of Florida. "What kind of a community and state do we want to live in?" he asked at the May 1978 anticasino gathering convened by Floridians against Casino Takeover (Askew 1978a). "Can government build economic strength by catering to people's weaknesses? Should government try to exploit the people? Is this any way to lead?" Askew called casino gambling an "illusory quick fix" for economic development in Florida. He touched on a number of points in his May speech and his June address, points that would later reverberate as the key themes of the anti-casino campaign.

First, legalization would lead to crime and corruption:

> If we take the wrong road and admit casinos to Florida, we will wake up one day to discover that they have infiltrated the politics and lifestyle of the state and have spread their influence to every corner of Florida. Casinos are an invitation to the further expansion of crime at a time when we are fighting to contain crime. It is said that organized crime can be kept out of casino gambling because the state would regulate it and inspect the background of everyone connected with it. Anyone who knows anything of Las Vegas knows that isn't nearly enough. The large amounts of fast money that are attracted to legalized gambling attract the criminal element in its turn like blood attracts sharks.

Next, legalization would damage Florida's existing tourist economy:

> Casinos may bring a certain kind of tourist to Florida, but they will just as surely keep away other families. The voters of Florida shouldn't recklessly exchange the stability that they cherish and that is becoming so attractive to the rest of an unstable world, for the sleazy carnival atmosphere of a gambling resort. Legalized casino gambling would seriously damage the tourist industry in Florida. And it would not replace tourism as a source of revenue or as a source of jobs.

The legalization would jeopardize decent economic advances and development potential:

> We have been trying to balance the Florida economy by recruiting solid business and industry. We want our new private corporate citizens to feel this is a state in which they want to invest their money. Miami is growing as an international crossroads of banking and commerce. The tarnished image of casino gambling is completely inconsistent and counterproductive with all our efforts.

The changes in Florida society would not be minimal. This was not an issue to be taken lightly: "These are not small changes. They are serious and drastic alterations in the future of Florida" (Askew 1978a, b).

Finally, Florida needed to act rationally, to weigh the costs and benefits of legalization, rather than be swept up in the gambling rush. Gambling experts seriously considered that Florida might burst ahead of Atlantic City in the casino business, as Sanford Weiner told the *Wall Street Journal:* "I wouldn't be surprised if we had two or three casinos in operation here before New Jersey has its second" (Koten 1978). New Jersey legislators had considered this possibility when constructing the temporary licensing provision. Askew sought to turn the rush rationale of "Why not have casinos?: beat the rush— get there before New York or New Orleans" on its head, and argue instead, "Why have it here? What will we gain?"

Perhaps the most crucial early signal of Askew's approach was his promise to separate his personal moral beliefs from his political and economic objections. Instead of concentrating on the inherent immorality of gambling as behavior, Askew turned his focus to "the criminal element that follows it, the social tragedy it creates among the weak-willed and the weak-minded, the fact that gambling is subject to manipulation and rarely produces as much tax revenue as promised by its advocates. It's one thing to visit Las Vegas and go on a spree, and it's another thing entirely to drag Las Vegas home with you and set it up in your own community" (Askew 1978a, b).

Askew was unable to affix his anticasino campaign to any political momentum generated by antilegalization sentiment. No major scandals had occurred in Nevada in 1978 to offset the growing respectability of the casino gambling industry there. The first New Jersey casino had opened on the Memorial Day weekend and was doing brisk business, and *Business Week* had published a cover story, "The Boom in Gambling," in which gambling was referred to as America's newest growth industry—at the same time that procasino forces were attempting to secure Florida signatures (*Business Week* 1978). Sentiment was building for the legalization of casinos in selected areas along the East Coast. New Yorkers and Pennsylvanians were considering legislation and referendum measures to permit the operation of casinos in resort areas in their states to duplicate Atlantic City's seemingly miraculous revitalization.

In the face of such momentum, Askew realized that a strong effort would be necessary to offset the attractive revenue and economic development arguments of casino proponents. In New Jersey, lack of opposition by prominent financial and political interests had created a void and led to the success of the procasino side. And, before Askew acted, the opposition in Florida was not off to an encouraging start. The prominent opposition group, FACT, a coalition of clergy, law enforcement agencies, and citizens' groups, had not stirred up any notable broad-based opposition to gambling—polls reportedly showed the measure even or ahead (Elfman 1978; Weiner 1978a, b; Krog 1979).

Then Askew began to mobilize forces at the June breakfast meeting. Ten of his closest friends and political allies were asked to contribute $25,000 apiece to offset the expected $1 million campaign chest of the proponents.

Miami Herald publisher Alvah Chapman, Jr., explained that he was willing to contribute the money and to encourage his associates to do so, because he realized that only a well-financed anticasino campaign would allow Floridians to make a reasoned decision (Chapman 1978).

The Legalization Measure

Proponents based their analysis of the economic impact of casinos on a number of assumptions.

(1) The constitutional amendment permitting legalized casino gambling in Miami Beach would be passed in 1978 and enabling legislation would be provided by the Florida Legislature in 1979.

(2) A state-controlled casino control agency, similar to the agencies in Nevada and New Jersey, would be in operation, and would receive applications and issue licenses in early 1980.

(3) By the period 1990–1995, approximately 15 casino hotels would have received licenses and would be in operation.

(4) Of the 15 licensed casino hotel operations, 8 would be newly constructed hotels and 7 refurbished hotels.

(5) Licensing requirements by the Florida casino control agency would call for a minimum of 400 to 500 hotel rooms and a minimum of 30,000 to 40,000 square feet of casino floor space, plus appropriate theaters, exhibition space and public areas. Freestanding casinos and other detrimental aspects of casino gaming would not be permitted.

(6) The gaming control agency would be self-supporting by annual license fees and investigation assessments. The fees were calculated at two percent of gross gaming revenues.

(7) Florida would receive six percent of the total gaming revenues, to be used for purposes to be identified in state legislation which would implement the results of the referendum. (Economic Research Associates 1978a; Let's Help Florida Committee 1978a)

The legalization model and the advertised benefits were generally similar to the successful New Jersey model. In New Jersey, a special fund provision of the legalization proposal had earmarked the state's tax revenues from casinos for senior citizens and the disabled. In Florida, the taxes were to be set aside for education and law enforcement. In this way, the prolegalization Let's Help Florida Committee hoped to counter a major source of opposition: that the increase in legal gambling would lead to a rise in street crime, organized crime, and public corruption, and that whatever revenues were produced would merely be offset by the rising costs of local law enforcement. The education and law enforcement provision had a special attraction for voters. The special fund would be divided into equal parts among all sixty-seven Florida counties (Let's Help Florida Committee 1978b). This meant that the population-rich south Florida area—particularly Dade and Broward counties, which include Miami, Miami Beach, and the surrounding suburbs—would receive the same share as less populated counties in the central and northern areas of the state. In this way, the casino proponents were promising those counties that would not directly benefit from casinos—by way of jobs, increased tourism, and construction—a greater share of the tax revenues.

For Dade County, there would still be enough of a reward, according to the procasino advertisements: a $147,734,000 increase in tax revenue to Dade County, with a 39.2% decrease in county property tax or an increase in services and a stabilization of rent; $37 million annually directly paid to the Dade County schools; 89,000 new jobs for Dade residents, and $1.7 billion in new payrolls; and $3.7 billion spent on construction of hotels, apartments, and houses (Let's Help Florida Committee 1978b). These features were meant to duplicate some of the successful steps in the New Jersey legalization process and the Nevada gaming control and taxation structure (Weiner 1978b). But if the success of New Jersey was to be duplicated in Florida, these measures would have to be sold to a population far different politically, religiously, and culturally in a state that was not suffering a fiscal crisis.

Florida's Economic and Political Profile

Florida is the eighth largest state, with a population in 1978 of 8,661,000. Its per capita income of $5,638 in 1975 ranked twenty-eighth in the country, in the middle of the fifty states, but second highest in the Southeast region, the poorest sector of the country (U.S. Department of Commerce 1976). The tax burden in Florida is relatively light, evidenced by its standing as forty-third for the percentage of personal income in support of government services. Even more significantly, this percentage was being reduced in the 1970s, at the same time that the national average was rising. Similar reduction in property tax burdens was experienced in only four other states— Idaho, Kansas, North Dakota, and South Dakota—none the size or stature of Florida (Greater Miami 1978). Between 1967 and 1975, Florida's per capita property tax revenues grew at an annual rate of 5.2%, 34% below the national average increase. Only nine states experienced lower annual increases. The property-tax burden in Florida remained relatively constant between 1942 and 1975, while the national average grew by 21.6%.

In 1974–1975, Florida ranked forty-first in the country per capita total general expenditures, forty-eighth in public welfare expenditures, thirty-ninth in funds spent on highways, thirty-fifth in aid to all education, twelfth in money spent for police protection and twenty-third in fire protection, and eighth in spending for health and hospitals. This last figure probably reflects the unique characteristics of the Florida population—Florida ranks first in the nation in the percentage of citizens over 65, with 15.7% of the population so classified, and last in the concentration of school-aged population (Greater Miami 1978). At the same time, Miami was just beginning to emerge as an important international trade and banking center, a development welcomed by the Miami Chamber of Commerce and leaders of the business community there (Chapman 1978; Hall Graphics 1978; Bomar 1979). Eleven U.S. banks had opened Miami branches during the last decade to cater to the Latin trade and eight foreign banks had opened similar branches; cargo shipments out of Miami—80% of which go to Latin American countries—tripled in the 1970s; Miami had become the key U.S. link with South America. Only New York, among U.S. cities, had more banks specializing in international transactions (Peterson 1978). Florida boasts more miles of coastline than any state except Alaska. This has meant historically that it enjoys a relative amount of autonomy from its southern neighbors, since it borders states only at its northern extreme. Those miles of coastline have also made Florida a most hospitable state for drug trafficking (*New York Times*, August 17, 1981).

Florida has been described as a combination of four relatively distinct social and political areas. The northernmost section—the Panhandle—stretches from Jacksonville on the east coast, through Gainesville and Tallahassee, to Pensacola—Reubin Askew's hometown—on the western side and is considered typically southern politically. It has been described as a rural redneck area and is heavily populated by strict Baptists who are largely registered as Democrats (Krog 1979). In an August 1978 poll, residents of this area opposed casino legalization by a fifty-nine to twenty-eight margin (Hamilton 1978a). The middle section of the state begins at Daytona Beach in the east, winds through Orlando, Tampa, St. Petersburg, and Sarasota, and ends in Fort Myers. It is often referred to as the "I-4 Corridor," from the name of the interstate freeway that connects those cities. This region contains about 50–60% of the eligible voting population in Florida and is the fastest-growing portion of the state, with a diversified economy. It was identified as the most important target area by the governor's no-casino committee (Markel 1979). Further south, on the east coast, are the affluent, condominium-laden suburbs of West Palm Beach and Fort Lauderdale, which are traditionally conservative. Ironically, residents of these upper Gold Coast suburbs favored the legalization of casinos by 50–45% in the August

1978 poll (Hamilton 1978a), suggesting inaccuracy or lack of conceptual clarity in the "conservative" label. Finally, at the southernmost tip of the state is the area that most outsiders associate with Florida—Miami and Miami Beach, which are heavily Cuban and Jewish, easily the most urban population in the state. Not surprisingly, this area, which would have the most to gain directly from legalization and included a high proportion of those voters—particularly Catholics and Jews—who were culturally predisposed toward gambling, favored casino gambling by a sixty-two to thirty-five margin in the August survey (Hamilton 1978a).

It was this southernmost section of the state that would be most directly helped by legalization of casinos, since the economic benefits of construction and service industry employment—and especially increased tourism—would go to southern Florida residents. The city that would be aided most was Miami Beach, a hotel resort area that, while in no way comparable in its decline to Atlantic City in 1976, was nonetheless fading as a premier vacation and convention tourist destination. To understand its decline, and its needed revitalization, we need to examine the wider context of Florida tourism, a relatively stable and healthy industry in the late 1970s.

The Southern Florida Tourist Economy

According to the figures of the 1972 National Travel Survey, Florida ranked third in the United States behind California and Texas as a travel destination (Economics Research Associates 1978a). When one considers only the number of person-nights that travelers spend, Florida ranked second, behind only California.

Miami Beach hotel trade depends heavily upon New York tourists. A survey conducted in 1975 by Florida International University researchers concluded that 28% of visitors to Miami Beach resided in the New York metropolitan area, while another 20% came from New England and other mid-Atlantic states (Florida International University 1975). Approximately 22% of the Miami Beach visitors were foreign, Latin America being most represented (Miami-Metro 1977). The long distance between Miami Beach and its prime market area of the Northeast is highlighted by the dependence of the Miami Beach trade upon air traffic—80% of hotel guests in Miami Beach arrive by airplane (Economics Research Associates 1978a). This also indicates a relatively high level of affluence of the clientele.

While the number of tourists visiting Florida increased through the 1960s and 1970s—Florida Department of Commerce figures estimate that 12.8 million persons visited the state in 1961, while 28.9 million came in 1976—the number of tourists arriving in Miami by automobile declined from 4.6

million in 1970 to 2.8 million in 1974 (Economics Research Associates 1978a). One explanation for this may be the increased air traffic, and another is the energy crisis of the winter of 1974.

In the 1950s and 1960s, when Miami Beach tourist and convention traffic was at its peak, the major resort hotels offered the best accommodations and convention facilities to be found in the world. Each of the area's largest hotels—the Fontainebleau, the Eden Roc, the Carillon, the Deauville, the Doral Beach, and the Konover, all built between 1955 and 1967 and all located on Collins Avenue between 44th and 69th streets—featured pools and private beach areas, fine restaurants, and ample shopping facilities.

The tourist season, because of Miami's southern location and climate, was at its peak in the winter months, when affluent tourists—mainly from the northeastern and north-central states, many of them Jewish, most of them middle-aged or older—filled the hotels. During the summer months, the clientele was younger, family-oriented, and more local southern. During the fall and spring months, convention business helped to fill in the tourist traffic. Miami Beach resort tax collections for 1976–1977 confirm this pattern: 42% of the resort tax was collected during the peak months of January, February, and March, and only 16% during August, September, and October (Economics Research Associates 1978a).

While Miami Beach still attracts a sizable number of tourist and convention visitors—in particular still holding on to its traditional base of northeastern middle-aged winter long-term visitors—it experienced a notable decline during the 1970s. Several reasons have been suggested to account for this decline.

First was the issue of competing tourist areas. One need not look beyond Florida to find reasons for a decline in Miami Beach's tourist volume. With the opening of Walt Disney World in Orlando in 1972, central Florida has become one of the most popular tourist attractions in the world. Some of the families and motorists who might have considered visiting the Miami Beach area may find that, after a few days at Disney World, they lack the desire and money to push further south.

With the advent of airline travel, several resort areas in the Caribbean as well as Europe, Hawaii, and Mexico are readily accessible and more attractive to the affluent winter visitor Miami Beach depended upon. Even some lesser-known resort developments in the South and Southeast have become increasingly competitive with Miami Beach because they offer new facilities catering to more active pursuits—golf, tennis, skiing, sky diving, and sailing—that are available to a lesser degree in the Miami Beach area. Even the convention traffic, which had remained relatively constant during the 1970s, began to show signs of decline in 1977. A reduced level of advanced booking indicated that Miami Beach convention activities could be facing a dramatic decline due to lack of first-class hotel accommodations and the increased competition presented by cities such as Atlanta and New Orleans, which have better facilities.

A second reason was the aging of clientele. It has already been noted that the Miami Beach tourists, in peak seasons particularly, were predominantly middle-aged or older. A 1975 survey found only 18% under 34 years of age, and only 49% under 49. After excluding the convention visitors, the figures are astounding: 64% of the remaining "pleasure" guests are over 50 (Economics Research Associates 1978a). As these tourists have grown older, many are unable to travel to southern Florida, for reasons of health or budget. These visitors are not being replaced by their children or by other young tourists, who are attracted to more active resort areas and who particularly do not want to vacation in what is seen as an "old people's" vacation spot.

The third factor was the decline in tourist facilities. The last major hotel constructed in Miami Beach was the Konover in 1967. Most of the major hotels, about twenty years old, are becoming obsolete. Some hotel owners have chosen not to invest in improvements. Several others were overextended in other investments, unable to afford suitable renovations. There is only one major hotel chain in Miami Beach—Holiday Inn. While the older tourist trade fails to replace its dwindling numbers with younger visitors, the lack of identifiable chain hotels serves to move the Miami Beach hotels one step further from potential clientele. The financial troubles are highlighted by the fact that, between 1974 and 1978, twelve Miami Beach hotels went bankrupt and seven were demolished (Economics Research Associates 1978a).

Given these factors, and facing an imminent decline, Miami Beach hotel officials and developers saw in the prospect of legalization a chance for southern Florida to regain some of its lost prominence in the resort trade. In view of the miraculous revitalization of Atlantic City, it was no idle promise. Entrepreneurs like Charles Rosen, the manager of the Marco Polo Hotel, embraced the Atlantic City model of resort redevelopment: "We deserve to be cut in. Tourists are standing in line in Atlantic City, but here they only trickle in" (Koten 1978).

The Economics Research Associates study commissioned by the Let's Help Florida Committee proposed the legalization of casino gambling as a natural remedy for the decline of Miami Beach: "As demonstrated in this report, Miami Beach has in recent years experienced a decline in its tourist trade. This trend is expected to continue, possibly at an accelerated rate. A major reason for Miami Beach's declining tourist appeal is the historical lack of reinvestment into the local economy, especially into the hotel/motel industry. The existing situation calls for policy stimulus to induce investment into the local economy, in order to upgrade Miami Beach's declining image. Without such a stimulus, private investors are unlikely to invest into the economy, leading to further deterioration in Miami Beach facilities, thus a further decline in tourist appeal, and so the spiral begins" (Economics Research Associates 1978a).

Let's Help Florida Committee

The key procasino campaign document involved a series of estimates prepared by Economics Research Associates that projected the amount of business that legalization would bring, directly and indirectly, to southern Florida. The legalization of casino gambling, under strict controls and a well-devised program, was said to be able to provide the best means for reversing the decline of Miami Beach, spurring significant new investments, and reestablishing its reputation as a premier resort on the southeastern seaboard. With the exception of $47,000 contributed by hotel service industries and $55,000 from assorted businesses, Let's Help Florida ended up depending exclusively on the financing by hotel interests: over $2 million (Let's Help Florida 1978c).

The increase in new hotel demand resulting from the legalization of casinos would be reflected by three figures: direct casino hotel demand; tourist-related nongambling hotel demand due to new facilities and increased tourist-oriented stock; and increases in new convention activities due to gambling-induced new attractions in Miami Beach.

ERA estimated that the number of daily visitors to casinos in Miami Beach in 1990 would be more than 22 million (Economics Research Associates 1978b). Adjusting for the percentage that would be staying overnight in Miami and other factors, ERA estimated that the influx of casino-related tourists would require the use of 27,000 more hotel rooms than current visitation patterns. Miami Beach's overnight tourism business had declined in real dollars. The rehabilitation of the hotel area, to a first-class competitive status, would encourage more business from tourists who visit the Miami area to enjoy the overall amenities, not just to gamble. The advent of legalized gambling would create both investments in hotel stock and the atmosphere and environment that would again place Miami Beach in a position to recapture the prominence it once held as a major convention city and replicate the enduring success of Las Vegas and the recent success of Atlantic City in gaining new convention bookings.

Overall, "given the advent of a positive casino gambling program with attendant investments in tourism support facilities and amenities," ERA predicted the following levels (which compared favorably with Las Vegas and Atlantic City levels) of annual visitation by the 1990–1995 period (Economics Research Associates 1978b):

Visitors Primarily for Casino Gambling	4,700,000
Convention Delegates	540,000
Visitors Primarily as Tourists	5,200,000
	10,440,000

The projection of increased room demand would lead to new investment potentials and additions to the hotel room stock as follows (Economics Research Associates 1978b):

New Casino Hotels	$320,000,000	4,000 Rooms
Refurbished Casino Hotels	70,000,000	2,800 Rooms
New Noncasino Support Hotels	244,000,000	8,000 Rooms

Excluding wages, estimated at $450,000,000 annually during the 1990–1995 period, ERA predicted that input into the Miami Beach economy during the 1990–1995 period would be $778,000,000 annually (Economics Research Associates 1978b):

Direct Hotel Employment	21,760
in Casino Hotels	
Support Hotels without Casinos	9,600
Service Employment	47,040
Retail Employment	10,400
	88,800

The ERA report concluded: "This compares to a current level of some 20,000 persons employed in the hotel industry on a seasonal basis and suggests that the average rate of unemployment, ranging from 9.2 to 11.6 percent, could be substantially reduced, given new employment opportunities accruing from the economic leverage of a casino gambling program."

Payrolls would increase (Economics Research Associates 1978b):

Hotel Transient Accommodations	$310,000,000
Service Sector Additions	329,300,000
Retail Additions	83,200,000
	722,500,000

Revenues would also increase: $54 million annually (6%, at $900 million gross gambling revenues); $18 million for administrative purposes (2%, excluding initial investigative fees—borne by casino applicants); and $8.2 million to Miami Beach property tax revenues, given new hotel stock—an increase of 40% over present levels.

After adding increases in sales and use tax, legalization would account for the following (Economics Research Associates 1978b:5–9):

Revenue	$54,000,000
Administration	18,000,000
Sales and Use Tax	48,100,000
	120,100,000

"Based on the foregoing analyses and projections of economic activity," the ERA report concluded, "a well-conceived gaming program with attendant stringent controls can be a major catalyst in reversing current trends and also be a major stimulant to the city and to the Dade County visitor industry" (Economics Research Associates 1978b).

This was the revitalization that the Let's Help Florida Committee envisioned when it began its campaign. Speaking to an audience gathered for a debate on the prospects of legalized casino gambling in south Florida, Sanford Weiner talked about the opening of the Resorts International Casino in Atlantic City the week before: "I saw a dream come true last week. I saw an economically deprived area come alive, people enjoying a legitimate and respectable activity" (Tobin 1978). Less than a year after his victory in guiding the New Jersey casino referendum to ballot success, Weiner had been invited to Florida by a group of Gold Coast hotelmen, including the Diplomat's Irwin Cowan, who promised to raise more than $1 million for a casino campaign that would attempt to sell Floridians on the same benefits that attracted the New Jersey electorate in 1976. Weiner's initial estimation was that casinos in Florida could produce from $80 million to $140 million annually for the state, depending upon the number of casinos and their hours of operation. To a Miami Beach area that was declining in ability to attract tourists, was in the process of "going condominium," and was experiencing a number of bankruptcies and receiverships among its hotels, the attractiveness of revenues, jobs, and economic development from casinos—the same magic that had turned Atlantic City into a boomtown—would be emphasized.

Weiner knew immediately that he was dealing with a problem of image: "The people of Florida have a terrible image of Miami Beach. But that cuts to a positive. People are going to say, 'If we're going to get gambling, let's stick it down there'" (Bearak 1978). His assessment was that there were polarized sides early in the campaign: that there were strong pockets of opposition—particularly among white Baptists—and pockets of support, from Jews and Latins. Weiner expected from the start to do poorly in the Panhandle area, but to do well in southern Florida. He acknowledged that the area to be won over was central Florida, and groups—like Florida's black population—that formed the undecided bloc. Weiner expressed initial optimism about the nature of the opposition to gambling. He felt that he had faced less church opposition in New Jersey, but acknowledged the potential power of attack from the media, especially the *Miami Herald*, committed to the fight against casinos. Still, Weiner felt that the changing face of the media, with the emphasis on television, would serve to minimize the effect of the *Herald's* opposition: "TV is more important. But TV editorials can be countered with TV spots" (Weiner 1978b).

The first step in the casino campaign for the proponents was to qualify an initiative for the November ballot. This effort required 255,653 signatures—8% of those Florida voters who cast ballots in the previous presidential election—on a "Constitutional Amendment Petition Form," to be filed with the Florida secretary of state. The petition would qualify a ballot proposition that called for the creation of Article X, Section 15, of the Florida constitution, which would permit "the operation of state regulated privately owned gambling casinos," within a specified area: along a narrow stretch in Dade and Broward counties, on one side of Collins Avenue, the main thoroughfare stretching north from Miami Beach, along the beach (Let's Help Florida 1978d). Taxes from the operation of gambling casinos would be appropriated to "several" counties for the support and maintenance of free public schools and local law enforcement.

Those voters who signed petitions were also provided with a series of questions and answers about the operation and impact of casinos. Some were distributed in newspaper advertisements, like the one reading, "Miami Beach Resort Hotel Association Says We Can All Be Part of Florida's Brighter Economic Future. Join Us . . . Let's Help Florida with Legalized Casinos along Florida's Gold Coast."

Q. How much money can the state make from taxes on casinos? What will be the total economic impact on the state?

A. The state will be collecting about $120 million annually just from the casino operations. Projections include 89,000 new permanent, full-time jobs; an increased payroll of $772 million, and nearly triple visitor levels for the state.

Q. Who will police the casinos? And who will pay for the policing?

A. The state will enact laws to license and regulate casino operations. Casino operators will pay for the cost of regulation—taxpayers will not. (Let's Help Florida 1978c)

Despite expectations that Governor Askew would oppose casinos, there was hope early in the campaign among Let's Help Florida strategists that the state Democratic party, at least in Dade County, would officially support casinos, an enormous boost in a state in which more than half the voters were registered Democrats (Elfman 1978). Above all, LHF's strategy was to establish projections about new jobs and increased tourism and about the strict controls that would be enacted. Proponents, recalling the 1976 New Jersey experience, might presume that the opposition would attack the morality of gambling and miss the mark by being overly emotional, in comparison to the rational fiscal arguments of LHF. Still, they had two primary fears: Askew's opposition and his power to mobilize others, and the organized crime issue. As the legislation campaign unfolded, it would become clear that these fears were far from unfounded.

Limited Opposition to Legalization

Gold Coast hotel owners were reluctant at the campaign's start to embrace casino gambling publicly. *Miami Beach Sun-Reporter* publisher Harry Buchel explained: "A lot of people have seen casino gambling just tied in with organized crime and there are a lot of people afraid to stand up and talk about the issue for fear of being painted with the same broad brush. . . . I think as Sandy [Weiner] becomes more vocal and visible and people realize a bolt of lightning isn't going to come out of the heavens and strike you dead because you spoke up for casino gambling, you're going to see more people be less fearful and speak up" (LaBrecque 1978).

Weiner had an answer to the fears: "Organized crime makes money where there's illegal—not legal—gambling" (Prugh 1978). He took a chance, presuming that Florida voters were willing, as New Jersey voters had been, to look the other way and not be concerned with organized crime participation in the legal casino industry or to dissociate organized crime from legalized gambling.

Casino advocates hoped that they would have to contend with a level of opposition that typified the church arguments: "Casino gambling will turn this area into a veritable cesspool of rot and filth" (Koten 1978). Weiner believed that his campaign could withstand the opposition forces if they were limited to ministers, or competing gambling interests, or the likes of FACT's chairman, who took to debates on legalization with a flashy style of argument and the prediction that the state would fall prey to an influx of organized criminals (Tobin 1978). Indeed, one slogan of FACT was "casinos corrupt" (FACT 1978). And Dade County public safety director (police chief) E. Wilson Purdy warned that "a vote for casino gambling will be a vote to turn this community over to organized crime" (FACT 1978). This was backed up with the analysis of Florida organized crime expert and author

Hank Messick, who wrote, "The whole history of gambling shows it is impossible to regulate and keep honest. The very nature of gambling attracts gangsters: a cash business, with odds favoring the house and money easily manipulated" (FACT 1978).

FACT emphasized the organized crime issue in its literature. Casinos will draw organized crime, "just like blood attracting sharks . . . there's no way you can keep them out" (FACT 1978). Although gambling backers said that casinos would be a bonanza for education and law enforcement funds, Dade County's annual share would not be enough to run the school system for half a day. FACT accused the procasino forces of promoting the image of Miami Beach as a dying resort to win the gambling fight. Miami Beach was not dying—much of its fading popularity was the fault of the same hotels whose owners were pushing for casinos: "It would be a tragedy to sell the soul of South Florida to fill 5 Miami Beach hotels" (*Oakland Tribune* 1978).

Sporting a button reading "Keep the Casino Mob Out," FACT chairman Jay Dermer said, "We will not allow the mob to wade ashore across the beaches of Florida" (*Oakland Tribune* 1978). Dermer and others concentrated on this idea of the "invasion" of organized crime into Florida and connected it with their criticism of Weiner and his chief campaign operative Sam Vitali as being "outsiders" and "hired guns."

One of FACT's problems, however, was its connection to Florida parimutuel interests. In Florida, unlike New Jersey, a well-entrenched parimutuel racing industry had much to fear from legalization of casinos. When the first forms of gambling were legalized early in the 1970s, there were few problems of competition for the legal gambling dollar. By and large, those states that legalized one major form of gambling did not also permit a second one that might divert some of the state revenues from the first. With the proposal to legalize casinos in southern Florida, however, there would be some problems, at least if one believed the owners and operators of Florida horse racing tracks. "No pari-mutuel could exist in the face of casinos," David Hecht, owner of the Flagler Dog Track, told the *Miami News*. "It would kill us" (Douthat 1978).

In light of this threat to their livelihood, pari-mutuel owners were among the largest contributors to the anticasino drive, in the organizational form of People against Casinos (PACT). While this was far from the most prominent or successful of the four opposition groups, it may have spent enough money on campaign television spots—nearly $700,000—to make a difference. The pari-mutuel issue became an important topic of debate. The Let's Help Florida Committee tried to reassure voters that the casinos would not cut into pari-mutuel earnings and subsequent revenues (Economics Research

Associates 1978d). The amount of money that pari-mutuels poured into the Florida economy in 1976–1977 was sizable (Economics Research Associates 1978d):

	Total Paid Attendance	Total Pari-mutuel Handle	Total State Revenues
Florida	$16,276,898	$1,244,159,788	$86,558,021
South Florida	8,799,290	738,782,729	51,404,650

Casinos would promise to be even more competitive with the frontons and tracks for several reasons. Unlike pari-mutuel systems, which keep 10%, casinos do not take a sizable bite out of each gambling dollar for overhead, administrative costs, and taxes; money won at a race track is immediately taxable by the IRS, making it more difficult for a winner to evade taxes on winnings; and casino patrons are attracted by the free admission, free drinks, and star entertainers.

The Let's Help Florida Committee did not evade the questions of the competition for gambling dollars, arguing instead that the horse tracks should be competitive to survive and that Florida should not engage in a form of protectionism by favoring the horse tracks through local state opposition to casinos. If bettors were to choose the casinos, the argument went, it would only be a matter of time before they left the horse tracks anyway. Let's Help Florida estimated in addition that the majority of the casino gamblers would be visitors, while the mainstay of the tracks were Florida residents, a contention supported by surveys that showed that 75% to 85% of the track bettors were Florida residents (Economics Research Associates 1978d).

Robert Shawn of Economics Research Associates, arguing from statistics gathered and estimates prepared for Let's Help Florida, predicted that casinos would have a ripple effect and contribute to a *rise* in pari-mutuel wagering. "Casino gambling and pari-mutuel wagering," Shawn said, "represent complementary forms of entertainment" (Economics Research Associates 1978d). To support his ripple effect, he referred to the report of the Commission on the Review of the National Policy toward Gambling, which had noted that gamblers do not restrict themselves to one game or another.

The issue of the pari-mutuels was not even raised in the PACT anticasino material. Their nine points for opposition were (People against Casinos 1978):

(1) Casino gambling would spread, like cancer, throughout Florida;
(2) Casino gambling promotes crime—and also human misery;
(3) Casino gambling is a breeding ground for organized crime;
(4) Casino gambling would destroy our quality of life;
(5) Casino gambling would be very costly to Florida's older citizens;

(6) Casino gambling will be bad for the young people in Florida;
(7) Casino gambling can be devastating to poorer and middle-class families;
(8) Casino gambling will darken the economic future of Florida;
(9) Casino gambling will cost Florida much more than it ever contributes.

PACT commissioned polls by President Carter's pollster Patrick Caddell that found the public's greatest underlying concern was a fear that organized crime would infiltrate the state. PACT's campaign spots would portray the coming of casinos as a near-apocalyptic disaster—hard-sell ads showing kids gambling at slot machines. PACT members would think that Askew's campaign was too middle-of-the-road (Krog 1979).

Legalization opponents dropped the pari-mutuel issue because they feared they would fall into the trap of having to defend a campaign that might be seen as protecting pari-mutuel operators, who could easily be portrayed as entrenched, powerful, anticompetitive forces. The director of Askew's No Casinos organization acknowledged that this was one reason for establishing a separate No Casinos group that did not, by policy, accept contributions from pari-mutuels (Krog 1979). Instead, track owners wishing to contribute were directed to PACT. In this way, Askew could be kept free of the pari-mutuel money and opposition. He had included the pari-mutuel issue in his earlier speeches—those prior to the June breakfast meeting—but dropped it later as a matter of campaign strategy (Askew 1978a).

Askew seemed to be either confused or ambivalent about the pari-mutuel issue, or at least tried to use the issue to attack the casino proposition from many sides. He tried to say that pari-mutuels were enough: "We have already crossed the bridge on the moral question of gambling with pari-mutuels. But that does not mean we have to go all the way" (Askew 1978a). Then, in the same speech, delivered in February to an "anticasino luncheon," he talked about the revenues that pari-mutuels contributed to the state—$87 million during the 1976–1977 fiscal year—and how little the state had to spend to regulate pari-mutuels—$1.9 million, less than 2% of what the state derived in revenue. Then he stressed the fact that pari-mutuels support other industries, particularly legal ones: "But pari-mutuels in Florida do not merely provide revenue for the state. They support a $300 million industry that breeds, raises, trains and trades greyhounds and horses. What kind of industries, I might ask, are supported by casinos?" All of this was within the logic of legitimizing pari-mutuels, especially captured by his summary description of Florida pari-mutuel wagering: "Carefully regulated and controlled pari-mutuel wagering has long been a reliable source of revenue and a familiar source of entertainment in Florida" (Askew 1978a).

Or, as Askew supporters put it, pari-mutuels are scandal-free and respectable.

Since PACT relied only on pari-mutuel backing, and FACT had accepted campaign contributions from pari-mutuel interests, these two organizations had to be distanced from Askew's new campaign so that he could "straight-shot" casino gambling. For that campaign to be successful, he emphasized, it needed to be well financed.

Well-Financed Opposition to Legalization

Aside from the pari-mutuel interests, Askew's campaign—through his No Casinos group and the Miami Chamber of Commerce's Casinos Are Bad Business organization—received contributions from four major sectors of the Florida economy (Division of Elections 1978):

Financial Institutions	$261,800
Tourist Attractions	50,000
Media	220,000
Other Business	160,000

Financial institutions were well represented in the anticasino fight; nine of them for over $10,000:

Florida Savings and Loan Association (St. Petersburg)	$25,000
First Federal Savings and Loan Association of Broward County	$25,000
Southeast Banking Corporation (Miami)	$25,000
First Federal Savings and Loan Association of Miami	$25,000
Chase Federal Savings and Loan Association (Miami)	$25,000
Freedom Federal Savings and Loan Association (Tampa)	$15,000
Flagship Banks, Inc. (Miami Beach)	$10,000
First Federal Savings of the Palm Beaches	$10,000
United First Federal Savings and Loan Association (Sarasota)	$10,000

Eleven others contributed $5,000 or more, and an additional fourteen gave between $1,000 and $5,000.

Three points should be made about Florida's banking community, and bankers in general, and their relationship to the legal casino industry. (1) They were associates of Askew, partners in his eight-year project to make Florida a thriving international banking and trade center for the western hemisphere; (2) institutional lenders had historically been reluctant to consider the casino gambling industry as less than suspect, because of its organized criminal roots and association, its propensity toward skimming in a business not unlike banking in its cash flow, and its lack of internal controls;

(3) casinos could rival banks as financial institutions—already drug importers were depositing large sums of money, mainly in $100 bills, in southern Florida banks.

In New Jersey, the indigenous media—especially Atlantic City newspapers—supported legalization. In Florida, by comparison, the media played a major and controversial opposing role. The print and electronic media of Florida were one of the major contributors to the anticasino effort, both in money and in time. Alvah Chapman, publisher of the *Miami Herald* and a friend and advisor of Askew, contributed $25,000 initially to the campaign and contacted friends and business colleagues to do the same (Chapman 1978). The fact that he was publisher of the state's major daily newspaper did not deter Chapman from taking a stand on the issue, and his stand infuriated the LHF group, which pointed to the influence—which they said was improper—of the media as a major reason for the defeat of the measure (Let's Help Florida 1978d). A total of $191,000 was contributed by major Florida newspapers.

No Casinos, Inc.

Time Publishing Company, St. Petersburg	$25,000
Tribune Company, Tampa	25,000
Florida Times-Union, Jacksonville	25,000
Wometco Enterprises, Inc. (WTVJ, Channel 4), Miami	25,000
Palm Beach Newspapers, Inc. (*Palm Beach Post-Times*) West Palm Beach	12,500
Sentinel Star Company, Orlando	12,500
Gore Newspaper Company (*Fort Lauderdale News-Sun Sentinel*)	12,500
Miami News, Miami	12,500
Miami Herald Publishing Co. (owned by Knight-Ridder Newspapers), Miami	10,000
James L. Knight (chairman of the board of the Miami Herald Publishing Co.), Miami	5,000
Bradenton Herald (owned by Knight-Ridder Newspapers)	3,000
Tallahassee Democrat (owned by Knight-Ridder Newspapers)	3,000
Boca Raton News (owned by Knight-Ridder Newspapers)	3,000
Mr. and Mrs. Alvah H. Chapman, Jr. (president, Miami Herald Publishing Co.)	2,500
Mrs. A. H. Chapman (mother of Alvah H. Chapman, Jr., president of the Miami Herald Publishing Co.), Columbus, GA	2,000
News-Journal Corporation, Daytona Beach	1,000
Dan Mahoney, Jr. (publisher, *Palm Beach Post-Times*)	1,000
Trend Publications	250
	$180,750

Chapman, who nearly sparked a mutiny of reporters and editors at the *Herald* with his action, expressed his rationale this way: he could not sit back and watch the well-financed LHF campaign change the face of Florida. As a publisher, he explained, he was a businessman—not a media mogul—and his financial contribution and activism represented his conclusion as a businessman that the introduction of casinos into the Miami area would be a serious threat to the south Florida economy and an equally serious threat to the future economic health of his publishing enterprise (Chapman 1978). He said: "Newspapers, in addition to their basic role of covering the news, are also business enterprises and have a stake in the community they serve" (*St. Petersburg Times* 1978). Chapman referred again to the New Jersey experience when he said that he was motivated in part by the need to educate the public to make a well-reasoned decision: this meant that the *Herald* was responsible not only for running a number of serious and balanced stories about the casino issue, but also for contributing to a fund against casinos.

The statewide steering committee chairman for the LHF, journalist and columnist Jim Bishop, filed a formal complaint with the National News Council, charging the *Herald* and Chapman with attempting to influence the outcome of the referendum issue through his direct contributions. Askew aides argued that Atlantic city papers had contributed to procasino efforts— The *Press* gave $45,000 in 1976—and said that the gambling referendum was not an ordinary issue. Chapman and other publishers argued that they supported candidates and other referendum issues and that their support for one side of an issue or for one candidate did not affect the coverage of the newspaper's editorial staff (Chapman 1978b). *St. Petersburg Times* and *Evening Independent* executive editor Robert Haimon said, "We endorse candidates all the time, and support or oppose referendum items, but that does not in the least inhibit our reporters" (McMahon 1978). Gore Newspapers Company (*Fort Lauderdale News and Sun-Sentinel*) president and chief executive officer Byron Campbell added: "We feel our news stories have been straight down the middle and they will continue to be, regardless of the contributions we have pledged." Florida Publishing Company (*Florida Times-Union* and *Jacksonville Journal*) chairman J. J. Daniel said: "The editorial pages are ours and the others belong to the public. We will continue to publish objectively" (*Valley Times*, August 31, 1978). Those in the editorial department who protested the *Herald*'s policies were more concerned that Chapman had undercut them by giving their paper the semblance of a slanted presentation.

John Lake, editor of the *St. Petersburg Times*, said in defense of his newspaper's contribution: "This campaign is unique. Newspapers take on a corporate responsibility in Florida that is different than in a heavily industrialized state. We are obligated to consider the long-range development of this state and convert this fragile tourist economy into something significant. Industrialization and casinos aren't compatible" (Prugh 1978).

The Organized Crime Question

Miami had been designated in the 1930s by organized criminal syndicate leaders as an "open city," not under the territorial control of any one organized criminal organization. Recent drug traffic estimates show it to still be—because of its proximity to South American drug sources and miles of coastline where boats can deliver contraband relatively undetected—a center of underground economic activity. Federal drug officials put a $4 billion a year estimate on south Florida's cocaine and marijuana imports, and south Florida banks have been called the "Wall Street" of the dope trade.

As a winter resort spot, Miami Beach became a favorite meeting place for America's most notorious gangsters, many of whom were anxious to escape the bleak climates of their native Chicago or New York environs. During the 1940s, mob-controlled casinos ran openly in Dade and Broward counties, with the cooperation of law enforcement officials. Because of its proximity to Cuba, southern Florida had been a natural meeting place and jumping off point for those organized criminal entrepreneurs—Meyer Lansky was a Miami Beach resident for many years—who had a financial stake in pre-Castro Cuban casinos.

Lansky's presence in Florida in 1978 was extremely important to the framing of the organized crime question. He had been indicted, along with other Miami Beach hotelmen, for conspiring to skim $36 million from Las Vegas casinos (*U.S.* v. *Meyer Lansky et al.* 1974); he was believed to be a driving force behind Miami-based Resorts International, the casino corporation that operates a Bahama casino and was suspected of controlling several influential politicians there—the prime minister among them—and had opened the first Atlantic City casino (Department of Law and Public Safety 1978); he was linked, through Miami restaurateur and businessman Alvin Malnik—referred to in law enforcement as Lansky's "lieutenant"—to Caesars World, the corporation that owned and operated Las Vegas's lavish Caesars Palace (Nevada State Gaming Control Board, Audit Division 1976). Lansky's opinion on legalization was actually made public in the Miami press: the mob would not infiltrate legalized casino gambling in Florida, Lansky explained, "because there is no such thing as organized crime" (Sosin 1978).

Florida law enforcement officials felt otherwise. A Florida Department of Criminal Law Enforcement report said legitimate casino operations would probably draw upon the criminal element for the management skills of running a casino. One drug enforcement official stated: "We have a whole lot of organized crime figures here who have the experience of running casinos in Cuba. It would be safe to say they already have their foot in the door (Messerschmidt 1978). Later in the campaign, when the polls showed that legalization would not pass, a bombshell was dropped in a Washington Committee hearing. On October 24, 1978, convicted narcotics smuggler John Charles Piazza III told the U.S. Senate Permanent Subcommittee on Organized Crime that in 1974 he had discussed plans with Meyer Lansky at a meeting at the Forge, Malnik's restaurant in Miami, to act as a front for a casino legalization drive—and to skim for Lansky, once casino gambling was legalized (Messerschmidt 1978).

In the meantime, the *Herald* brought the organized crime question to the forefront, with articles that examined the potential for organized crime growth and accompanying political corruption as a result of casino legalization. Whether or not these articles reversed public opinion on the legalization issue, they did add an important element for the success of the anticasino campaign. Well-reported, clear, and professional, the articles provided a low-key informative background for the anticasino campaigns to draw upon when they raised the organized crime issues as a present, rather than a future, problem for Florida voters.

Effective Opposition: No Casinos and Casinos Are Bad Business

This section examines the ways in which the anticasino forces coalesced, decided on the level and issues of argument, and proceeded to campaign.

First, the opposition groups needed to identify those sections of the population that were predisposed to opposition and to determine the basis of their disapproval of legalization. A poll taken for the No Casinos group provides a look at the Florida population and their positions (Hamilton 1978a, b). Early indicators led opponents to select some of the population subgroups most likely to oppose casinos. Religious differences seemed marked: Catholics favored legalization by a fifty-four to forty-two margin, Jews by an even larger sixty-nine to twenty-four spread, while Protestants opposed it by a sizable fifty-seven to thirty-nine.

There was an increasing tendency to oppose casinos as one moved up the age ladder. The youngest age group, those 18 to 34, favored legalization by a fifty-nine to thirty-eight margin. Middle-aged voters, those between 35 and 49, were split, with opponents holding a slight forty-nine to forty-seven edge. Finally, those over 50 came down strongly in the camp of the opponents, by a fifty-nine to thirty-six margin.

Gender differences were significant. While men tended to favor legalization, fifty to forty-eight, women overwhelmingly opposed it, fifty-six to thirty-eight. White voters and black voters were close in their opposition—the former opposing legalization by fifty-two to forty-four, and the latter by fifty-seven to thirty-seven. Only Hispanics were shown to hold a preference, by fifty-five to forty. The strength of opinions was noteworthy as well: four out of five voters on each side held very strong opinions on the subject. One of the most important findings in this poll is the breakdown of reasons for opposition. The importance of morals and crime to opponents of casino gambling was measured by the question: "Are you mainly opposed to casino gambling on the moral issue—because it's not right—*or* because of a fear of the possible influx of organized crime?" Statewide, those choosing the moral issue alone amounted to only 14%, supporting Weiner's contention about the size of the morally opposed group. A much larger number—44%—noted "fear of crime" as their main reason for opposition. Given the option of combining the two, another 40% considered both the reason for opposition.

The ambivalence that has been noted historically in Americans' treatment of gambling surfaces again in the findings among the Florida electorate. Both proponents and opponents of the measure held positive *and* negative views of the issue. Statewide, more than 70% of those responding to the Hamilton poll volunteered a positive comment. However, the complication is in the crossover or ambivalence reflected among those who supported or rejected the idea. Among those favoring casinos, almost half—47%—mentioned some sort of disadvantage, primarily the potential for organized crime infiltration of the legalized casino industry or that legalization would attract "bad elements" generally. On the other extreme, about a third—32%—of those who opposed casinos volunteered a positive comment—such as generating revenue, lowering taxes, or creating jobs.

The Hamilton survey, commissioned by the forces seeking to defeat the casino gambling initiative, made several conclusions regarding campaign strategy. First of all, it indicated the magnitude of the task ahead and stressed the power of a well-financed procasino campaign: "with such a well organized and well financed proponent campaign, defeat on revision Number 9 will be tough." Next, it recommended a range of appeals to the various publics that should be approached on the issue. After consulting the figures for ethnic, racial, sex, and religious breakdown, the No Casino staff decided that the bulk of the campaign effort should take place in the following locations, listed in the order of importance: the lower West Coast, Hillsboro and Pinellas counties, the west central region, the east central region, and the Panhandle, and should be keyed to blacks, women, those over 50, retirees, and Republicans.

The analysis provided by the Hamilton staff about the debate concerned the two major issues: revenues and organized crime: "The proponents," they wrote, "can effectively use the Proposition 13 concept to wean away some of the opponents' base unless the beneficial economic aspects of casino gambling are discredited. At the same time, opponents of casinos should concentrate on explaining (or documenting) the various ways in which organized crime will be allowed to flourish and/or expand" (Hamilton 1978a, b).

The single aspect of increased or spreading criminal activity was the opponents' best issue on which to wean away proponents of the proposal. Only 7 to 8% of the voters volunteered that they thought casino gambling was evil and immoral; to a direct question about the relative importance of morality or fear of crime as the basis of their opposition, more than three times as many choose the crime factor rather than morality. While the morality issue might work through various opponent organizations, the pollsters noted, "it is the fear of crime which can have the broadest impact."

With this information in hand, legalization opponents established their campaign strategy. Askew's campaign manager figured that they needed between $650,000 and $800,000 for a successful advertising campaign. They started in July with a close vote in the polls, and also a discrepancy, which indicated some amount of confusion among the voting population. Casino opponents saw the need for an "education" process. They observed that the proponents had seven months of lead time in publicity. They stated that their earliest goal was to make it socially unacceptable for prominent Floridians to support casino gambling. They decided to concentrate on fund-raising and moving opinion leaders. The governor had to raise money early and spend it early. The campaign managed to buy prime TV spots— even over gubernatorial candidates—and decided to start early in the ads with the governor setting the moral tone (Krog 1979; Markel 1979).

Askew presented casino gambling to business leaders as a critical issue; he reminded them that the Florida economy was strong and that they really had no need to bring in another industry, particularly one with an unsavory reputation and financial history. The best issues, from the start and throughout the campaign, were crime and the effect of the economy, according to Askew's strategists. They felt that the proponents "led with their chin" with the economic figures they emphasized and that the best strategy the opponents had was to neutralize the proponents' economic arguments (Krog 1979). The opponents' decision not to launch a moral attack on the casinos was also well thought out and crucial. Askew's strategists acknowledged later that a moralistic appeal by Askew might have backfired. Consistent with that opinion, No Casinos strategists criticized PACT commercials for coming on too strong, with a style that no longer was convincing and would have overheated the issue.

A sample of a PACT TV commercial (October 19, 1978) gives an indication of why the Askew people feared the PACT attack would open the opponents to charges of exaggeration: "Florida, brace yourself. Las Vegas is closer than you think. Casino promoters are telling us just how great casinos will be, but there's a lot they're not telling us. Like the fact that Las Vegas ranks first in the nation in murder, suicide, alcoholism and personal bankruptcy. Or the fact that Las Vegas has prostitution that got so out of hand they had to legalize it. And skimming. And loan sharking. And the mob."

On the whole, Askew's reputation as a conscientious person helped. He was described by friends as a person whose opponents, even though they might dislike him, felt he was honest—it was agreed that he could be a significant moral force (Colson 1979). Askew was also an adept political operator. He had political credit stored up, and although he could not promise any future favors to friends from the governor's office, he chose to expend those credits on the casino campaign.

No Casinos and CABB (Casinos Are Bad Business 1978a) raised a number of arguments against casinos.

First was the argument that taxes wouldn't be lowered, emphasizing the minimal difference that gaming revenue would make in the Florida budget. As the literature put it, "It does not make sense for Floridians to risk a higher tax bill for the promise of a return equal to less than one percent of the total state budget (No Casinos 1978). This argument was based on the proposition that there were legalization costs to the Florida community, in the form of increased law enforcement surveillance and social costs—"When you add on the actual cost to the community of the increased social burden we wind up as losers." The decision to divide the revenues among all sixty-seven counties in equal portions opened the way for arguments by the opponents that Dade and Broward counties would bear the burden of the increased costs and problems, while sharing only $\frac{1}{67}$th of the revenues. Thus, a special appeal to Dade and Broward residents tried to convince them that their area was being shortchanged, forced to bear the burden of legalization (CABB 1978a).

Second was the argument that Florida's future was bright—that Florida was fortunate to have so much going for it. Legalization was portrayed as a shift to a gambling-based economy, which would shatter Florida's potential for new industry. Casino gambling was contrasted with the "stable, consistent and productive" industries that Florida was beginning to attract. Tourism was increasing, south Florida was developing as an international trade and banking center, and casino gambling was portrayed as a new development that would counteract Florida's progress in both spheres. The average Florida tourist, according to campaign literature, spent fourteen days in the state, while the average Las Vegas tourist spent two to three days. Legalization of casinos would not make Florida more competitive for the family tourist dollars. Moreover, casinos would destroy the image of Florida and would adversely affect the quality of life—what Dermer emphasized as the watchword of the campaign (Dermer 1979). "We have worked hard for Florida to maintain a clean wholesome image," No Casinos literature read. "Let's not throw it away." The climate that accompanies gambling was described as one that promotes cheap thrills and immorality—the state's image would become one of sanctioned greed (CABB 1978a).

Next was the argument that casinos invite organized crime. "No matter how tightly regulated casinos are," CABB literature argued, "they foster *related* activities which are uncontrolled, in which the underworld abounds." Testimony of the Dade County Organized Crime Bureau was used in support of this plea: "There are already 20 organized crime 'families' here. We expect others to move in. There's no way we'll be able to regulate casinos to keep them out of the action" (CABB 1978a). FACT, using the slogan "Casinos Corrupt," included a copy of the headline from a *New York* magazine article, "The Mob Wades Ashore in Atlantic City," which detailed how organized crime families had infiltrated the ancillary businesses that supply Atlantic City casinos with provisions and services (FACT 1978). Moreover, the ripple effect of legalization was cited by gambling opponents: "Florida can even expect an increase in illegal gambling if the casinos come here" (No Casinos 1978).

Next was the argument that casinos would spread beyond Miami Beach due to the power of the gambling operators. This argument emphasized the power of the casino industry: "Once a foothold is gained by the casino interest, the pressure on local and state officials will be tremendous" (CABB 1978a). This sentiment was echoed by one of Askew's close friends and advisors, attorney William Colson of Miami (Colson 1979). He commented that his most significant observation on the legacy of casino gambling in Nevada was the way in which the political power of the casino industry exerted itself in Nevada—primarily through contributions to candidates for political office, but also in lobbying for legislation favorable to gambling interests. The dog track lobby already was powerful enough in Florida. The "cancer" analogy was used as well, mostly to explain that casinos started out in Las Vegas in a few large hotels—now slot machines proliferate in supermarkets in residential areas.

One memo to CABB members suggested that the committee emphasize the detrimental effects—preying upon the poor and working class, in particular—that legalization would bring. The memo recommended language for a brochure that sketched a scenario of life with casinos and slot machines: "Husbands would cash their paychecks and lose their money to slot machines or betting on horse races and football games in casino bookie joints. Wives would feed grocery money to slot machines. This would mean heavier welfare costs to taxpayers" (CABB 1978b).

Next was the argument that legalization would only benefit a handful of promoters. The picture that accompanies the copy for this point in the literature is of a Cadillac parked in front of a Miami Beach hotel (No Casinos 1978). One consistent charge that the casino proponents were unable to shake was that their campaign was financed by entrepreneurs utilizing an outside political consultant, who sponsored a campaign that would benefit a small number of greedy Florida businesspeople.

Finally, there was the argument that there would be a detrimental impact upon senior citizens. One of the salient arguments of the New Jersey legalization campaign had been the provision for a special fund for relief for senior citizens and the disabled into which state taxes from casino gambling revenues would flow. Unfortunately for gambling's sponsors, by the summer of 1978, the gambling rush that had engulfed Atlantic City had also caused the property values to skyrocket there. This had the effect of raising the cost of rent that many low-income senior citizen residents of Atlantic City paid, thereby driving them out of their homes (CABB 1978c). This argument also was concerned with the fund for the elderly that pari-mutuel revenues went into in Florida. If pari-mutuel revenues were to diminish because of legalization—which many opponents predicted—then state aid to the elderly would diminish twofold, since the federal government matched that money. The opponents built a case around this issue, a case of broken promises in New Jersey, which they predicted would be repeated in Florida.

These issues were emphasized in the series of letters to Miami area businesspeople, speeches before interested organizations, and advertisements sponsored by CABB. Opponents promoted the image of Miami Beach hotelmen as greedy entrepreneurs who had let their properties run down and milked them for money and now were hoping the state would increase their property values without any effort on their part.

CABB's message to southern Florida businesspeople carried the urgency of this message, stressing that the effect of Florida legalization of casino gambling would not just be changes in the style of living in the area, but in the prosperity of their individual businesses and the south Florida economy as well. A letter from CABB chairman Tom Bomar to the business community emphasized the potential for noncasino development in the south Florida area and urged the participation of business leaders in the anticasino campaign.[1] The CABB radio and television spots carried the message further, echoing the urgency and economic messages that Bomar had expressed in his letter.[2] Television stations also picked up on these themes.[3]

The CABB effort was highly organized, with a number of committees taking responsibility for various planning activities, holding meetings weekly, or more often if necessary. Included were a legal committee, which researched legal attacks on the ballot measure—such as a contribution limitation question; a finance committee; a public relations committee and issues development committee; a speakers' bureau, which both responded to requests for anticasino speakers and attempted to stimulate a demand for those speakers; an associated organizations committee that planned the statewide coordination of different groups in opposition to the ballot measure; a research committee; and a position development committee (Hicks 1979; O'Neill 1979). The plan was to spread the message and engage support early. Each member of the Greater Miami Chamber of Commerce—500 in all—was to write to 5 business contacts, suppliers, or customers, and send each of them CABB fact sheets. Then each of those 5 was to write another 5, and the message would spread accordingly.

Each committee member was required to take a strong public position against gambling casinos and to ask his or her trade organizations and all others with whom they came in contact to voice their opposition, in the hope that a counterposition to the progambling forces could be developed. CABB speakers were told to emphasize the small amount of direct revenue relief that would go to Florida residents—the tax revenues estimated would amount to less than $10 per person—and that revenue to the state treasury represented less than 2% of a present state budget of $5.5 billion. The effect on employment was also emphasized, since Let's Help Florida had made much of the argument that jobs would be created for the south Florida economy. CABB argued that those new jobs would be menial—porters, maids, busboys—and that the skilled jobs would go to trained casino personnel from outside of the state and even the country. In their attack, the CABB speakers repeated a number of attacks on the LHF position. CABB argued that only a small, limited group would benefit and supported this point by asking the audience to take a look at the supporters and opponents of casino legalization. CABB speakers were advised to establish themselves as longtime residents and volunteers, with no hope of gain except a better community in which to live, and to show their opponents to be in the opposite situation (CABB 1978f).

Regardless of the audience, the list of active opponents of legalization was considered impressive, and the CABB brochure presented a similar study in contrast:

> "You can judge casinos by the company they keep"
> Look who supports casinos:
> * A few wealthy Miami Beach Hotel interests
> * Hired out-of-state political arrangers
> * The behind-the-scenes underworld. (CABB 1978g)

In those few lines, we have a portrait of the proponents that was crucial to the opposition campaign. First, the proponent group was limited, both in number and geographically. The negative image of Miami Beach was emphasized even by Weiner, who acknowledged that the hotel owners there were not popular throughout the state. FACT had portrayed them as a group of entrepreneurs who had overseen the decline of the Gold Coast through policies of extracting profits without putting them back into the local economy or into the hotels themselves. The argument about the out-of-state political arrangers is similarly significant. Because the campaign could be accurately portrayed as being conducted by non-Floridians, it could be easily dismissed as something out of step with the local population.

The rehabilitation of Atlantic City after 1976 was nothing short of a miracle, some contended, while others noted the rising real estate values and questioned whether the increased employment and construction only benefited a few speculators or the entire city. With Atlantic City established as an example of a resort in desperate condition, Florida casino opponents proposed that New Jersey voters were not in a position to scrutinize what they were getting into—they were making a pact with the devil. The Florida casino opposition posed the question: was Miami Beach so desperate as to embrace gambling, or was legalization only deemed necessary by outsiders and rapacious hotel interests? Weiner was portrayed as a political arranger, a term that connotes corruption and deals cut in back rooms removed from public scrutiny and accountability. The fact that he was a bona fide political consultant, basically the same sort of professional the opposition itself would hire, was overlooked.

Finally, the issue of the impact of the underworld and the covert nature of its interest and control cannot be overlooked. Here the casino opponents did not get as specific as they could have, for they declined to argue along the lines of the *Herald*'s investigation. They might have emphasized that the New Jersey legalization campaign was in large part financed by a Miami-based casino corporation that had long been suspected of ties to Meyer Lansky and stood accused of many improprieties—charges of skimming and of political corruption—in its Bahamian casino operations. Overall, though, the depiction of the proponents as a small out-of-state group might have fit with the public's conceptions of the conspiratorial nature of organized crime—a murky collection of economically interested criminals who operate in the shadows and control politicians and public officials through their influence.

On the other hand, those who opposed casinos were listed as:

* United Council of Churches
* Rabbinical Council
* Law enforcement agencies—at all levels

* Governor Reubin Askew
* The responsible business leadership of Dade County and the rest of Florida
* Every major newspaper across the state
* Greater Miami Chamber of Commerce
* Senior Citizens Groups
* Archbishop McCarthy
* Tenants' organizations (CABB 1978g)

CABB speakers were told to ask the final hard question: what are the costs and what are the benefits? The referendum, they argued, failed to consider the costs and the loss of growth potential suffered by a state that relies on an activity with significant negative social implications. Pari-mutuels are clean and pump money into a senior citizens fund, while Nevada—again, the Gomorrah image was cultivated—ranks first in the nation in suicide, personal bankruptcy, and murder.

The important question, CABB speakers were told to ask, was:

Would . . . mob influence, prostitution, personal bankruptcy, suicide, murder, divorce, loansharking, police corruption, political corruption, judicial corruption, traffic congestion on Miami Beach, pornography, extortion, narcotics traffic . . . decrease?

Would the image of Florida as a place to visit and a place to live be better or worse? Would the overall quality of life for the average tourist and residents improve or decline with legalized casino gambling? Casino gambling, the speakers would state, produces no product, provides no service. It coldly and with mathematical precision separates the gambler from a fixed percent of his money every day, every month, every year. This is not the type of industry that South Florida needed more of. (CABB 1978g)

The speakers emphasized crime, both corruption and street crime: "As a community who believes in law and order, we should strive to reduce the influence of organized crime, not present it with additional opportunities to carry on its anti-social activities." Relying on the negative aspects of the Atlantic City experience, CABB speakers reminded voters of the price to be paid and that the same recurring mob patterns seemed to be reappearing in Atlantic City.

The negative economic side effects were the second emphasis of this strategy.

* The new image of South Florida can be shattered
* The business climate would be tainted
* Florida would get: tawdriness, cheap glamor, inflated prices, and the undesirable element
* All as a result of a few people whose interests didn't coincide with that of the state

* Legalization would lead to or encourage:
  greed on the part of local merchants
  real estate speculation
  displacement of people
  increase in hotel rates (CABB 1978f)

In all its literature, speeches, and appeals, CABB came back to one key argument: the incompatibility of gambling casinos with the long-range objectives of Miami and Florida.

In conclusion, the CABB attack echoed the sentiment of Miami Chamber of Commerce president Jeanne Bellamy, who wrote in a June letter to all members: "Miami's future is brighter today than at any time in the last 15–20 years. This surging revival is due largely to the cooperation of governmental and private developers who are creating a New World Center. The Board feels that casino gambling would undermine all the good and positive action that was taking place" (CABB 1978h).

Conclusion

Polls showed that opinion on the legalization issue was evenly divided as late as August; the issue was up for grabs until the campaign began. Despite some analysis that mentioned the "Bible-belt mentality" of the largely Baptist Florida population, the proponents had written off that small minority adamantly opposed to gambling for religious reasons. One could not say, then, that Florida was necessarily headed toward defeat of the measure because of religion.

It might well be that the Florida opposition to gambling was mobilized for legitimate economic reasons. But it might also be argued that the opposition was no different than that in New Jersey, only more sophisticated and cognizant of the fact that a morality-centered opposition had failed in that state. For this kind of argument, we might want some evidence that showed that Askew and some of his allies, similarly strict religious believers such as Chapman, were actually objecting to the nature of gambling itself and were using the economic arguments to dress up their very deep-seated personal moral and religious antagonism to gambling.

Such evidence appears in one passage from an article Askew wrote for *Presbyterian Survey,* which appeared in October 1978 under the title "Casinos in Florida: A Bad Gamble" (Askew 1978b). In it, Askew is described as follows: "The author has been governor of Florida since 1971, and is an elder in First Church in Pensacola, Fla." Early in the article Askew asks

How can we combat the gambling ethos in a society that is regularly propagandized to think that: (1) the consumption of material goods is the key to happiness, and (2) people who are daring, clever, or lucky have a shot at getting those goods without having to waste their lives working for them? The fantasy of the gambling life attracts not only the trapped and desperate, but the affluent and the mildly bored.

Even those of us who oppose gambling find it difficult to oppose it directly. In Florida, we have already lost the fight against legalized gambling. The question is whether to expand from pari-mutuel gambling to casino gambling. (Askew 1978b; italics added)

Even if it was popular among the opponents of legalization, this sort of argument was carefully kept out of the No Casinos and CABB campaign literature, commercials, and presentations. There were many who might oppose gambling and the "outlaw businessmen" who would be legitimized by legalization, but the No Casinos campaign was carefully aimed at the latter. For both sides knew that the minds of those voters with strong moral objections to gambling were made up and that it was a wasted effort to appeal to the electorate on those grounds.

So what did work? Several things can be seen as crucial in the success of the anticasino groups. Most importantly, the governor committed his time and influenced others to make this a priority issue, to donate, and to work in the casino opposition effort. What exactly was it about Askew's performance that led to the defeat of the measure? We should probably rule out the impact solely of his personal endorsement. A poll taken for No Casinos showed that Askew's opposition was likely to cause only 5% of those initially favoring casinos to change their votes. The key benefit derived from Askew's wholehearted dedication to defeat of the gambling measure was not the number of "turnarounds" his support provided, but rather the legitimacy and access to the media that his support offered his opponents.

The business community, led by the CABB group and allied with Askew's confidants, coalesced around the issue as their counterparts had not in New Jersey. The anticasino forces were well financed, united in their strategy, and organized in their operation. Unlike New Jersey, where only $20,000 was spent, opponents among the four groups spent some $1.6 million. And they used it effectively—professional polls, low-key literature, timely and persuasive television and radio spots. They were able to attract many businesspeople, politicians, media executives, and prominent decision makers and policy shapers to their side, and to neutralize others—something Weiner had been successful at in New Jersey. In fact, they made it unpopular for any opinion leaders to support casino gambling.

The tone of the anticasino campaign shaped the nature of the debate. From the start, the proponents were described as outsiders and the campaign itself was linked to Weiner as a political consultant/hired gun from out of state. The implication was that the proponents were people out of touch with the real needs, beliefs, and desires of the Florida population. They were

portrayed as promoters, and this coincided with the portrayal of the actual
Florida backers—millionaire Miami Beach hotelmen who expected to make
a killing with the increased tourism, hotel construction, and property values
along the Gold Coast. The idea that the price would be paid by all the
Florida residents while the benefits would accrue to a few millionaires, who
would become multimillionaires, was an attractive theme. When combined
with the neutralization of opinion leaders, this "outsider" label served to
alienate the proponent group from any powerful base of political or financial
support, save for those hotel interests that would directly benefit.

Much of the success was attributable to Askew. He was popular, widely
regarded as a moral person with a great deal of integrity. He had introduced
reform legislation during his administration, and he was never suspected of
involvement in any scandals. During the campaign, he was careful to keep
the pari-mutuels and their $750,000 campaign fund at arm's length, so that
he would not be tainted by the charges that he was fronting for other
interests, who might already be exerting influence in his administration.
Askew made casinos his number one priority, a commitment that had been
underrated by the proponents.

Askew's timing, ability to encourage large donations from powerful contributors, and emergence as the central organizing point for the coalition of
interests must be considered the first crucial activity. As a popular governor
not standing for reelection, Askew had the luxury of making such a principled stand. The leading gubernatorial candidates, by comparison, did not
back the legalization measure, but promised not to veto enabling legislation
if the initiative did pass. Chambers of Commerce across the state were asked
to take a position. It was the prime issue of concern of the greater Miami
Chamber of Commerce.

By October, according to No Casino strategists, they had achieved their
goal of making gambling a serious question of debate: 25% of the population
identified it as the most important issue in the election. Taxes, by comparison, ranked next at 5%. This was a success of the No Casino plan, which
had been to make the legalization question an overriding issue and then get
the vote out (Krog 1979; Markel 1979).

Florida was among a handful of states—most of the others small—where
the tax bite was being reduced, instead of expanding ahead of or at the same
rate as the national average. Thus, a prolegalization argument that a fiscal
crisis, combined with the deterioration of Miami Beach as an attractive
resort town, compelled Florida to accept this innovative plan for economic
development and a relaxation of the tax burden was presented to an electorate that was not as desperate as residents of New Jersey had been. While
Atlantic City's problems may have typified New Jersey's crisis, Miami
Beach's decline was at odds with the relative prosperity of the Florida econ-

omy. Las Vegas and Atlantic City were used as negative examples for the opponents. Atlantic City's early success with casinos never became a strong point for the proponents. The problems of legalization were emphasized by anticasino advocates—senior citizens kicked out of their inexpensive housing to make way for speculators, the problems of uncontrolled growth, the attendant police expenditures for increased law enforcement. Askew argued that, in Nevada, casino industry money found its way into the political process and predicted the same—with dire consequences—for Florida. Nevada was shown to have high crime and suicide rates—not the "quality of life" that Florida projected and hoped to share in through legalization.

There had been illegal casino gambling in Florida before, and it had flourished as a result of public corruption. The ties of organized crime to Florida were legendary, and the increased drug traffic from South America was noted prominently in Florida news reports. Another opening for organized crime-affiliated businesses was not especially welcomed by certain powerful sectors of the business community and the state—a situation that contrasted with that of New Jersey. The Florida media opposed casinos and contributed heavily to the opposition campaign, even risking charges of improper influence. The legalization issue was presented in full coverage by the *Herald,* one of the nation's premier dailies, in a series of investigative articles that concentrated on the roots of the legal casino gambling industry in organized crime.

The proponents never recovered from the anticasino groups' challenge to the accuracy of the data base and assumptions employed by the firm that did the Let's Help Florida projections. This had not occurred in New Jersey, where the benefits were defined by the proponents and went unchallenged.

The problems of the Let's Help Florida campaign were noteworthy. Proposed gambling control legislation had been used in New Jersey to assure voters that the state would enact the world's strictest gaming control regulations. In Florida, the proposed legislation was changed in mid-campaign, to allow as many as forty casinos on the beach, when earlier drafts had specified only seven possible casinos.

The moral-economic tone of the opposition was crucial. Unlike New Jersey, where a church-led opposition had sounded an anachronistic religious and moral opposition to gambling, Florida's opposition was geared to possible negative impact on business, especially tourism, international trade and finance, and new industry. Florida's current tourist industry, Miami Beach's decline aside, was large and healthy and catered to a different clientele than casinos would. Much was made of this in the opponents' literature—casinos were portrayed as inimical to family tourism and to the strength of the Disney World–led rise in Florida's tourist economy.

Miami Beach was, at the time of the election, being presented as an international trade and finance center, and this had several complications. For one thing, the opponents could point to the rise of Miami as a hemispheric capital and show that the economy of south Florida was healthy and thriving. The anticasino assertion that "Miami's future is brighter today than at any time in the past 15–20 years" seemed to deflate the desperateness issue. Instead, the question was posed another way: "would the taint of the organized crime–associated casino gambling industry actually *impair* Miami's ability to attract new visitors?" One observer remarked after the campaign was over that it had come down to the "big promise" versus the "big scare." If that was true, the manner in which the "scare" took shape undoubtedly accounted for the results. The characterization of legal casino gambling as "painless prosperity" never took hold—opponents challenged the notion that it was painless, due to the many offsetting costs of legalization, and they even questioned the basis of the prosperity argument.

The Florida anticasino campaign proved the value of effective mobilization around a perceived threat. The mobilization of the local power elite around a well-financed and professional low-key campaign gathered those whose real interests might be threatened by legalization of casinos there. Given the state of the Florida economy, Florida voters could be approached with the argument that their material interests were threatened, rather than served, by the integration of a potentially lucrative—yet financially suspect— legal casino industry.

In the end, the power structure of Florida coalesced around Askew's leadership to oppose casinos. In the words of Tom Bomar, president of First Federal Savings and Loan Association and chairman of the Miami Chamber of Commerce's Casinos Are Bad Business Committee, the opponents' success was predicated upon nothing less than the coalescence of the power structure under the governor's leadership (Bomar 1979). A few days after the election, Sanford Weiner told the *Miami Herald* that, indeed, his opposition had proved more formidable than anticipated. "The power structure," Weiner charged, "has been orchestrated against us. They mobilized the full circle of the Establishment. Our weakness was a lack of prominent people to represent us" (Morin 1978).

Notes

Note 1.

"Dear Sirs,

The threat of casino gambling is the most serious economic issue to face Dade County in many years. The development now underway in every part of the county is unprecedented. Unless it is sabotaged by something like casino gambling, the economic base for the community will soon be diversified and balanced as never before.

In finance, education, medicine, transportation and international commerce, Greater Miami can become the new World Center. Beach Restoration, Southshore redevelopment, Watson Island and others are strong positive forces to rebuild family tourism. We have it within our grasp to reach these goals. Or we can turn our future over to the roll of the dice.

Make no mistake. This will be a hard fight. The promise of an equal share in tax revenue will sound good to people in other parts of the state. The story that the casinos will be confined to one small strip of Miami Beach will make it sound like gambling is Dade's problem only. To defeat casino gambling will require all the strength and unity that Dade county business leaders can muster.

The purpose of the meeting will be to present the issue to you briefly and factually and to ask for your personal help and for your firm's financial support. I feel very strongly that Greater Miami's economic health and quality of life depend upon defeating casino gambling. Come hear the facts on September 13, and I believe you will share my concern and determination that it must not happen here" (CABB 1978c).

Note 2.

"Casinos are good business, for a handful of profiteers, for prostitutes, and for parasites who don't care what happens to the fiber of our community. But casinos are bad business for South Florida, and the majority of our business community is against casinos. For many reasons, casinos bring in criminals. Criminals breed corruption, and corruption carries its forms of destruction. Behind the glamour of Las Vegas is a high crime rate, rampant prostitution, a high suicide rate, and an alarming number of bankruptcies. Casinos generate big money, the kind that corrupts public officials and creates a harmful atmosphere in which to raise families. And that discourages new business from locating here. Also, South Florida will get all the problems of casinos, and only a fraction of the taxes. Let's not cloud our bright future or contaminate our healthful environment with the polluting influences of casinos. Vote against casino gambling" (CABB 1978d).

In contrast to CABB, the bulk of the No Casinos efforts were spent in television and radio spots and on campaign material. Most of the spots took the form of "slice of life" 30-second and 60-second commercials in which a hidden camera zeroed in on the conversation two people were having about legalization. The following nine highly professional spots, produced at the Criteria Studios—where the Bee Gees had only recently recorded their platinum albums—were "meant to reinforce people we knew were against casinos and show them there are other folks out there who feel the same way" (Krog 1979; Markel 1979).

Number 1. Governor Askew on Taxes

Narrator: Some people think casino gambling will cut our taxes.
Askew: Casinos will not provide tax relief. Wherever you live in Florida, casinos will end up costing you money. More payrolls, because new industries and tourists will go somewhere else. Increased government spending caused by casino gambling and money wasted promoting Florida as a haven for gamblers. The odds on casinos are stacked for the promoters, not for the taxpayers.
Narrator: Who needs casino gambling? We don't. Vote no November 7th.

Number 2. Husband and Wife—Aid to Schools

Father: What's the matter, honey?
Mother: Johnny's unhappy about school. He says it's so hot he gets sleepy.
Father: Well, if casinos come, maybe schools will get air conditioning.
Mother: Casinos pay for school improvement? Some joke. What we'll get will pay less than one day's county school bill. And who'll pay for the sewers and roads that they'll need? Us, that's who. We'll be ripped off again, just for a bunch of promoters who fouled up the beach in the first place. Who needs casino gambling? We don't.
Narrator: You've got to vote no to stop it, on November 7th.

Number 3. Father and Daughter—Jobs

Daughter: Gee, Dad, don't I need to look up North, where opportunities are?
Father: Honey, opportunity is where growth is. That's here in Florida. Homes are selling at a record rate. The international banks, electronic firms, theme parks—that's growth.
Daughter: But, Dad, I can't see casino gambling bringing in good companies, or investors, or anything.
Father: That's true, they never have elsewhere. But it's not passed yet. After all, who needs casino gambling? You certainly don't, sweetheart.
Narrator: You've got to vote no to stop it, on November 7th.

Number 4. Governor Askew—The Possibility of Casinos Spreading throughout Florida

Narrator: Some people say casinos will be all right as long as they stay in Miami Beach.
Askew: Once casinos get a foothold in Florida, their well-fi-

nanced lobby will be pushing for more and more territory. For two years during the depression we had legalized casinos, but it took us years to get rid of the harmful effects all over the state. If you don't want casinos or slot machines in your backyards, don't put them in Miami's front yard. Like weeds, they will spread to wherever you live.

Narrator: You've got to vote no to stop it, on November 7th.

Number 5. Governor Askew—Tourism

Narrator: Some people say casinos will be good for Florida tourism.

Askew: Casinos can permanently damage our tourism. While some new visitors will come to the casinos, many old friends will choose someplace else. The average casino tourist spends only four days gambling. The average Florida tourist spends thirteen days in a wide variety of activities and shopping. We're one of the top tourist areas in the world. Let's not spoil a good thing.

Narrator: You've got to vote no to stop it, on November 7th.

Number 6. Two Women in a Supermarket—Inflation

Woman 1: Prices are just terrible.

Woman 2: Casino gambling may help. There'll be more money.

Woman 1: Did you read about Atlantic City? Everything's higher. Casinos are inflationary.

Woman 2: Casinos say they'll bring a lot of jobs.

Woman 1: Jobs at casinos? How about jobs lost when businesses or people won't come because of higher costs? They don't subtract jobs lost. Gamblers spend their money gambling. They're gamblers, not tourists.

Woman 2: Makes sense. Who needs casino gambling?

Woman 1: We sure don't.

Narrator: You've got to vote no to stop it, on November 7th.

Number 7. Two Black Law Enforcement Officers—Crime

He: Jan, do you think this casino thing will pass?

She: I sure hope not.

He: Even if it pays for more law enforcement?

She: You'll get more crime. A guy loses, borrows, loses that. He has to get it from somewhere. Maybe from a holdup, or a mugging. And maybe you'll have to chase him.

He: We've got our hands full already.

She: Well, think twice. You want more tourists or more gamblers in this state? Who needs casino gambling? We don't.

Narrator: You've got to vote no to stop it, on November 7th.

Number 8. Narrator—Florida's Image of Itself

Narrator: Florida is looking hard at itself these days, at what it wants to be, where it wants to go. Most people know that casino gambling just doesn't fit in with those plans. People and promoters who want it for their own benefit will vote for it. You just can't be against it, you've got to *vote* against it. Here's how. Look for Amendment 9 on your ballot. And vote against it. You've got to vote against casino gambling to stop it.

Number 9. Narrator—Legalization Promises Suspect

Narrator: Florida has looked hard at its own progress, and has looked hard at the casino gambling promises, and found the promises bigger than the facts. Not quite 89,000 jobs. Not quite $120 million. Not quite 10 million tourists. And maybe not quite only in Miami Beach. They've tried to fool the people. There's one way to stop the false promises. Let them know on your ballot. Look for Amendment 9, and vote against. You've got to vote against casino gambling to stop it.

Note 3.

May 26, Channel 4: Atlantic City Fever. Miami Beach is not a down-and-out resort area like Atlantic City—the future of South Florida is linked to many positive and constructive things which don't involve casinos. Before you jump on the casino bandwagon . . . remember the price to be paid . . . and it's a very heavy one for a decent community to bear.

June 8, Channel 10: The issue is whether South Floridians want to sacrifice their clean family atmosphere in order to make a handful of casino operators rich.

August 9, Channel 10: Many people don't think the fastbuck, something-for-nothing philosophy is a healthy basis for long-term prosperity.

October 11, Channel 10: The truth is that casino gambling would benefit a handful of entrepreneurs at the expense of just about everybody else.

October 12, Channel 7: As a practical matter, the casino is where the bucks would stop. Resorts—just one casino—is shown to have raised considerable problems already in New Jersey.

October 24, Channel 4: With the change to 8 story instead of 500 room requirements, it is estimated now that 30 or more beachfront hotels would be eligible. Instead of a few, well-regulated casinos in the largest hotels, we now have the group advocating 'no holds barred' . . . a 'let 'er rip' attitude which removes any semblance of logical restraint.

October 27, Channel 4 (From a Tampa station): Would you trade Disney World for Las Vegas? Florida already has gambling, and a much safer type that's easier to regulate. As for new jobs, those created by new businesses and industries are worth a lot more. They pay better and are more permanent, and they attract a better class of citizen. There is a lot more room for new offices and factories in Florida than for casinos.

4 ～ Explaining Casino Outcomes: The Gravity and Veto Models

Casino gaming will expand to other states. The other states will be attracted to casinos by the widely and regularly publicized success of Atlantic City. Legislatures will be motivated by the prospects for substantial new employment, new hotel-casino construction projects, protection or improvement of existing tourism, general economic improvement stemming from a new industry, and increased state revenues. . . . By the end of 1984 there could be eleven states with casino gaming legalized; by the end of the decade there could be as many as eighteen.

—Public Gaming Research Institute 1980

. . . from coast to coast, state and city officials are turning an eager eye on legalized gambling as a profitable and politically palpable way to raise money. . . . But the growth in legalized gambling has its limits. Casino gambling, for example, was approved for Atlantic City but is routinely defeated in other states whenever it is suggested.

—*New York Times*, May 3, 1984

Legalizing Gambling

To understand the forces at work in the New Jersey and Florida campaigns, and to construct a model necessary to allow for the outcomes in the other casino campaign states, it is necessary to understand the range of legal reform situations related to vice in America. While gambling has historically enjoyed a unique position, it nonetheless shares certain features in common with other vices concerning the movement toward legalization.

Recent studies of the decriminalization and legalization of formerly prohibited activities have shown that the normalization of deviant behavior, or its redefinition as an acceptable variation, a private behavior, or a nonthreatening activity, precedes decriminalization or legalization. The most recent American example concerns the widespread use of marijuana among white middle-class youth and its effect upon marijuana laws. Bonnie finds that the scientific propositions attending the attachment of deviant status to marijuana use have always been assumptions tied to broader social perceptions of the using class (Bonnie and Whitebread 1974; see also Kaplan 1971; Musto 1973; Grinspoon and Bakalar 1976; Grinspoon 1977). The basic propositions—for instance, that use inevitably led to abuse—were quickly challenged when use of the drug was taken up by society's privileged classes. When the consensus against marijuana lost its sociological support, it immediately lost its scientific support as well (Bonnie and Whitebread 1974:225).

While studies of criminalization have identified the role of economic interests in the criminalization of certain behavior and classes of offenders, the literature on decriminalization has tended to embrace a perspective more closely aligned with a consensus view of formulation of the law—generally asserting that legal reform finally occurred when prudent and tolerant policymakers recognized the errors of past criminalization efforts. The basis for legalization is usually presented either as a reaffirmation of traditional values or as the realization that new mores are necessary to confront new social realities (Allen 1964; Schur 1965; Kadish 1967; Packer 1968; Skolnick 1968; Geis 1972; Levi 1973; Schur and Bedau 1974; Israel and Mogill 1975; Kaplan 1975; Jennings 1976).

In the literature on decriminalization, there are some findings that are pertinent to this study and to the analysis of the economic interests that structure campaigns and movements surrounding decriminalization attempts. Galliher (Galliher et al. 1974; Galliher and Basilick 1979) in a series of studies on the sources of impetus behind decriminalization of marijuana, found in at least two cases that liberal and conservative opinion converged; together, the two forces were responsible for the decriminalization of possession of small amounts of marijuana in what are generally considered conservative states—Utah and Nebraska.

Rothman proposes that the coerciveness of the state in areas of morality is limited not by principled opposition to specific policies, but rather by the unwillingness of legislators to spend taxpayers' money: "It is an odd but perhaps accurate conclusion to note that the dependent and deviant may owe what freedom they have more to the fiscal conservatism of elected officials than to the benevolent motives of reformers" (1978:81). Steinhoff and Diamond (1977) found, in a study of abortion law repeal in Hawaii, that it was not the efforts of proabortion groups campaigning for change that prompted repeal of that state's abortion laws. Instead, they maintain, repeal efforts succeeded because they were proposed as a conservative issue, one that appealed to traditional values already supported by the middle class.

Lempert's discussion of the goals of groups involved in campaigns to sway public opinion on issues of law and morality makes the same point:

> Generally speaking, disputes between groups with conflicting moral claims will be decided by the relatively uncommitted, typically the bulk of the populace and political elites not tied to committed groups. The struggle for the support of the uncommitted will often appear as a more or less rational battle between conflicting groups to convince the uncommitted of the correctness of their preferred moral positions since, by definition, the uncommitted see neither position as clearly correct. Groups often attempt to tie their preferred positions to issues on which the public morality is clear. (1974:4)

Ranulf (1964) proposes that lower-middle-class indignation and the tendency to inflict punishment rise as the result of economic depression. While he and others have found support for an increase of moralization in the face of economic depression, there is evidence to support the opposite contention: that, in times of economic crisis, the state cannot afford to waste resources and lose revenue sources through the decision to control marginally condemned activities.

This was the major argument in the repeal movement during Prohibition, and the success of that position was due in large part to the way in which that argument was accepted and promulgated by significant and powerful sectors of society, including many industrialists who turned from Prohibition advocates to repeal supporters (Sinclair 1962; Burnham 1968; Engelmann 1979). In the face of the Depression, it became more difficult for supporters of Prohibition laws to support the continuation of legal policies that were ineffective in destroying the market for alcoholic beverages, removed tax revenues and jobs from the legitimate economy, and encouraged the rise of a powerful underground economy of vice. In times of economic crisis, the morality of Prohibition seemed ridiculous. Repeal, its supporters proposed, could help fight the economic slump, through the reincorporation of the liquor industry—which would lighten the load on other sectors—and through the redirection of tax revenues away from organized criminal interests and back to the state. Repeal became equated with prosperity.

The ideology of the repeal supporters, particularly those industrialists who had supported Prohibition and then advocated repeal, included a number of points that referred directly to the failure of the policy of criminalization. They sought to correct a misguided law that was a clear failure, had caused new problems, and represented a dangerous overextension of the law. Repeal supporters explained that they were not attacking the social ideals of Prohibition laws, only that they were dismayed by the actual results. The Depression was presented as a strategic event that made Prohibition policies outdated and called for an adjustment—with the adoption of new ideals and a new order of values (Sinclair 1962).

These studies indicate that the convergence of certain social forces, or the coincidence of various social movements, produces conditions under which reform of laws governing morality is likely. The extent to which those conditions are conducive to the formation of successful movements and organizations, however, is in turn dependent upon those groups' maximization of certain resources and strategies. In the negotiation of deviance outcomes, these studies agree, the possession and wielding of salient resources is most crucial. The socioeconomic position or class background of an individual deviant or class of deviants has a direct bearing on the ease with which one can be branded a deviant. One important focus, then, is on the power of one group to impose its definition, as Rock notes: "Deviance flows from the successful imposition of unwelcome status. The study of definitional processes must therefore be wedded to an analysis of the power structures which realise definitions in action. More particularly, it must focus on the groups which have the power to award lowly status and on the processes whereby such awards take place" (1973:122).

Schur makes an observation about the process of *undeviantizing* that is central to this study—the other side of the definitional process of deviantizing is the process by which former or potential deviants manage to avoid or reject labeling as stigmatized or disreputable:

> If deviantizing involves an assertion of social power, so too does the avoidance of stigma that others might seek to impose. The success of those who—while engaged in wide-spread problematic behavior that could be defined as deviant, is thus the other side of the social relations or definitional thesis regarding deviance. . . . Both stigma and non-stigma outcomes reflect the same basic self-fulfilling mechanism in official deviance processing through which power is confirmed and reinforced. (1980:168)

Those who have been successfully designated as deviant may seek to protect their culture by influencing the process of designation. Four possible responses of the deviant to stigmatization have been identified by Shoham (1970): concealment; acceptance of labeling and subcultural withdrawal; neutralization; and repudiation and politicization (Davis 1961; Goffman 1963; Dinitz et al. 1969; Matza 1969; Shoham 1970).

Concealment would include processes that divert attention away from the deviance; consequently, it does not include a societal response based on deviant identity. Withdrawal to a subculture serves as a means of support for the deviant group, but with the isolation comes the expense of perpetuating the self-identity as deviant. Neutralization involves a direct interaction between the labeled person or group and society. It is an attempt on the part of the deviant to alter his or her conception of self as being unacceptable. It can be similarly described as normalization, defined by Davis: "the term 'normalization' denotes a process whereby [someone] for whatever reason comes to view as normal and morally acceptable that which initially strikes him as odd, unnatural, 'crazy,' deviant, etc., irrespective of whether his perception was in the first instance reasonable, accurate or justifiable" (1961:126n). The neutralization of the shame that accompanies stigma is achieved through the redefinition of the activity involved as acceptable, tolerable, or, at least, a private matter.

Neutralization has another side to it, tied to the attempt to influence the designators. One way to influence the process of designation is to join some movement to redefine the deviance. Another is to attempt—directly, through bribery, or indirectly, through the use of influence attained through cultural affinities—to influence the decisions of legal authorities (Gusfield 1967). This method is particularly suited to the deviants considered in this study—organized criminals, whose structurally induced proclivity to corruption as a method of protecting their enterprise is a central defining characteristic of their activity (Bell 1962; Cressey 1969; Albini 1971; Schelling 1971; Ianni and Reuss-Ianni 1972; Ianni 1974; Smith 1975; Chambliss 1978).

While the attempt to influence the decisions of legal authorities may be considered a political act, the fourth category—the politicization of deviance—refers to a more separable phenomenon. While all deviance issues can be reviewed as political issues, since the relative balance of power influences the ability of a dominant and powerful group to impose definitions on a less powerful one, stigmatized individuals may in a narrower sense seek to politicize their deviations, to alter existing deviance definitions, reactions, and policies. Through politicization, deviants hope to narrow or overturn dominant definitions, to "undeviantize" existing deviance categories, to combat collective disvaluation and stigmatization (Kitsuse 1979; Schur 1980).

However, the political act that *demands* recognition of deviance as acceptable may have some side effects or unintended consequences. Because politicization is a more militant tactic, it may have one important short-term disadvantage: even as they seek to legitimize the deviation, such efforts necessarily give great primacy to it.

What, then, are the important variables in the successful mobilization of sentiment? The first point to emphasize, Gusfield notes, is that deviance designations can be very fluid: "deviance designations have histories; they are changeable and subject to political reversals, the vagaries of public opinion, and the development of new social movements and moral crusades. Such changes have often been associated with the symbolic functions of law for the participating parties, whatever the effect of law in controlling deviant behavior" (Gusfield 1967:72). Gusfield's study of temperance politics and other studies of the social movements and crusades that surround deviance-defining struggles have identified a number of variables that account for the successful imposition of deviant status and legal definition as criminal.

Becker (1963) emphasizes the role played by moral entrepreneurs, those individuals who develop a strong stake in moral crusading and devote abnormal amounts of time and energy to the problem. Such actors shape what Fuller and Myers (1941) term a "problem consciousness." One goal of deviance theory, Cohen (1965) writes, is to determine under what conditions feedback circuits promote change and under what conditions they inhibit change in the normative structure. There are several stages of interest to us in the deviance-defining struggle. Earlier studies cited concentrated on the role of threatened economic interests in furthering definitions of activity as deviant or criminal. But these studies have also attempted to identify the conditions under which such deviance struggles take place. There are conflicting theories on this—is stigmatization more likely to occur under conditions of prosperity or during economic depression? Ranulf (1964) proposes that during times of fiscal crisis and economic depression, the lower middle class exhibits tendencies toward disinterested punishment of deviators. Bonnie and Whitebread's study of marijuana criminalization supports this:

> drug use or other minority behavior is more likely to be viewed with anxiety and to be indicted as a "menace" in times of social malaise than in times of social stability and optimism. When the dominant order is thought to be threatened—by economic woes, by internal disruption or lawlessness, or by external aggression—policy-making is likely to be defensive, lashing out at behavior perceived to be associated with the general societal fears. (1974:30–31)

This theory is at odds with the conclusions of others who propose that status politics are more likely during times of prosperity, because it enables the upward mobility of certain groups that may pose a threat to the established status groups, who fear the effects of integration. In addition, other scholars (Kitsuse and Spector 1973, 1975; Schur 1980) have pointed to the need for deviance theorists to consider the broader societal importance of deviance and to examine the development of problems at a societal level. While not dismissing the importance of examining the role of gambling and its legalization for society generally, this study is concerned with more "micro"-level issues in the development of conducive environments and effective campaigns for casing legalization.

This study attempts to resolve the conflict between these two competing theories of conduciveness by suggesting that the proper focus of a study of deviance struggles is on the processes through which threat is perceived, amplified, and diffused. More important than the identification of a number of conditions prompting legalization is analysis of the processes by which ambiguity is resolved into certainty. The importance of the moral entrepreneur, for instance, lies in his or her ability to spark a problem consciousness, rather than just to represent certain material interests. Thus, the manipulation of political symbols and the use of propaganda in stigma contests take on importance beyond the merely threatened material interests that may be involved. We can envision a situation where clearly aligned and orchestrated material interests fail, when they cannot counter the allegations of a powerful symbolic appeal: in fact, the 1974 New Jersey legalization campaign demonstrated this (Weiner 1978a).

This thesis proposes that it is misleading to concentrate on static conceptions of moral crusades or legal reform movements as contests where either side gathers obvious support, then battles for the undecided vote. Instead, the nature of the deviance struggle is of a battle for definition of the central attributes of an activity or of people participating in that activity. Therefore, this thesis proposes a more dynamic conception of the role of material and symbolic interests—in the formulation of criminal law, issues of morality are always present, and therefore debates are likely to take the form of symbolic disputes. The ambivalence of societal responses to gambling and to organized crime results in a stigma contest where both sides can call upon existing value systems to support their arguments—either to further tax relief or to prevent disreputable economic elements from being integrated.

This study concentrates on the primary determinants of movement success in campaigns—the important factors in generating effectiveness in deviance struggles—while restating the proposition that, in negotiating deviance outcomes, salient resources count most. The concluding chapter discusses how certain social movement variables—the mobilization of resources, the articulation of political symbols, and the access to key decision makers—account for the success of the casino legalization campaign in one setting and its failure in another.

Florida and New Jersey

Florida is a conservative state, but that fact alone could not explain why Florida voters turned down casinos by a three to one margin in 1978. Rather, the ability of Florida opposition groups to prevent a fiscal conservative prolegalization sentiment from developing was notable. With conservative positions blocked for the proponent forces, the opponents of casinos could attract voters to the notion that legalization would irreparably damage Florida's economy and society. The influential groups were not only threatened. They also depicted that threat in a manner that translated into a threat to the general population. Governor Reubin Askew was able to convey to influential Florida economic interests his sense of trouble about the issue.

Florida opposition forces exhibited superiority on three levels: their resources, their strategies, and their access to decision makers. Opponents were able to raise money quickly, after Askew asked for $25,000 donations, and they were able to reserve valuable television advertising space. Still, the 1974 New Jersey example—where proponents outspent opponents by twenty-five to one in an unsuccessful effort—indicates that the material advantage of resources is not sufficient to ensure success.

In Florida, the casino opponent groups employed a low-key strategy and aimed their critique at the economic program of the legalization proponents. Without losing their conservative and Baptist support, they gained votes among the "conducive middle," those middle-class homeowners who, while not avid gamblers, were tolerant enough to consider allowing casinos in their state if legalization meant tax relief, increased tourism, economic development, and strict state control of the presumed negative effect of legalization—rampant prostitution and an increased organized crime presence. Casino opponents coalesced behind the leadership of Governor Askew at an early and crucial point, a June 1978 breakfast meeting, and set out to make gambling an important election issue. They carefully deployed their physical, organizational, political, and motivational resources. In New Jersey, the campaign had been run on the momentum of the proponents' definition of the issue. In Florida, this situation was reversed.

The question persists: did New Jersey voters approve casinos and Florida voters reject casinos for reasons peculiar to those two states? In what ways are elements of other states' failure to welcome casinos foreshadowed by the Florida action? What explains this unpredicted rejection of casinos so soon after *Business Week* heralded legal gambling as America's hottest growth industry and gambling stocks paced the stock market (*Business Week* 1978)? The remaining sections of this chapter consider the utility of two competing models.

Predictions of Casino Growth

When casinos were legalized in New Jersey in a 1976 referendum vote, it appeared to many observers that the third wave of legalized gaming in America was still approaching its crest and would soon bring a flood of casino legalizations across the land.

In 1977, Duane Burke, director of the Public Gaming Research Institute, predicted that casino gaming would be legalized in six states by 1980 (Burke 1977:4–5). Michael Donohue, chairman of the Washington State Gambling Commission, thought that his state would certainly be one of those six (Donohue 1977:8). In 1978, Walter Tyminski wrote in *Gambling Times* that "informed observers see an explosion of interest in casino gaming as additional states bless the industry with votes of confidence" (1978:19).

In 1980, Lee Isgur, vice-president of Paine, Webber, wrote, "Over the next four to five years, I think that we will have at least two more states in the United States which will legalize gaming. Over the next decade, I believe anywhere from 10 to 20 states will legalize gaming" (*Gaming Business* 1980:24). His sentiments were echoed in the words of Victor Lownes, president of Playboy Clubs International: "As moral attitudes toward casino gaming change, no state is going to sit idly by and watch millions of dollars earned at home drift to neighboring states. Ultimately, I foresee that casino gaming will come to practically every state in the union" (*Gaming Business* 1980:25). Even the usually reticent organized crime financial genius Meyer Lansky made predictions, telling a trio of Israeli journalists:

> Today, with the opening of casinos in Atlantic City, I think the American government has realized that you can't stop people from gambling. Now I read that Japanese businessmen are buying their way into hotels in Atlantic City, and that *Penthouse* magazine has acquired another hotel on the Boardwalk, and I can't help smiling. . . . It seems a long time ago that Bugsy [Siegel] and I were driving back and forth across the desert trying to get the first casino built. (Eisenberg et al. 1978:269)

Robert Shawn, vice-president of Economic Research Associates, also wrote in early 1980 that casino expansion into New York and Pennsylvania was favorable within two to three years, with mixed chances for casinos in Massachusetts and Connecticut. But not all shared these positive prognostications for the legalization of casinos (Shawn and Root 1980:7). Gamer Si Redd, former president of Bally Distributing of Nevada, said in 1981, "I don't think we will see casinos legalized in very many states. Certainly not in Florida. The state of Washington strikes me as the best possibility" (*Gaming Business* 1980:25). However, among knowledgeable observers, Redd seemed to be in a very distinct minority.

In April 1980, the Public Gaming Research Institute issued a report entitled "Further Legalization of Gambling in the United States in the Decade of the Eighties." The report stated in part,

> Casino gaming will expand to other states. The other states will be attracted to casinos by the widely and regularly publicized success of Atlantic City. Legislatures will be motivated to approve enabling legis-

lation by the prospects for substantial new employment, new hotel-casino construction projects, protection or improvement of existing tourism, general economic improvement stemming from a new industry, and increased state revenues. . . . By the end of 1984 there could be eleven states with casino gaming legalized; by the end of the decade there could be as many as eighteen.

New York . . . will very likely approve a casino gaming measure in this session of the legislature in order to put the state in the position of voting on the issue again in 1981 when the new legislature convenes. The proposal is very likely to be approved by the legislature again in 1981 and by the voters that November.

Most of the other eastern states, with a tradition of depending on gaming revenues from racing or lotteries, will be looking at casino gaming. . . .

Overall, the growth of casino gaming should be a very positive force in U.S. society in this decade. (Public Gaming Research Institute 1980:8)

The report and its conclusions were based upon several hundred telephone interviews with legislators and political executive in all the states. The institute discerned two biases in the nation: the general public had a distinct bias in favor of gaming, while political leaders had a bias against gambling. Therefore, the institute saw that the expansion of legal gaming would occur more rapidly where changes could take place with referenda that did not require legislative action.

In its 1980 report, the Public Gaming Research Institute predicted gaming expansion activity in all fifty states by adding the positive and negative scores allotted to each of twenty-one different factors. A total of balance of positive points was presented as evidence that the state would be a likely place for casino legalization. These factors included the method of legalization to be followed in the state, funding for support of gaming, funding for opposition forces, economic conditions, employment potential presented by the gaming activity, potential tourism benefits, proximity to existing commercial gaming, the reputation of gaming, policy positions of political leaders, religious and social bias, and public sentiment. Legal casinos were projected for nine states by 1984, with another nine predicted by the end of the decade. The institute's model was essentially a gravity model. Evidence for or against legalization was weighed. If the "preponderance of the evidence" fell toward legalization, legalization was predicted.

The factors presented in the institute's analysis certainly would have totaled a positive result had they been applied to New Jersey in 1976. Political leaders there favored casinos; economic interests favored casinos. New Jersey had already adopted other forms of legal gaming. Supporters of casinos were well funded, and opponents were poorly funded. The tone of the campaign was controlled by the proponents. The debate focused on economic factors, not on crime or the intrinsic value of gambling. The gravity model triumphed—or did it? Is there perhaps another model to explain the New Jersey vote and to predict other results in campaigns for casinos?

Florida was only the first major case in a growing succession of failing campaigns for casinos. All of the other cases are examined in the chapters that follow. The recurring failures, especially in the face of predictions of success, cause us to search for a new model for explaining results and predicting results of future campaigns. The gravity or "preponderance of the evidence" model appears weak. Other campaigns have been conducted in an atmosphere of economic hardship, two most evident cases being those of Detroit, Michigan, and Pueblo, Colorado. Other states had favorable experiences with forms of legalized gaming and witnessed popular sentiment in favor of casino gaming. Major politicians supported drives for casinos at certain vital stages. Major casino interests expressed desires for new markets, as did Resorts International in New Jersey. Yet all the major campaigns have failed until 1989 when small-scale gambling was headed toward operation in Deadwood, South Dakota, and on Iowa riverboats—hardly the densely populated or wide-open scenarios predicted for New York, Florida, Massachusetts, or other large states.

Are we then faced with rejecting the gravity model? In searching for another explanation, we must determine if there were peculiar aspects of the New Jersey campaign that could explain the unique results there. Was the economic situation in Atlantic City and New Jersey so desperate that this could propel success for a casino drive only there? The answer is clearly no. As indicated, Detroit suffered a more devastating recession; so did Pueblo. Michigan, like New Jersey, increased taxes. The entire northeast corridor of the nation felt the hard times that New Jersey felt. Was the Resorts International involvement unique to New Jersey? Did the campaign succeed because a major casino interest promoted New Jersey casinos? Such involvement was not unique: MGM sponsored a Massachusetts effort, while major casinos were certainly interested in New York and Florida campaigns. We reject the notion that New Jersey was unique because of any single factor. Rather, casino campaigns turn on patterns of events. By reviewing the results of the New Jersey and Florida campaigns and examining other campaigns, we must consider whether another model is in operation.

One such model can be called the veto model. It contains a set of critical factors that determine the results of casino campaigns. In this study, we advance the notion that there are four sets of such critical factors. We call these veto factors. The sets encompass items identified by the predictive model utilized by the Public Gaming Research Institute as well as other items of consideration. Our basic thesis is that all sets of factors must be favorable for a casino legalization effort to be successful.

Predictive Factors in Casino Legalization

We call our first set of factors political environment factors. In analyzing particular campaigns for casinos, we look closely at what has become the central justifying reason given by proponents of all legalization drives during the third wave of legalizations—the improvement of the economy. The question we pose is simple: what was the economic condition of the local area designated for casinos and of the state as a whole? Additionally, specific attention is given to the question of the adequacy of governmental revenues and the taxation burden on the citizens of the state. The political environment set also includes questions about the nature of gambling in the state at the onset of the casino effort. Did the state have other forms of legalized gambling—lottery, horse racing, dog racing, jai alai, charity gaming, Indian reservation gaming? Also, was the state's experience with those forms of gaming favorable? Did the gaming activity produce desired revenues? Did it aid the economy? Was the gaming activity free from major scandal or suspicion of scandal?

The second set of factors is labeled political elites and active interests. Here specific attention is given to the role played by certain key actors in the political processes surrounding the drive for casinos. The governor's role deserves individual attention in each case. How did he or she participate?— as a supporter or an opponent? Was the governor a leader in the struggle or a follower? We also look at state attorneys general and other major political leaders—key legislators, judges, state executives. The role of the business community is important, since businesses are purportedly the benefactors of the casino movements. Business activity supposedly increases with casinos in communities, along with an increase in circulation of revenues. Also, the tax burden that often falls greatly upon the shoulders of businesspeople is supposed to be eased with casino legalizations, as well as other gaming legalizations.

Another interested party in the casino struggle is the competing legalized gaming industry in a state. Most prominently, this industry participation is by horse track interests. If other gamers are actively engaged in operations in the state, we ask what role they foresee for casinos in the state's gaming economy. Are casinos viewed as rivals that will take away gaming action from the tracks or bingo halls? Will casinos deprive tracks of their spectator gates? Or will horse race or other gaming interests be content that the casinos will not hurt them? Maybe they even see possible benefits with casinos, since many more tourists might visit their facilities. Whether they are active in opposition or support or whether they are passively neutral makes a difference.

The third set of factors consists of campaign sponsorship factors. Here two concerns are addressed: credibility and financial resources. Did the campaign sponsors have credible standing in the state's political community? Were they people of stature who were connected to the power structure or were they individual political actors without such connections? Additionally, were they perceived to be legitimate actors? Were their motives confined to casino gaming or were casinos just part of a larger agenda? Did the sponsors operate wholly within the law? Were they engaged in illegal or questionable gaming activities? The second concern is campaign financing. Did the proponents of casino legalization command adequate financial resources to wage their campaign? Did they have sufficient money to meet the rival campaign chests of opponents of casinos?

The fourth major factor is campaign issue dominance. On which battlefield was the campaign for legalization fought? Did proponents and opponents focus their debate on economic questions, thereby giving an overall emphasis to the positive side of casino gaming? Or was the campaign dominated by themes of crime, social deviance, and quality of life, the "bad" side of casino gaming? One theme propels casino advocacy toward success, while dominance of the other theme in a campaign effectively kills the casino drive.

These four sets of factors are presented in our model. A positive rating in the political environment area would be warranted by the existence of a positive experience with other forms of legalized gambling in that state. Another item causing a positive rating would be the presence of a weak economy. In the area of political elite involvement, an active supporting interest by the governor and attorney general are strong positives, as are the involvement of key business elites. Two issues in the campaign sponsorship area merit positive ratings: strong funding and credibility of sponsors. Finally, a positive rating in campaign issue dominance is given when legalization proponents are able to turn debate topics to their central issues. If a campaign exhibits positive results for all of the four sets, the campaign will be successful. If one set of factors is negative for casino proponents, the campaign will fail.

In this suggested model, as we examine each of eighteen campaigns for casinos, we need not mark each factor with a plus or minus sign and then total the results. All we must do is find the significant negative factors in the list that cause the entire issue to be subject to failure. Any critical factor can veto the legislation effort. For legislation to succeed, therefore, every critical factor must be supportive of legislation. All such factors were positive toward legislation in New Jersey, and the proposition carried, still only by a margin of less than 13%. In the face of overwhelming support by political and economic elites, 44% opposed.

If the veto model applies, a campaign for legalization of casinos can be likened to a campaign for an expensive bond issue that will have the effect of significantly raising property taxes. The issue will succeed only if all major forces are coordinated in a positive effort for passage, and all negative issues are repudiated or neutralized. Schur (1980) argues that a primary concern of a "stigma contest," which these campaigns essentially resemble, is the struggle to define the central definitional issues of any debate over legal reform concerning vice. The following chapters show that the most salient negative issue is crime—both organized crime and street crime. The appearance of any strong negative force will spell defeat for the measure. Moreover, the ability of casino opponents to determine the parameters of the legalization debate has been significant in all states since New Jersey.

Our model was derived from an in-depth analysis of the Florida (1978) and New Jersey campaigns (1974, 1976), and its efficacy as an explanatory as well as a predictive tool is tested below by an examination of case studies across the United States. We have tried to be all-inclusive in the sense that we have examined each casino legalization effort that has emerged with at least some serious content since the onset of the third wave. For background reasons, our study also reaches back to two campaigns in the early 1960s. The bulk of attention, however, is given to efforts to secure casino legalizations in the years since the successful drive in New Jersey. The depth of treatment given to each study was determined by our assessment of the degree of seriousness of the campaign. Most attention was given to the jurisdictions experiencing actual referendum votes, especially at the state level, or where advanced legislative activity was witnessed. With 1989 cases, we analyze them to the extent possible as this book goes to press.

Where we could not discern any activity for casino legalizations in a state, we considered that fact alone to be conclusive that the state should not be treated in the study. If our veto model is an effective tool for explaining the defeat of campaigns, we can be so bold as to advance the notion that, where no campaign existed, we might also find our veto factors manifesting themselves. Campaigns are generally lacking in mountain and southern states (Florida, Colorado, Louisiana, and Arkansas being exceptions). These states, while they may experience economic downturns with the rest of the nation, have not suffered the pains of public budget crises as extensively because they have not established as strong a pattern of public expectations for social services as in other states. For the most part, these states have not accepted other forms of legalized gaming to the extent that the campaign states have. These states do not for the most part have developed tourism industries that would seek gaming in order to attract patrons. They may also have the strongest religious-political lobbies that would stand ready to invest or be catalysts for investments of resources in campaigns against gambling. It is likely that such interests could dominate themes examined in casino campaigns. At the onset, then, we would conclude that the veto factors may be effective in vetoing the establishment of campaigns for casinos.

The following chapters present case studies from the eighteen casino legalization efforts conducted in the United States since 1964, aside from the Florida (1978) and New Jersey campaigns. Some of the cases include public referenda, others only legislative studies. In some of the states profiled, enormous sums of money and other resources were spent on either side of the casino issue. In other states, relatively modest funds were deployed. Some efforts were among the most publicized issues of that state's election or legislative session. Other efforts were of secondary importance. Some of the states concerned are in the industrial Northeast or Frostbelt; others are in the Sunbelt.

In presenting the cases, we have tried to bring forth the individual features of the efforts in each of the states. In doing so, we have consciously sacrificed an approach that would have presented cases as mere recitations or listings of the factors that have been identified in the model presented. We save such an analysis for the concluding sections of chapters 5 and 6 and for the concluding chapter of this study.

The most striking similarity among these eighteen cases is that the outcomes, except for New Jersey, were the same: defeat for casinos. The third wave of legalized gambling included jai alai, horse racing, off-track betting, bingo, legal numbers, and lotteries among its successes. Only casinos were a failure, and only in 1989 did this pattern begin to shift on a limited basis.

5 ~ The Frostbelt States

The Northeast, suffering from industrial relocation and fiscal crises in several states, and with the highest national proportion of citizens who gamble, was naturally the first region seriously to consider legalization of casinos. The New Jersey experience had prompted several states to consider casinos after 1978, whether to emulate Atlantic City's success or as a defensive reaction. New York, Massachusetts, New Hampshire, Connecticut, Pennsylvania, Michigan, Illinois, and Rhode Island all debated the casino issue between 1978 and 1984. Several of these states, with large markets of potential gamblers within easy driving distance of their proposed locations, would present strong competition to Atlantic City for a share of the regional casino gambling dollar. While New York was not the first to act, it was the most serious effort, and therefore we turn to that state's consideration of casinos first.

The Major Efforts:
New York, Massachusetts, Michigan, Pennsylvania

New York: "Let the People Decide"

Casino gambling for New York State died in Albany this week for the fourth time since 1972. It was done in by religious opposition, racetrack money, the spectre of organized crime, inept lobbying and lukewarm backing by state leaders.

—Ackerman 1981:1

Political Environment

Prior Experience with Gambling. New Yorkers like to gamble. According to *Gambling in America,* the 1976 report of the federal Commission on the Review of the National Policy toward Gambling, New Yorkers ranked first in the nation in gambling experience. The state also ranked first in legal gaming revenue in 1980.

New York has also led the way in legalizing many forms of gambling. In 1971, it became the first state outside Nevada to permit off-track betting on horse races. OTB, the Off Track Betting Corporation, grew quickly in volume, revenue, and popularity. By 1976, its fifth year of operation, gross revenues were over $100 million. Like several other northeastern states, New York has also legalized various forms of lottery and number games. All of these were passed by both houses of the state legislature, with the support of the governor and the mayor of New York City. During the 1970s, while these new forms of gambling were prospering, the New York horse racing industry had fallen on lean days. Attendance and wagering at New York's thoroughbred and harness tracks were declining when inflation was accounted for. Horse racing, the sport that had been the gathering place for New York's elites, was slipping relative to newer forms of wagering.

On the illegal side, estimates from government agencies on the amount of illegal betting in New York City alone range from $800 million to $1 billion annually. Two social scientists who studied the size and function of illegal gambling markets in New York City estimated annual illegal gambling at $800 million (Reuter and Rubinstein 1982). Whether legally—in OTB parlors or at drugstore LOTTO machines—or illegally—in any of New York City's illegal casinos or with the numbers games that proliferate in the lower-class sections of the city—New York City and state residents are avid gamblers.

When Resorts International Hotel and Casino opened its doors in Atlantic City on Memorial Day weekend in 1978, legal casino gambling had moved within a few hours' drive of New York City. Legal casino gambling, the one form that New York had not yet adopted, was within a day's trip of millions of New York residents. To some New York state legislators, who had witnessed the economic decline of the state during the early 1970s, the potentially revenue-rich casino industry in New Jersey looked attractive. Many had lived through the fiscal crisis of New York City in 1975, and its nearly miraculous recovery at the hands of Felix Rohatyn and the Municipal Assistance Corporation.

Economic Situation. New York politics was not a stranger to the use of legalized gambling as a revenue-raising mechanism. OTB had coincided with the fiscal crisis of 1975. And, while New York City had bailed out of that ordeal, restoring its bond ratings and fiscal stability, there were indications that the state was continuing to be affected. The state's labor force, like that of neighboring Northeast industrial states, had been shrinking as outdated industrial plants were closed down and as major manufacturers sought conditions more favorable to growth and business concerns. Between 1970 and 1976, the labor force in New York had shrunk by 700,000 workers. The

Economic Development Board, established by Governor Hugh Carey to protect the health of the private sector, advised him that the state's economic decline and loss of jobs were its foremost concerns. In fact, New York took some forceful action to improve its business climate, including the passage of incentives for business expansion and the delaying of environmental impact statements.

To some New York City hotel executives, Atlantic City gambling would soon pose a threat to the convention business that Manhattan enjoyed. To some upstate New York resort hotel owners in the Catskills and city officials in Niagara Falls, Atlantic City provided a model for legal casinos in their areas. Both the Catskills and the Niagara Falls areas were established resort areas, the latter slowly declining, facing a direct challenge for the tourist dollar from the more exciting Atlantic City casinos. Niagara Falls was experiencing an economic downturn, as was much of the Frostbelt or Rustbelt, as the industrial Northeast was called. The state of New York had already done the groundwork, commissioning a number of studies to assess the feasibility of legalized gambling in the early 1970s (Hudson Institute 1973). At that time, casinos had been thought to be riskier and more cumbersome to regulate than lotteries or off-track betting. However, when Atlantic City casinos opened in 1978, interest in New York casinos was sparked.

Proposals for Casinos. Unlike New Jersey, New York offered no obvious single location for the operation of legal casinos. While Atlantic City had been a fading resort town, only the Catskills among potential New York sites easily fit that image. The Catskills provided one of the strongest arguments for an Atlantic City–type legalization in New York. The once thriving area, located a few hours by car from New York City, had been a major resort for many years. The clientele upon which the Catskills had depended was largely middle-class and Jewish, groups who could easily patronize either Atlantic City or Massachusetts casinos. When the issue of casinos first arose in the New York legislature, Catskills hotel owners were among the first proponents of bills that would include their area in any legalization scheme.

The Catskills was an area, like Atlantic City, that had faltered when relatively inexpensive airline travel made the Bahamas and other Caribbean islands competitive with the local automobile-oriented resorts. However, the Catskills did change its appeal in the 1970s. The predominantly Jewish clientele changed to include a larger gentile population. Still, the age factor remained. The Catskills had definitely lost the market among younger people and hoped that the excitement of casinos would restore that age group to the Catskills' clientele.

The social benefits of casinos in the Catskills were keyed to the ease with which casinos could be made operational. The existing hotel stock there was reasonably good. In addition, casino supporters argued, it could be easily converted to casino and hotel room specifications. Several large hotels were likely candidates for casinos. They could be divided into three categories. At 1,200 rooms, the Concord was probably of the size and stature to make the easiest transition to a casino hotel. At the second level, there were eight or nine sites that had around 600 rooms, which would qualify if New York adopted a 500-room minimum for casino hotels. Among these were Grossinger's, Kutscher's, and the Nevele. In the third group were hotels with around 300 rooms. This third group could hope to benefit from legalization only if there was some sort of grandfather clause in the enabling legislation. Such a clause would permit already existing hotels to include casinos, even if they did not meet the room requirement, while forcing newly built structures to adhere to the limitation.

The Catskills hotel owners were definitely interested in casinos. They viewed legalization as the only way to keep their area competitive—for both tourist and convention business—with Atlantic City. While the occupancy figures and convention bookings shortly after the advent of Atlantic City casinos did not reflect damage to Catskills business inflicted by Atlantic City, the promoters of legalization explained that the correct figure to focus on was advance convention bookings, which they claimed were beginning to drop and would eventually result in a downturn in the Catskills economy.

Like the Catskills, Niagara Falls presented the model for the renovation of a decaying resort with the economic boost of casinos. However, in Niagara Falls the model was mixed. The area was dependent on more than tourism, unlike the Catskills, and it was suffering from the economic decline that had beset other Frostbelt cities. In fact, the executive director of the procasino lobbying organization, the Coalition for Casino Gambling, Inc., David Wrona, was the assistant general manager of the Niagara Hilton. He took a leave from that hotel, one of several in the area that were interested in being transformed into casinos. Wrona worked through a group formed and funded by the Niagara Falls city council and the Greater Niagara Job Development Corporation.

A few New York City locations were mentioned prominently as possible sites for legal casinos. Among these, the Rockaways, at the tip of Brooklyn, was considered a strong possibility because of the strong championship of legalization by Assemblywoman Gerdi Lipschutz. As the chair of the Assembly subcommittee on gambling, Lipschutz was in a position to keep her area's interests in prominent position in prospective legalization bills. In the Rockaways, a city-owned site of 150 acres, near water, was considered the leading candidate for a casino. Legalization was supported by the borough president, Donald Manes, and local residents of the area with a hard-core unemployment problem expressed support.

Coney Island advocates argued for their area's inclusion. Together, the Rockaways and Coney Island would have provided for a sizable presence of legal casino gambling adjacent to Manhattan, but in an area that could nonetheless be considered beachfront or resort area property. Niagara Falls supporters boosted that area's inclusion, as would some Buffalo residents. Finally, there were proposals including Manhattan, which generated no little controversy. Those who wrote about gambling preying on the imprudent judgment of the working class could hardly find a more densely populated area than Manhattan.

Added to the problem of location of casinos was the idea that publicly owned casinos were a possible way for New York government officials strictly to regulate an industry known for its attractiveness to organized criminals. This increased the difficulty of discussion of the casino issue when New York legislators turned to it in 1980. In addition, the state constitution required that any change such as that contemplated to allow casinos required passage of a bill by two consecutively elected legislatures, followed by state-wide voter approval and then local approval for the area in question.

Public Opinion. A poll taken for *Cue* magazine by Penn and Schoen Associates in September 1979 produced some interesting results that helped shape the casino legalization debate in New York. From a scientific sample of respondents in New York City, responses were categorized as to strength of attitude toward legalized casino gambling, location of potential casinos, organized crime, and the image of New York City, as well as the best reasons to support or oppose casinos for New York City.

On the question of which was the best reason to support casino gambling, asked only of those who expressed support for casinos, two responses brought overwhelming support: "it will bring jobs and business" received the support of 67%, and "increased tax revenue" received 65%. Lesser rated responses included "will bring people to New York" (26%), "other forms of gambling should be allowed" (24%), and "I like to gamble" (14%).

For the responses to the best reason to oppose, asked only of those who opposed casinos, only one response stood out—"it will bring organized crime" (62%). Lesser responses included "encourages prostitution, etc." (37%); "I oppose gambling" (32%); "it will hurt the moral climate" (28%); "casinos hurt the poor" (28%); and "I just don't like casinos" (14%).

Strong support of casinos in New York was expressed by 29% of the respondents, and some support by another 34%. Strong opposition was expressed by 18%, and some opposition by 15%. On specific locations, the respondents gave the following answers:

Location	Percentage in Favor	Percentage Opposed
Catskills	65	27
Niagara Falls	49	35
Manhattan	42	54
Your neighborhood	27	71
Rockaways	45	49
Long Beach	49	40
Coney Island	45	52

On the issue of organized crime, the following question was asked: "If casinos are legalized, will organized crime's influence in New York State increase?"—60% agreed, while 31% disagreed. On the question of whether the image of New York City would be affected if casinos were permitted, 33% thought that the city's image would be hurt, and 52% thought it would be helped, while 16% didn't know. In addition, in respect to the strong negative response toward organized crime, the pollsters placed the issue in perspective. In New York City, they argued, as far as crime is concerned, the primary issue is street crime, the second is subway crime—organized crime would be a remote third place.

From these findings, and similar results statewide, proponents and opponents fashioned slogans and appeals that were similar in style but divergent in substance: "Casinos Mean Jobs" and "Casinos Mean Mobs."

The Role of Political Elites

Among the New York officials whose support of casinos was decisive, several were notable. Even though the governor's signature would not be required on any enabling legislation for a referendum, Hugh Carey's support when casinos were first proposed was obviously important to the legalization proponents. In January 1981, at the outset of the legislative session, Carey's office expressed its support for casino gambling and its willingness to work for enabling legislation. "We will affirmatively support casino gambling," Carey's office told reporters, "on the grounds of economic competition, and equality with New Jersey" (*Newsday*, January 4, 1981). Carey was also subject to influence from New York's horse racing interests. In response to New York Racing Association concern over competition for a limited number of "leisure dollars," Carey reportedly told his commerce secretary to figure out which of the eight bills passed during the 1980 legislature would have the least impact on the racing industry and recommended that bill for passage.

Later Carey would confound the issue with several other proposals. Once, in 1981, he supported publicly owned casinos. Another time, in place of casinos, Carey offered instead the notion of legalizing slot machines, installed in specified hotels, bars, and transportation terminals. He said at a news conference early in 1981 that legal slot machines were to his liking (John Omicinski, "Gambling Effort Floundering," *Elmira Sunday Telegram,* February 1, 1981). The idea was attacked by Assemblywoman Lipschutz, the ardent casino supporter, who claimed that poor people would be more likely to play slot machines and computer games than to gamble in casinos.

Like Carey, attorney general Robert Abrams had expressed his support for casinos when they were proposed after Atlantic City casinos opened in 1978. Abrams had explicitly endorsed casinos in 1978 when running for attorney general. In August 1979, after taking office, Abrams stated that gambling was a fact of life, and that New Yorkers should take advantage of the revenues available with legalization. So it was a stunning blow to legalization hopes when Abrams distributed an official report (Abrams 1981) that announced his firm opposition to casinos in New York. He said it was a host of problems with New Jersey gambling, especially casino-related crime, that changed his opinion. In his report, he cited three major factors: possible increases in street crime, organized crime, and political corruption. On street crime: "The evidence from Nevada and Atlantic City conclusively indicates that legalized casino gambling in New York would be accompanied by a debilitating upsurge of crime in areas where casinos are located" (Abrams 1981:2). On organized crime: "Gambling casinos are a magnet for organized crime and New York lacks the sophisticated law enforcement system required to keep organized crime out of the casino gambling industry" (Abrams 1981:8). On political corruption: "Legalized casino gambling poses a danger to the integrity and credibility of government institutions and public officials" (Abrams 1981:18).

Abrams's statement made him the first statewide elected official to express opposition to casinos (*New York Law Journal,* May 21, 1981). Assembly Speaker Stanley Fink had been supportive of legalization efforts, but had advocated publicly owned casinos as the only way to prevent infiltration by organized crime. He said about the report: "Casino gambling was down for a nine count, and the Attorney General just kicked it in the head" (*New York News,* May 21, 1981). At that same time, a spokesman for Republican State Senate leader Warren Anderson said that the upstate New York senator was not enthusiastic about casino gambling and remained ambivalent on the several enabling bills before the legislature. The Senate, in 1981, as in previous years, proved to be the biggest obstacle to the legalization of casinos in New York. Before Abrams's statement, concern with organized crime had been diffuse, even if it had been prominent in the 1979 Penn and Schoen poll. After the report became a lightning rod for the organized crime issue, potential organized criminal involvement in the legal casino industry and possibilities of corruption became stumbling blocks for casino legalization in New York.

In addition to attorney general Robert Abrams, Dr. Gerald Lynch, the president of New York City's John Jay College of Criminal Justice, became an important actor in the casino story when he chaired Governor Carey's panel that studied casinos and issued a report in 1979 listing the costs and benefits of various legalization schemes and location proposals. While the mandate of his 1979 panel had not been to decide whether or not to legalize casinos, Lynch made his opinions known during the crucial stages of the 1981 debate as well. With the legislature poised to act on one or several bills in June 1981, Dr. Lynch made his first public statement in opposition to casinos. Appearing with Manhattan district attorney Robert M. Morgenthau, Lynch announced his opposition on the basis that casino gambling would promote crime and corruption. Lynch referred to his examination of the regulation of casinos in London and Atlantic City and noted that "the thread of casino money influence was woven throughout the fabric of ABSCAM" (*New York News,* June 25, 1981).

In London, Lynch said, "where the controls and limitations were far more stringent than would be possible under our constitutional form of government, 'casinos' . . . have been decimated by organized crime" (*Rochester Democrat and Chronicle,* June 27, 1981). Copies of Lynch's statement, as well as Morgenthau's, were duplicated in Albany soon after the two spoke in New York City and were distributed to Republican senators as they met in a closed-door caucus session.

None of the eight bills reached the floor of the Senate, and the legalization effort was dead for 1981. Proponents would claim later that casinos had never been voted down in New York, a technical truth that belied the reality of the failed effort. The biggest push in New York for legal casinos had come to a halt, the victim of several factors. Opponents would argue over which of those factors and which networks of contacts or strength of public appeal had triumphed against casino legalization. Only one thing could be said with certainty: the No Dice leaders had stated that they could not afford to compete with casino proponents in a referendum campaign. "We've got to beat it in the legislature," former state senator Thomas LaVerne told a reporter, "because we don't have the resources to beat it at the polls" (*Buffalo Evening News,* March 15, 1981). Whether LaVerne, who represented the interests of the race track owners, spoke for the other opponent groups was unclear. However, the effort to bring the issue of casino legalization to the state's voters had failed and would not succeed again in the next three years.

Issue Dominance: "Mobs" or "Jobs"?

Because of the New York requirements that mandated that a legalization bill be passed by successive legislatures, interesting jockeying arose around the importance of the referendum. With eight bills approved in 1980, allowing for any of a number of sites, lobbyists for the Coalition for Casino Gambling began in 1981—the year of the crucial second vote—to encourage legislators to approve one or more of the bills and let the voters make the ultimate decision at election time. This strategy attempted to sway some of the votes of key state senators who were wary of the legalization bills, but who might consider voting for a bill and submitting it to a popular vote. In a letter to several newspapers, Albert Formicola, the Coalition for Casino Gambling's vice-chairman and the president of the New York City Hotel-Motel Association, warned that "procrastination will only give a further edge to Atlantic City and three years from now it will be too late. . . . Casinos mean jobs. Let the people decide" (*Mount Vernon Argus*, April 10, 1981).

To the antilegalization group No Dice, a public referendum would have favored the proponents of casinos in several ways. Most important of these would be that voters might interpret, with the help of proponent commercials, the positive legislative vote to "let the people decide" as an actual vote in support of casinos.

While the *New York Times* continued to oppose casinos in New York as it had in Atlantic City, other New York newspapers joined it in editorial opposition to the various legalization bills. In an editorial entitled "Bad Bet on Casinos," the *Buffalo Evening News* (June 29, 1981) warned that any benefits from legalization were likely to be temporary. The *Rochester Democrat* wrote on June 27, 1981, that "arguments for casinos are fading fast." The same newspaper had cautioned the week before that "casinos' social effects mustn't be downplayed" (*Rochester Democrat*, June 27, 1981). In general, the newspapers took the "high road" of opposition to casinos by arguing that the casinos were high-risk, low-yield ventures. In that way they disputed the projections of a consultant group, Program Planners, and the New York State Department of Commerce, which estimated that a number of sites and casinos could be profitable and contribute to a rejuvenation of the local economy where they were placed. The newspapers' efforts could be contrasted to those opponents, like the New York Racing Association, who feared competition, or who found gambling morally objectionable, or who stressed the crime issue, organized or otherwise. *Newsday*, the leading Long Island newspaper, took a moderate position, supporting state-owned casinos built on a modest scale and modeled after Puerto Rican casinos, with prescribed hours of operation, no advertising or neon signs, and a discreet atmosphere, rather than patterned after Atlantic City or Las Vegas (January 4, 1981).

Public officials in the areas to be affected spoke up and were generally favorable to the idea of legalization. The mayor of Buffalo believed that casinos would not be disruptive to that city's economy because Buffalo was diversified (*Buffalo Business Review,* May 11, 1981). Both he and the Niagara Falls mayor lobbied in Albany in the spring of 1981 for the passage of the gambling bills. Of the hotel owners who stood to benefit, the general manager of the Niagara Hilton was representative when he claimed, "we are in dire need of an economic stimulant, and casino gambling is the only one around the corner" (*Niagara Gazette,* May 21, 1981).

In January 1981, Mayor Edward Koch of New York City reaffirmed his support of casinos. In a letter to State Assembly leader Stanley Fink, Koch said he would back casino gaming if privately owned casinos were allowed in New York City and if the city would receive at least 12% of casino revenues—a significant increase from the 8% that New Jersey casinos paid to that state's treasury. Koch explained that he supported casino gambling "solely for economic reasons" (*New York Times,* January 19, 1981). In addition, Koch said he would support a plan that included New York City only if it came with legislation that allowed the residents of each of New York's five boroughs to decide whether to permit casinos in that borough. Koch's problems with casinos extended to his own cabinet. Bernard Rome, Koch's advisor and head of OTB, had been outspoken in his criticism of developing plans for New York casinos. Rome refused to back Koch's announced policy supporting casinos and was asked to resign. He continued to oppose casinos, including a notable *New York Times* Op-Ed page article.

With all this activity keyed toward the second year's consideration of the eight gambling bills in 1981, there was still no indication of how the state's political leaders would assert their respective influence. Only one thing could be said without dispute in early 1981: as Stanley Fink indicated to the *New York Times* (May 21, 1981), there was no clear consensus in the Assembly and Senate on how casinos should be run or where they should be established.

Conclusion

After the failure of the 1980–1981 bills, legalization momentum in New York subsided. But there were still surges of movement among casino supporters. Proponents claimed that their bills had never been voted down and sought to recharge the elements that brought them close to passage, as well as removing some of the obstacles. The governor's support was one key factor. Mario Cuomo, lieutenant governor and Democratic candidate for governor, said during his campaign in 1982 that casino gaming was an issue that the people should decide in a referendum. After Cuomo had won the election, his press secretary said that the governor-elect personally opposed casinos, but felt that one or two should get underway on a trial basis if approved by a popular referendum, with a special board appointed to pinpoint the areas of location.

In 1983, four legalization measures were introduced in the New York legislature. Assemblywoman Lipschutz's subcommittee passed a resolution to allow casinos in Niagara Falls, Sullivan and Ulster counties (the Catskills), and the Rockaways. That same year, the Catskills resorts' interests hired one of the most prominent lobbying firms in Albany—Condello, Ryan, and Piscatelli. For the one client, and the one issue, the firm was paid an estimated $50,000 annually for three years (1983–1985).

According to No Dice lobbyist Charles Kriss, casino proponents in 1983 stressed the controllability of casinos. Such an approach was tied to a statement by New Jersey Gaming Control official Martin Danziger in *Public Gaming* that casino gambling is controllable and to claim otherwise is a subterfuge. According to Kriss, significant interest was generated in casinos in New York in late 1983. In 1984, Assemblywoman Lipschutz filed a bill to legalize slot machines only in resort areas of the state. The supporters of the slot legislation made much of the argument that slot machines were more easily controlled by the state because of sophisticated electronic mechanisms. It was not clear whether any of the well-established casino interests in New York—the resort owners, the labor unions, the businesspeople and the retailers—would remain happy in the future with a shift toward a slots-only development.

Massachusetts: "Over My Dead Body"

Introduction

The Commonwealth of Massachusetts acted prior to New York in following the lead of Atlantic City and proposing the legalization of casino gambling. This was not because Massachusetts had access to a larger tourist market than New York or had resort areas in more depressed conditions. Because of constitutional provisions that would permit the legislative sanction and legalization of casinos with county referenda rather than a statewide vote, Massachusetts might have been able to move quickly on the casino question in 1978, when efforts began to surface there.

Political Environment

In the wake of the defeat in Florida in November 1978 of the campaign patterned after the successful 1976 New Jersey campaign, casino legalization became an active issue in the Bay State. Two locales were prominently mentioned—the communities of Hull and Adams. Hull is a seaside community close to Boston. It had experienced economic decline during the 1970s and was suffering from an unemployment rate higher than that of the rest of the state. The second suggested location, Adams, is a resort town of several thousand in the Berkshire Mountains west of Boston, about as accessible from New York as it is from Boston. One prominent casino corporation— Metro-Goldwyn-Mayer—was involved in promotion of the legalization effort, as MGM Greylock. MGM, once a motion picture giant, had been more recently known for its successful operation of the MGM Grand Hotels in Las Vegas and Reno.

The change in strategy by Massachusetts casino proponents could focus attention on the residents of the immediate area to be impacted by casino legalization, rather than convincing voters in the entire state on the advisability of improving the economic condition in one or two areas. By so doing, they enjoyed one point of support while encountering one obstacle. On the positive side, local residents stood to benefit most from the economic development surrounding casinos. This was not necessarily true of tax benefits, which would actually have been divided among all the counties in the state. In New Jersey, New York, and other states considering legalization, state tax revenues from legal gambling were earmarked for the state general fund, in some cases being set aside for support of programs for the poor, aged, or disabled. On the negative side, polls from New Jersey and elsewhere showed that citizens were more supportive of casino proposals when it was clear that such casinos would not be located in the respondents' home communities.

In both Hull and Adams, local residents had voted in favor of casinos for their home areas. In 1978, 70% of Berkshire County residents who cast votes in a referendum to allow casino gambling were against the proposition, although the question carried in Adams, the proposed site of the casino facility (Legislative Research Bureau 1983:307). Hull's vote was on a strictly local referendum, in which the non-Hull residents of Plymouth County did not participate (Legislative Research Bureau 1983:307). The nonbinding votes did not provide the Massachusetts legislature with a mandate to act in accordance with the results of the referendum. But it is significant to note that sizable opposition forces arose within the two regions.

In the Berkshires, the first negative report came from the Casino Study Committee of the Berkshire Hills Conference in October 1978. With the action of MGM Greylock, the introduction of House Bill 1398 in 1977 by an Adams representative to the state legislature, and the impending ballot question, the study committee analyzed the costs and benefits of casinos for the region. The report stressed both the positive aspects and negative findings from other studies of casino impact. The negative list included increased crime and prostitution; increased organized crime; impulsive gambling; land speculation and tenant dislocation; and negative effects on the area's existing tourist economy. Positive issues included the lack of a large, modern, first-rate convention facility in New England; the job production potential of casino development; the inevitability of some casino legislation within five years in Massachusetts and throughout the United States; tax revenues for the state and local entities; and general nonseasonal multiplier effects.

Still, the study committee's recommendation, unanimously adopted by the Berkshire Hills Conference's Board of Directors on October 19, 1978, was: "Given the probability that casino gambling would have a negative impact upon the arts, the image and quality of life of the Berkshires; and given that the final language of casino enabling legislation is undetermined and subject to change, the committee feels that the element of casino gambling should not be introduced within Berkshire County" (Casino Study Committee 1978:7).

In the report's appendix, the committee indicated it had spoken with prolegalization interests, but also with the organized opposition in the Adams area—Voices, Not Vices. That group could claim some responsibility for the 1978 vote in Adams being close (2,218 to 2,067), even while it was positive in favor of legalization. The countrywide vote had been 31,835 against and 13,665 for (*Boston Globe,* August 2, 1979).

The casino issue took on a new life when the House of Representative's Committee on Government Regulations recommended that a bill permitting casino gambling in Berkshire and Barnstable (Cape Cod) counties be passed. "When people go somewhere, they want to go for some action. And we're not providing that action. We've been too conservative," said Robert Ambler, the committee's chairman (*Boston Globe,* August 2, 1979), in approving for the first time legislation that would bring casinos to Massachusetts. Under the Ambler bill, the state would have received 1.4% of the gross revenues of the casinos and would regulate gaming. The local community where the casino was located would receive 5.6% of the casino's gross income.

While some speculated that Ambler's intention was to prepare the way for a 1980 push for legalization, he said himself that the issue had been over-studied and that it was time to act. Legislators from the counties to be affected complained that they not only did not support the legislation, but had not been consulted regarding the approval by Ambler's committee. While the idea that New York might act first and beat Massachusetts to the opening of a legal casino worried some, the 1979 bill died in the legislature, only pointing the way to an eventual showdown over the casino issue.

That showdown arrived in 1981, when Hull began to appear as a second site to accompany Adams. MGM began negotiations in 1980 to buy land at Hull, when indications were given in the legislature that bills to permit gambling in those two areas were to be reintroduced in the 1980 legislative session (*New York Times*, March 13, 1981). The same article indicated that Greylock Associates was interested in casino properties in Connecticut and New Hampshire.

The Role of Political Elites

The fiscal crisis that had engulfed New York in the mid-1970s and the decline of the economic base that was affecting the industrial Northeast had caused particular problems for Massachusetts. The Reagan budget cuts had caused some fiscal problems for the state, and a tax-cutting referendum, Proposition 2½, was overwhelmingly approved by the state's voters in November 1980 (*New York Times*, March 13, 1981). At that point, Governor Edward King appeared noncommittal about the casino issue. That position changed in September 1981 when King committed his office to a drive to defeat legalized casino gambling in Massachusetts. "I am absolutely opposed to casino gambling," the governor said. "As far as I'm concerned, the only way you are going to get casino gambling in Massachusetts is over my dead body" (*Boston Herald American*, September 13, 1981). In June, King had said he favored an areawide vote on the legalization issue and, while neutral toward the idea, had indicated he might sign a bill if the legislature passed it. He apparently cooled on the casino idea after he attended the Governors' Conference in Atlantic City in August 1981 and after New York state attorney general Robert Abrams issued his report that indicated a 180-degree shift in his view of legalization.

King pointed to what he called the "seamy bedfellows of casino gambling"—increased crimes of violence, corruption, drug traffic, prostitution, family instability, alcoholism, and organized crime—as reasons for his disapproval. About Atlantic City, he said, "Corruption and crime is all you read about down there. I know about the new hotels, the payrolls, the taxes. I'm for business, but not that kind of business . . . it's something we can do without. We're doing quite well. We've got a strong economy. The social cost would be too high" (*Boston Herald American*, September 13, 1981). With that, King promised to veto any bill that reached his desk permitting legal casinos in Massachusetts.

In staking out his position, King wanted to correct the misconception that he was "nothing more than a bottom-line man" (*Quincy Patriot Ledger*, September 17, 1981). In opposing casinos, he joined the attorney general of Massachusetts, Francis X. Bellotti, and the lieutenant governor, Thomas P. O'Neill III, who had gone on record in opposition earlier in the year. King also called on newspapers, radio stations, and television stations to join his attack on casino gambling.

While King's staunch opposition indicated that effective legalization would be thwarted in Massachusetts for the rest of his term, the forces that coalesced in favor of the idea planned to wait King out and hope that the next governor might be more neutral toward their plan, as King himself had once been (*Quincy Patriot Ledger*, September 14, 1981). The election in November 1982 was projected to present a new political picture.

Issue Dominance: Dubious Economic Benefit

In the meantime, other forces in opposition and new state studies of the legalization issue were put in motion. Important labor organizations in the state were described as "putting on a full court press" on the issue (*Quincy Patriot Ledger*, September 17, 1981), a statement of some meaning in a traditionally Democratic state with a history of championship professional basketball.

Another local report, this one more detailed than the Berkshires' report of 1979, was issued by the South Shore Chamber of Commerce in December 1981. The report accompanied announcement of the Chamber of Commerce's decision to oppose introduction of legal casinos in Hull. The chamber referred to earlier supporters of legalization in New Jersey and their contention that casinos should be used as a last resort by an area with serious economic problems and no other prospects for development (South Shore Chamber of Commerce, press announcement, December 18, 1981). Their area, the South Shore group stated, was not in such a desperate condition. Indeed, the case pointed to an interesting physical issue with the location of casinos in Hull. Since it is at the edge of a peninsula, tourists planning on gambling there would have to utilize a road that passed through a wealthier area that, unlike Hull, was not itself in economic decline. The other option, considered marginally practical, would be for a hydrofoil to bring customers from the Boston area to Hull.

The chamber's decision was considered bad news for those who favored legalization, since it was felt by some observers that the report would influence the opinions of area legislators (*Quincy Patriot Ledger*, December 18, 1981). In the report, the chamber compared casino legalization as a policy option to the use of cancer drugs: "It may be necessary as a last effort to revitalize an area, but it will have strong negative side effects." The task force did not believe that the MGM proposal "is safe enough medicine for the region, the state and probably Hull to warrant its adoption at this time" (Casino Gambling Task Force 1981:5).

At the same time, Carol Oteri, vice-president of the Massachusetts Citizens against Casinos, and later an articulate member of the LANCE group (Legislators against New Casino Expansion), continued to lobby against casinos. She mentioned the blizzard of 1978 as a possible contributing factor to the legalization debate, since it might have "set up a disaster mentality ready for exploitation" (*Yankee,* March 1982).

But by far the most comprehensive analysis of the benefits and costs of legalization was being conducted by the Legislative Research Bureau of the legislature, which began its work in November 1981. It undertook what is arguably the most thorough analysis of the casino question by any state that considered casinos in the 1970s and 1980s. The report, prepared by Charles R. Ring and Robert D. Webb, would not be issued until April 1983; but by virtue of its research, it prompted formal position statements by various state officials.

The United States attorney, requested by the Legislative Research Bureau to comment on legalization proposals, responded in September 1982 with a six-page statement that drew heavily on the Abrams report from New York and dwelt on negative factors associated with casinos in New Jersey and Nevada: increase in street crime, public corruption, and organized crime. He wrote: "we believe that the experiences of Las Vegas and Atlantic City demonstrate that dramatic increases in violent crime, organized crime, and public corruption are the natural corollaries of legalized casino gambling. We would expect similar effects if casino gambling is legalized in Massachusetts" (Weld 1982).

The attorney general for Massachusetts also registered his suspicion of the economic benefits that would result from legalization. "It has never been shown," Bellotti argued, that "the vast amounts of money generated by casinos have ever brought any economic benefit to anyone other than those directly involved in the operation." Massachusetts residents, Bellotti further argued, would be the primary patrons of any legal casino establishments, and legalization would therefore be a regressive tax. In addition to questioning the possible benefits of casino gambling, Bellotti repeated warnings of increased street crime, organized crime, and public corruption. He also expressed fears that the increased law enforcement expenditures to contain such crime might be so substantial as to offset what he called the "illusory financial benefits identified by the proponents of legalized gambling" (Belloti 1982).

The Legislative Research Bureau's report, issued on April 13, 1983, is a 355-page document that surveys most of the relevant material on the subject of casino legalization. Because the bureau was not supposed to make a recommendation, there are no explicit directions given to the legislature. However, if one wanted to make a case for casinos from the report, one would have to sidestep the voluminous analysis of the problems associated with legalization. The report is balanced, but, on the whole, one might say that the costs of legalization seem clear, while the benefits are speculative—exactly the situation that spelled defeat for casino proponents in Florida. In any case, Michael Dukakis, who succeeded Edward King as governor (and who had preceded him as well), did not have to make a decision whether to sign a bill or not. There was no momentum in the legislature to pass any of the legalization bills, and the tide that seemed to be growing in the late 1970s in the Northeast did indeed ebb in Massachusetts by 1984.

Conclusion

While the Reagan budget cuts and the state tax relief measure hampered some Massachusetts efforts for fiscal solvency, by 1984 Massachusetts had weathered the storm of economic decline far better than some of its Frost-belt neighbors (*Los Angeles Times*, November 30, 1984). Even as the casino bills were debated, Massachusetts was intent upon developing its high-technology sector, which had been growing steadily for some time. The transition from heavy manufacturing to more contemporary methods and products had been handled successfully in Massachusetts, to the extent that, combined with demographic factors, high-tech and service sector growth made Massachusetts in 1984 the industrial state with the lowest unemployment rate, 3.7% (*Los Angeles Times*, November 30, 1984). The idea that Massachusetts was in dire straits and that gambling casinos were indeed a last resort for a desperate state was difficult to establish during the 1979 and 1980s debates over legalization. By 1984, it would be impossible.

Michigan: Another Plan to Save Detroit

Political and Economic Environment

Economic Situation. No state suffered through the recession of the early 1980s with as much economic despair as Michigan. The automobile industry witnessed a high rate of unemployment. Industry cities such as Detroit and Flint have seen unemployment rates reach 25%. Added to this cyclic economic calamity were massive problems of urban decay and a population that was heavily taxed. Michigan has searched for solutions and few have been found. Economically, the state has been ripe for any gimmick or serious plan that might ease the pain. Detroit has looked to inner city structures such as hotels, convention centers, new stadiums, and trolley cars—and to casino gambling.

Casino Proposals. The third wave of legalized gambling hit Michigan in 1972, as Michigan voters approved both a lottery and charity gambling. The constitutional amendment that was ratified in the vote also removed prohibitions against other forms of gambling. The legislature therefore gained the power to legalize casino gambling. Soon casino advocates had a sponsor for such legislation, Democrat Casmer Ogonowski, a state representative from Detroit. Ogonowski was first elected in 1968 and was appointed to the tourism committee of the House of Representatives. By 1975, he was the chairman of the committee and regularly introduced bills for casino gambling. In April 1975, Ogonowski sponsored a successful resolution that called for the creation of a special casino gambling study committee, of which he was made chairman. Ogonowski's committee held nine public hearings throughout Michigan and gathered information from Nevada and foreign casino jurisdictions, as well as from surveys of tourists and members of the Michigan Travel and Tourist Association. Respondents favored limited casino gambling in Michigan. The members of the tourist industry favored the idea by a two to one margin. Major reasons cited in favor of casinos were the creation of additional jobs and boosts to tourism and convention business (Michigan House of Representatives 1976:3–8).

Nonetheless, when Ogonowski introduced House Bill 6078 in 1976, he found that the idea of selling casinos was made no easier because of his surveys. His bill, which provided for casinos just in Detroit, was defeated in his own committee. Ogonowski had claimed that four casinos in Detroit would produce about $58.4 million in taxes and that 70% of this amount would come from visitors to the state. His colleagues argued that they could not support his bill until the voters of Detroit indicated their approval for the idea. This sentiment was also expressed in the 1975 hearings. Several people indicated that casinos should be approved only after a referendum vote, not by legislation alone. Therefore, Ogonowski and other casino supporters persuaded the Detroit city council to place the question of casino gambling on an advisory ballot in the November 1976 election. The campaign of 1976 won the support of Detroit's mayor, Coleman Young, but the campaign did not have any focal point of leadership. Very little media attention was given to the cause. It was defeated by a three to two margin at the polls.

In 1977, casino supporters gave it another try. Several downtown business investors spearheaded the drive. Brothers John and J. Michael Hughes joined with Dr. Eugene Horrell in purchasing the defunct 800-room Tuller Hotel in downtown Detroit. They made an alliance with real estate developer Jerry Luptak and began raising funds for a campaign. They hired a Washington-based political consulting firm for a lobbying effort in Lansing. However, the lawmakers again balked at a bill introduced by Ogonowski. Attention was then given to winning another advisory vote in Detroit. The Hughes group drew support from the Central Business District Association and the Metropolitan Detroit AFL-CIO Council, but the attempt fell short.

The city council did not want the question on the ballot. Mayor Young was running for reelection in 1977, and he did not want to risk any votes on an issue that was roundly defeated just one year earlier. Ogonowski kept at it. In 1978, he regained the mayor's support along with the support of William Ryan, Speaker of the Michigan House. However, Republican William Milliken and his Democratic opponent in the 1978 governor's race, state senator William Fitzgerald of Detroit, indicated strong opposition. Horse track interests also voiced concern about casinos. Ogonowski's bill floundered once again.

The story was repeated in 1979 and 1980. Ogonowski's 1980 bill had twenty-four cosponsors. However, one of these, Mary Brown (Democrat of Kalamazoo), indicated that she had cosigned the bill simply because Ogonowski sat next to her in the house chambers. She said that the legislators could not give the matter serious attention until a specific casino corporation or interest stepped forward and stated its desire to come into Detroit. "Until that happens we will not have any idea about what we are considering," she said (Brown 1984).

But even after the 1980 defeat of the bill in his own committee, Ogonowski persisted in the effort. The Public Gaming Research Institute indicated that his bill "is picking up momentum with the bad economy. It will be reintroduced in 1981" (Public Gaming Research Institute 1980). It was—and it failed again. But there were other failures in 1981 for Ogonowski. The casino forces won another advisory vote for the issue in Detroit. But they lost a lot of credibility in the process. First, Ogonowski was arrested, indicted, and later convicted and sentenced to a term in federal prison for accepting a $4,000 bribe for efforts to gain a lottery sales license for a grocery store owner. Second, direction for the advisory vote campaign somehow fell into the hands of Tom Wishart, a self-appointed promoter who had previously crossed paths with the law over his pornographic bookstores. Among other things (claiming support from national hotel chains and indicating large financial backing), Wishart selected a Committee for Hotel Casinos and Tourism. He placed prominent Detroit businesspeople in leadership roles on the committee. However, after he bandied their names around, it was revealed that they had no knowledge of the committee or of Wishart—and they indicated that they opposed casinos. Restaurateur Joe Muer III, co-owner of the famous downtown seafood restaurant that bears his name, claimed, "It's one of the most dishonest things a man can do, to use someone else's name. I totally and vehemently object to casino gambling" (*Detroit News*, October 2, 1981). Wishart's fund raising didn't go much better. He attempted to raise $300,000 in a gala event at the Renaissance Center but lost money instead. His campaign spent close to $10,000.

The opponents did somewhat better. The Jackson Trotting Association alone gave the opposition campaign $10,000. Other racing interests also contributed, as did a large group of black clergy in Detroit. The ministers also utilized their pulpits against casinos.

Before the campaign had gotten under way (the measure was placed on the ballot at an August city council meeting), Governor Milliken attended the governors' conference in Atlantic City. He returned to Michigan as a more vigorous foe of casinos. He called casino gambling "the plague" and vowed to veto any casino bill passed by the legislature. Mayor Young faced another reelection campaign in 1981. While he had publicly endorsed casinos, he did virtually no campaigning on behalf of the proposition and kept his distance from Wishart. Casinos did not have a chance. Detroiters cast 161,000 ballots against casinos, and 96,000 in favor. That vote along with Ogonowski's departure slowed down the campaign for Michigan casinos considerably.

But the issue will not go away entirely. A new state representative, Thomas Scott, Democrat of Flint, introduced legislation for state-owned slot machines to be placed in bars throughout the state. His efforts, however, did not gain the support of any of his colleagues. In 1984, new promoter groups, led by developer Patrick Meehan, focused attention on Detroit's Belle Isle, a pleasant park in the middle of the Detroit River, near downtown. Their plans received encouragement from the fact that William Milliken retired from the governorship. His replacement, Democrat James Blanchard from the Detroit area, understood the grave economic conditions of the region perhaps better than his predecessor, who was from the far northern reaches of the state. However, Blanchard took a "wait and see" attitude toward casinos. But in 1983, with the Republican party reemerging as the majority contingent in the state senate, passage of a casino bill became very difficult.

Nonetheless, Meehan's group reached an agreement with Resorts International to push his plans. In 1985, state Senator Jackie Vaughn took up the cause and introduced two bills for local-option casinos for hotels. There was little support for such legislation. House Speaker Gary Owen, like Vaughn, a Democrat, said he would oppose any attempt to authorize casinos. He saw little support in the House for the idea. Senate Majority leader John Engler, a Republican, said "the Detroit religious community has some very serious concerns, and I don't see the Detroit delegation in the Legislature united on this. That causes some problems right off the bat" (*Detroit Free Press*, February 27, 1985). The proposals did not receive a hearing.

Two years later, the mayor of Detroit, whom many considered to be the politically strongest mayor in the country, came off the fence. He endorsed casinos, and in December 1987 he persuaded the city council to appropriate

$150,000 to support the work of a "Blue Ribbon" commission of sixty-eight citizens which he would appoint to study the question of casinos.

The commission began work in March 1988. Most members claimed to be neutral on the subject of gaming, but few believed that. One skeptic was Thomas Barrow, formerly a candidate for the mayor's job. Barrow formed a rival group called Citizens for Detroit's Future (*Detroit News*, February 13, 1988). The group opposed casinos and immediately began a petition drive which placed a proposal ordinance on the August 1988 ballot banning casino gambling in Detroit. Young vigorously fought the placing of the negative question on the ballot, however, election authorities and state courts found no reason why the voters could not vote on such an ordinance (*Detroit News*, June 10, 1988). Before his commission could seriously ponder various options for casinos, the opposition had therefore seized the initiative and had begun its campaign in earnest. Ther were aided by several ministerial associations, by the horse-racing industry, and also by the Detroit Chamber of Commerce.

Polls indicated that casinos had little chance to win popular support within the city. An early *Detroit Free Press* poll found that 62% of Detroit residents opposed casinos in their city (*Detroit Free Press*, February 21, 1988). The poll also found that, statewide, Michigan citizens opposed casinos for Detroit by a 53% to 39% margin. A later poll showed statewide opposition to be much greater: 65% to 25% (*Detroit Free Press*, July 19, 1988). Legislators took heed, and very few expressed a willingness to support casinos. Governor Blanchard refused to endorse the idea, saying he remained "skeptical but open-minded" (*Detroit Free Press*, February 22, February 28, 1988).

The commission went about their task, issuing a report in June which called for ten to twelve casinos, which would provide 50,000 jobs for Detroit-area residents. The casinos were to be in hotels that would be constructed on land set aside for the purpose. Suggested areas would be removed from other commercial and residential areas by land and street barriers. While the commission had considered a smaller "European-style" casino arrangement, the mayor rejected that approach out of hand. "We ain't in Europe. Who the hell would come in here for something like that? I'm not going to get my head flattened for something like that. It doesn't make any sense." The voters of Detroit didn't find much sense in his plan either. The mayor loaned the campaign against the city ordinance banning casinos $287,000 from his personal campaign funds. But it was not enough. The voters said no to casinos on August 2 by a 62% to 38% margin. Young gave the epitaph for the casino movement in Michigan. "It's certainly dead for the moment. I may be hardheaded, but when you hit me on the head three times, I think I begin to get the message" (*Detroit News*, September 8, 1988).

Pennsylvania: Regional Competition

Pennsylvania had joined with other northeastern states in welcoming the third wave of legalized gambling. A lottery was established in 1971, and charity bingo was legalized in 1981. These programs have not been without their problems. The Keystone State lottery suffered a blow to its credibility when a numbers drawing was rigged and later exposed (*Christian Science Monitor*, March 31, 1982).

The effects of Atlantic City's amazing casino growth on East Coast tourism have certainly been felt in Pennsylvania. Residents of Pennsylvania account for nearly one-third of the revenues in the New Jersey casinos (*Sunbury Daily Item*, April 27, 1984), and many recreational businesses in Pennsylvania have suffered as a result. It has been reported that on-premise consumption of beer in Philadelphia area bars dropped dramatically as regular patrons took their business instead to the Atlantic City casinos (*Business Digest Monthly*, August 1984). These views were prominent soon after New Jersey's legalization of casinos, when a Pennsylvania legislator introduced casino legislation and argued for its passage as a way of beating other northeastern states to the casino dollar (Garzia 1977).

The brunt of the competition from Atlantic City has fallen on the tourist resorts of the Pocono Mountains area, specifically in the counties of Monroe, Carbon, Wayne, and Pike. Not surprisingly, this area has been the major target for Pennsylvania casino promoters. These proponents argue that the Poconos are losing more than $35,000 a day to Atlantic City and more than 300 jobs a year because of lost business (*Lancaster Sunday News*, December 18, 1983). Those pushing gaming have also sought to see casinos and slot machines established throughout the state, with attention given to Pittsburgh and Philadelphia.

Political Environment

Proposals for Casinos. The interest in the Poconos has been highlighted by the fact that major Las Vegas investors purchased resorts property. Caesars World acquired four properties, the first one in 1969. In 1982, Las Vegas entertainer Wayne Newton gained title to another resort. Both Newton and Caesars denied interest in using the properties for casinos. However, their mere presence allows others to speculate that, with legalization, major casino companies would invest in the Poconos resorts—the area is within a two-hour drive from New York City and Philadelphia and is less than five hours from Boston, Baltimore, and Washington, D.C. Two airports in the Poconos area are served by Eastern, United, and US Air airlines (*Meeting News*, February 1984).

The case of the Poconos campaigns presents a reversal of other campaigns in several respects. First, although Atlantic City has taken its toll, the resorts of the Poconos area are economically strong. In 1983, gross revenues grew over 8% to $200 million. Several properties were undergoing major renovations and expansions (*Meeting News*, February 1984). It is the economy of the whole state of Pennsylvania that has been hurting. Second, those promoting the legalization of casinos are politicians, for the most part from outside the resort area. Unlike the locals of other states who have had to struggle to convince those in other parts of their state that they should be allowed to have casinos, the locals of the Poconos area have had to struggle to persuade the outsiders that they do not want casinos.

Pennsylvania law allows casinos to be established there by simple legislative action. Legislation for the Pocono casinos was first introduced in 1977, but the resorts responded in the negative. The Pocono Mountains Vacation Bureau polled its 300 resort members and concluded that casinos were not welcome because they would conflict with the dominant family-oriented activities of the area (*Easton Express*, January 15, 1983). The area Chamber of Commerce also voiced opposition (*Leighton Times News*, April 21, 1981). And in an advisory referendum in 1977, the voters of Monroe County rejected a casino proposal handily, 5,060 to 1,320 (*Quakertown Free Press*, April 29, 1983).

Two years later, after Resorts International's Atlantic City casino had proved successful, a state senator conducted a feasibility study and introduced another bill for Poconos casinos (Shawn and Root 1980:7). After that bill died, Philadelphia legislators sought casinos with tax revenues earmarked for schools, but that proposal also failed (Klein and Selesner 1981:10).

Several bills in 1981 sought expansion of gaming in Pennsylvania. One effort, supported by legislators in Pittsburgh and Philadelphia, provided for the establishment of county gaming commissions by local option votes. The commissions would then regulate gaming activities approved by the counties. State senator James A. Romanelli, a bill sponsor, said, "Gambling is a willing tax. It's something the people want to do. Why shouldn't the government reap the benefits?" Allegheny County police superintendent Bob Kramer endorsed the proposal with the comment, "People by their very nature are gamblers. If it's going to go into illegitimate hands, why not channel some of it into doing some good for the people?" He claimed that his department did not have sufficient officers to "do the job on gambling violations that we should be doing" (*Pittsburgh Press*, September 20, 1981). Other political voices urged casinos as a way of restoring revenues to local governments that have been shortchanged by policies of Richard Thornburgh's gubernatorial administration. But the superintendent of the Pittsburgh Police Department, Robert Coll, was not totally convinced. He saw the revenues from the casinos as being "a drop in the bucket" when compared with other tax revenues. But he added, "If it's done properly and the right people are involved, it's o.k. with me" (*Pittsburgh Press*, September 20, 1981). However, the plan did not win wide-based support. The governor and key legislative leaders were in opposition. The bill died, as did other legislation in the 1981–1982 session that would have allowed sports betting and slot machines (*Wilkes-Barre Times Leader*, January 6, 1983).

Role of Political and Economic Elites

During the 1982 campaign year, both Governor Thornburgh and Lieutenant Governor William Scranton II stated that they were "flat out" opposed to casinos (*Easton Express*, October 6, 1982). However, as 1983 began, Pennsylvania faced some rather bleak economic forecasts. Cuts in federal programs culminated in a state budget deficit of $164 million. The unemployment rate for the state was 12.9%, the third highest among the industrial states.

For a moment, Thornburgh had second thoughts about gambling. He indicated a willingness to consider gambling as a potential revenue source. One high-level state political source indicated that Thornburgh might support slot machines or electronic poker in Pocono resorts. While his willingness to push strongly for legal gambling was in doubt, Thornburgh's remarks stimulated an avalanche of legislative proposals calling for casinos, sports betting, charity sports pools, punch boards, slot machines, and electronic poker games.

The legislation in turn stimulated much political and interest group maneuvering. As in all other jurisdictions, the clergy consistently opposed gambling. The Reverend Paul Gerhis, lobbyist for the Pennsylvania Council of Churches, attacked gambling in a January 1983 statement. "Gambling is a quick fix and doesn't solve any of the state's problems. We have a deficit of $164 million, and the lottery did better on a revenue basis than we thought. It made no dent in illegal numbers operations. It was a very slick sell." Gerhis revealed that he was working with the Tavern Association to fight a slot machine bill. The taverns were afraid that slots in private clubs would hurt their business (*York Dispatch*, January 28, 1983). Later in the year, the Pennsylvania Tavern Association favored a bill for slot machines in all establishments with liquor licenses (*Easton Express*, July 1, 1983).

Other ministers may have been more careful in their associations. United Methodist minister Mark King asserted the view that gambling was "a menace to society, deadly to the best of interests of moral, social, economic and spiritual life, and destructive of good government." His stance was strictly religious. "As a Christian and a minister of the gospel of Jesus Christ, I have a responsibility to Christ and to my conscience" to oppose gambling (*Hazelton Standard Speaker*, February 4, 1983). King had plenty of company in the pulpit. The Lehigh Presbytery cast a unanimous vote for a resolution opposing Pocono casinos. Representatives of thirty congregations in the Northeastern Pennsylvania Lutheran Synod unanimously opposed casinos. So did the Lutheran Church Women and the Penn Northeast Conference of the United Church of Christ (*Leighton Times News*, June 15, 1983).

With the introduction of multiple pieces of legislation in 1983, the Pocono Mountains Vacation Bureau decided to review the attitudes of its members once again. A June survey revealed some changes in feelings: members favored slot machines by a 277 to 154 margin. They continued to oppose casinos in the Poconos but only by a close margin of 226 to 207. On the basis of this survey, the bureau went on record favoring slot machines for the four county areas (*Easton Express*, July 1, 1983), at the risk of upsetting some member resorts. One, the Skytop Lodge, was so bothered that it withdrew its membership. Lodge manager Donald Biles said the "gambling with its well known and well documented evils would result in the worst possible catastrophe imaginable" in the Poconos (*Easton Express*, September 2, 1983).

Other tourist associations were divided in their opinions. The Luzerne County Tourist Promotion Agency members voted seventeen to fourteen to support casinos on a county option basis throughout the state (*Wilkes-Barre Times Leader*, September 23, 1983). The Pennsylvania Dutch Visitors Bureau went on record against any additional gambling legalizations in the state (*Lancaster Sunday News*, December 18, 1983). The Economic Development Council of Northeastern Pennsylvania also opposed casino legislation. Roy Martin, the council president, said they had examined the issue from an economic point of view. He concluded that casinos would cause substantial problems for economic development over and above any positive effects that might accrue as a result of permitting casino gambling. He observed that casino gambling would provide construction jobs, but that it would undercut opportunities for industrial development and add greatly to costs of local government services (*Allentown Morning Call*, January 8, 1983).

The Pocono Mountains Chamber of Commerce surveyed its membership. It found that 63% were opposed to any new gambling in the state (*Scranton Times*, November 19, 1983). Prior to the survey, the chamber conducted a three-year study of the impacts of casinos on the Poconos

(*Allentown Morning Call,* April 24, 1983; *Quakertown Free Press,* April 29, 1983). The Monroe County Commission also authorized an economic impact study. The two studies projected an additional 9 million visitors for the area. Between 18,000 and 27,000 new jobs would be generated. Real estate values would double. So would criminal activity. This would necessitate an increase in taxes of $6 million to pay for police services. Hospital costs would increase by $16 million, schools by $90 million, solid waste facilities by $30 million, and a new highway bypass would require an additional $339 million. To offset these costs, the casinos would generate from $252 to $430 million in annual revenues. The Monroe County Report asked: how much is the state going to give to the Poconos if they accept the burdens? "In Pittsburgh, there is no burden" (*Pittsburgh Post Gazette,* October 12, 1983).

In response to the pressures on Harrisburg legislators from gaming proponents, the opponents in Monroe County persuaded the county commission to place the question of casinos on the ballot. The commission agreed. "We think it's the best protection we can have, because you can never be sure what will happen in the Legislature. We're sort of forearming ourselves," said commission chair Nancy Shukaitis. The Reverend Thomas Richards, an active gaming opponent, acknowledged the possibility of a tactical error in calling such an election. But he led the Monroe County Clergy Association in a vigorous campaign that secured the results he desired. On May 17, the opponents of casinos garnered 10,019 votes. Only 2,537 voters (20.2%) favored casinos (*Quakertown Free Press,* April 29, 1983; *Easton Express,* July 1, 1983).

Despite the ringing defeat in Monroe County, campaigns for legal gambling continued through 1983 and 1984. In the fall of 1983, two legislators from parts of the state well outside the Poconos introduced a bipartisan bill for slot machines in the Pocono resorts. They were recruited by a political consultant with ties to gaming machine manufacturers. However, the bill failed, as did other bills introduced in 1983. Contributing to the defeats was the renewed opposition of both Governor Thornburgh and Lieutenant Governor Scranton (*Middletown Times Herald Record,* September 23, 1983; *Washington Observer Reporter,* October 27, 1983).

Issue Dominance: Rejecting the Inevitability of Casinos

The fall also saw the formation of a legislative coalition of fifty-five members pledged to oppose casinos and aligned with LANCE, the interstate group of public officials (*Bethlehem Globe Times,* October 12, 1983). In November, they took the offensive by pushing for a constitutional amendment to ban all new gambling legalizations. Coalition leader Joseph Battisto said, "The gambling interests would like everyone to believe that it's just a matter of time until casino gambling is in one state or another. Our answer to that insult is that we emphatically won't allow an outside force to upset our social order to the extent that it will produce an irreversible decline in our quality of life" (*Allentown Morning Call*, November 1, 1983; *Wilkes-Barre Times Leader*, November 11, 1983).

In 1984, over twenty gambling bills were introduced in the Pennsylvania legislature. The three most active bills provided for Pocono slots, slots state-wide on a city option basis, and charity games such as fishbowls and punchboards. For the most part, the proponents and opponents were the same as before, wielding identical arguments. Churchmen conducted sign campaigns as hearings were held on the bills. The Pennsylvania tavern owners again said that they "needed gambling revenues as a pick-me-up. The buses are leaving everyday taking thousands of dollars to New Jersey" (*Observer Bi Weekly*, January 23, 1984). Backers said a Poconos slots bill would bring $210 million in revenues to the area. A group called Concerned Citizens against Gambling challenged the claim, saying the people would have to lose $3.5 billion in the slots for the state to achieve such revenues. At a take of 17%, this would amount to play of $2,480 from every citizen of Pennsylvania (*Erie Daily Times*, January 17, 1984).

The executive director of the Pennsylvania Crime Commission testified that "organized crime elements will be attracted by the legalization of casino and slot machines. They are attracted by the opportunity" (*Sunbury Daily Item*, April 27, 1984). Local officials in the Poconos area remained opposed. The Kidder Township Supervisors (Carbon County) passed a resolution in opposition (*Hazelton Standard Speaker*, April 21, 1984). The Monroe County Commissioners succeeded in having the Pennsylvania State Association of County Commissioners pass resolutions opposing gaming and demanding local option referenda for any further gaming authorized by the legislature (*Allentown Morning Call*, August 3, 1984). The governor remained an opponent. "I can't muster much enthusiasm for gambling in the Poconos. [I have] spent too much time in law enforcement as a U.S. Attorney in Pittsburgh to want to import gambling into Pennsylvania," Thornburgh explained (*Bethlehem Globe Times*, February 5, 1984).

The minimal popularity of the gambling bills was revealed in a comment by one of the slot sponsors, Representative Gaynor Cawley of Scranton. In late March, he all but conceded defeat, saying, "It's an election year and many members of the Legislature are facing tough uphill fights to keep their seats. They can't afford to have their opponents using the gambling issue as a club against them" (*Scranton Tribune*, March 30, 1984). Supporting expanded gambling had become a political liability throughout Pennsylvania.

The single Poconos area legislator who cosponsored a slot bill for the region withdrew his support in February. He indicated that he did so because it had not received support in the Poconos area and had little chance for passage. It was observed that he faced a strong primary challenge from a candidate who was running on an antigambling platform (*Allentown Morning Call*, February 27, 1984).

Other candidates followed suit. Former congressman Allen Ertal had run for governor in 1982. At that time, he did not take a position on gambling, whereas his successful opponent, Thornburgh, had opposed gaming. In 1984, Ertal, a candidate for attorney general, opposed Poconos gaming because "people in the Poconos do not want it." He added, "I think it would change the character of the Poconos. The Poconos are a family resort and a honeymoon resort area, and to put gambling there would change the character. If they don't want it there, and they are the ones that live there, then why should the rest of the state foist it upon them? I don't think we ought to do that" (*Scranton Tribune Review*, August 20, 1984). Ertal's sentiments dominated Pennsylvania thinking in 1984. The League of Women Voters released an unfavorable report on gambling in April, pointing out environmental problems with gambling, such as pollution, road decay, and water shortages; social problems like compulsive gambling; and economic problems such as the regressive nature of gambling as a form of taxation (*Wilkes-Barre Times Leader*, April 25, 1984).

Only one of the gambling bills had even a glimmer of hope in 1984. The small games of chance (fishbowls) bill was amended to provide for local referenda. It then passed the House by a vote of 139 to 57. However, the Senate Finance Committee did not allow the bill to surface for Senate floor action (*Observer Bi Weekly*, August 29, 1984). No other bill survived a floor fight.

While there was genuine concern that outside gaming interests and supporters might be maneuvering for casinos in the Poconos and elsewhere, the business community of Pennsylvania was not enthralled by the idea. The directors of Herco, Inc., a Hershey-based firm that owns lodging facilities in the Poconos, announced that they would not allow any gaming in their resorts, whatever direction the law took (*Pittsburgh Press*, April 12, 1984). A survey of 305 Philadelphia companies conducted by the First Pennsylvania Bank found 70% opposed to the notion of casinos in the Philadelphia area; 62% felt the issue did not warrant further attention. Crime was seen as the major drawback to casinos. While 48% were indifferent to whether their company was located near a casino, 42% preferred a distant location. Several harsh negative comments were offered on gambling. Some saw their employees being hurt by gaming; others saw the image of the city being tarnished. One offered that "we might decide to move our company to the South if casino gambling comes" (First Pennsylvania Bank 1984).

Conclusion

There was also a turnabout in state fiscal affairs in 1984. While a deficit of nearly $500 million had been projected for the state in 1984, an actual surplus was being realized in the state budget (*Sunbury Daily Item,* April 27, 1984). The principal rationale offered by the outsiders for gambling seemed to have vanished. In 1985, casino-style gambling arrived in Pennsylvania by means of overlooking wording in a rider to a state law regulating liquor licenses. Little noticed when it was approved, the law permitted anyone holding a liquor license—bars, restaurants, or hotels—to sponsor card "tournaments" with cash prizes (*Las Vegas Review Journal,* February 10, 1985). In addition, the state's regulatory role was expressly limited by the approved law. Pennsylvania legislators soon enacted a new law removing the loophole, but for a while taverns in the region of Pennsylvania most adversely affected by Atlantic City competition had enjoyed a sizable increase in business. It was still not expected that the interest in gambling would lead to legalization of casinos in Pennsylvania, but, at least for a time, Pennsylvania had competed with New Jersey for the legal casino dollar.

Other Campaigns: New Hampshire, Connecticut, Illinois, Rhode Island

New Hampshire: Crest and Trough of the Third Wave

By Professor I. Nelson Rose's account, the upsurge of interest in legal gambling over the past two decades has been the third wave of gambling legalization in American history (Rose 1979). Beginning with the New Hampshire lottery in 1964, legal gambling grew in popularity as an alternative mechanism of taxation and as an attractive means of economic development. In New Hampshire, any momentum for casinos in the early 1980s was stilled by a report from the Commission on Gambling established by Governor Hugh J. Gallen. The commission had been constituted in July 1982 and had studied the potential impact of state legalization of jai alai, casinos, and off-track betting. The report did not single casinos out: it rejected all three forms of gambling as a prudent policy choice for New Hampshire. Gambling, the report concluded, "whether for the purposes of raising money for government or charities or for the sake of private business, is a corrupting enterprise. . . . Expansion of state-sponsored gambling, despite its beneficent rationale, is inevitably accompanied by a substantial increase in crime and its consequent violence" (Commission on Gambling 1983:2).

The commission's ultimate question about casinos was: do the benefits claimed to derive from legalized casino gambling outweigh the known social costs? The commission's overwhelming answer was no. This position was based on several separate conclusions. The first rationale was that casino gambling was not an economically sound source of public revenue, since New Hampshire casinos could not hope to draw upon as large a market as Atlantic City. The second point raised in opposition was that casino gambling would not invigorate the New Hampshire economy. The report cited the inapplicability of the Nevada experience to New Hampshire, and the limited success of casino development in Atlantic City spilling over into the noncasino sector. Finally, the report emphasized the problem of casino-generated crime. The long association of legal casinos with organized crime and the creation of an atmosphere in which street crime thrives were presented as the major points in opposition to casinos, with Las Vegas and Atlantic City supplying the prime examples.

Casino gambling, the report concluded, "for the little promise it holds out as a source of state revenue, will bring with it serious disadvantages. It will burden the state government and local communities with the cost of policing its operations and providing municipal services for the mass of patrons needed to make it run on a paying basis. It will devastate the existing family-oriented vacation industry" (Commission on Gambling 1983:24).

By 1983, LANCE was active in the Northeast and casino proposals no longer went unchallenged. It is not clear that New Hampshire's commission and governor singled out casinos for disapproval. What is clear is that the recommendation for casinos was a resounding no, a trough in the state where the third wave had begun twenty years earlier.

Connecticut: "Desperate to Raise Money"

The third wave of legalized gaming engulfed Connecticut swiftly and almost completely. In 1971, the Nutmeg State legalized a lottery, off-track betting, and betting on horse racing all at the same time. In 1972, dog race and jai alai betting were legalized (*New York Times*, February 1, 1981). Only casinos and sports betting remained, and campaigns for action in these areas began. Some legislators saw the financial success of the legalized games as evidence that the state could venture into casino gaming and also reap large returns. The 1980s brought the state financial problems that called out for solutions. The state faced a $50 million deficit as 1981 began (*New York Times*, January 31, 1981). The year also brought legislation for casinos. Proposed bills were introduced to allow a casino in the depressed community of Bridgeport. Most prominent among the supporters of the Bridgeport casino idea was the Connecticut Leisure Corporation, which wanted to build an $80 million casino in the city. It saw the single facility bringing in 2,400 jobs, state tax revenues of $12.4 million, and city tax receipts of $6.3 million. The corporation was affiliated with Greylock Associates, which had joined together with MGM Grand, Inc., to sponsor gaming propositions in Massachusetts (*New York Times*, March 1, 1981).

Not everyone was happy with the prospects of more gambling in Connecticut. Revenues had come from the legal games already in place. However, the story was not all positive. Connecticut has a history of clean government, relatively free from corruption. Nevertheless, gaming has taken its toll. Jai alai games were rocked by a scandal involving bribes to players, rigging of odds on games, and contacts with organized crime associates. The scandal brought twenty-six indictments and thirteen convictions (*Wall Street Journal*, November 7, 1978; *Christian Science Monitor*, March 31, 1982). Gaming also had administrative problems. A gaming commissioner was hired by an off-track betting company, raising conflict of interest questions (*New York Times*, January 28, 1979). A study called for restructuring the process of gambling regulation, because the existing commission lacked expertise in gaming or accounting (*New York Times*, March 23, 1979).

The late governor Ella Grasso was adamant in opposition to casinos. "I would be very pleased personally if we had no more gambling in this state," she claimed (*Wall Street Journal*, November 7, 1978). Bridgeport residents did not feel much better about casinos in their community. Church leaders complained, the Chamber of Commerce said gaming would destroy the work ethic, and the prosecuting attorney saw it bringing crime (*New York Times*, March 1, 1981). The city council voted down a proposition endorsing casinos (Klein and Selesner 1981:10). The city council of Milford was concerned that casino forces might look at their jurisdiction. "In a state desperate to raise money to offset deficits, casino gambling could become a reality," according to alderman chairman Alfred Ahreus, Jr. Therefore, Ahreus led a move to adopt an ordinance that would ban any potential casinos from his city (*New Haven Register*, March 26, 1981).

Nevertheless, the proponents of casinos were optimistic during the 1981 legislative session. Recently elected, Governor William O'Neill appeared open-minded on the question. A subcommittee made a unanimous recommendation for passage. However, the full Public Safety Committee voted fourteen to zero to kill the bill. There had been no ground swell of support for the casino (*New Haven Register*, February 27, 1981, March 31, 1981). The defeat of the measure for casinos was so sound that the General Assembly also decided to place a moratorium on all new gambling licenses until

1983 (*New Haven Register,* January 31, 1982). In 1983, the moratorium was extended to 1985.

The *New York Times* opposed the legalization movement in Connecticut by referring to the lack of social success surrounding gambling in New Jersey, the ABSCAM scandal, an economic boom that bypassed Atlantic City residents, prostitution and other crime, high unemployment, and severe problems for senior citizens and also referred to the jai alai scandals (*New York Times,* January 31, 1981, February 1, 1981). In 1982, a *New York Times* survey found that 56% of the residents of Connecticut opposed casinos, while only 36% favored them. Opponents cited prospects of increased crime and betting by poor people as reasons for opposition (*New York Times,* October 17, 1982). But the proponents kept trying. In 1983, the state still faced a taxation and budgetary crisis and casino advocates tried seizing the moment. They proposed bills for a pilot program of casinos in Bridgeport and Hartford.

Public Safety Committee co-chairman Senator Steven C. Casey led the charge against gambling each time. Addressing the subcommittee handling the legislation, he asserted that "the problems of crime, the corruption of public officials, deterioration of the quality of life due to congestion and other problems and the exposure of our citizens, especially the young, to the lure of gambling in casinos are too high a price to pay" (*New Haven Register,* January 31, 1982). Casey was so vigorous an opponent that he reached out to other northeastern states' legislators and formed an interstate lobbying group against casinos. He called his group LANCE, Legislators against New Casino Expansion. Thus far, the group's efforts have been successful. The Connecticut casino bills were again killed in legislative committees in 1983. By 1984, the Connecticut economy was recovering and the state enjoyed a big budget surplus. The momentum for casinos was gone.

Illinois

The severe snowstorms of 1979 and incumbent mayor Michael Bilandic's inability to provide necessary public services helped elect Jane Byrne mayor of Chicago that year. As Byrne's term of office began, she realized that the snow and its removal, her political "blessing," had also left the city with a major budgetary imbalance. One answer to the fiscal problem appealed to her: a "Monte Carlo type casino." Citing the success record of Atlantic City, she voiced hopes that the doors of a legal casino could be opened in 1980 in time to balance her first city budget: "If it's done right, done properly and certain strict enforcement policies are put through, I would like to see a gambling casino" (*New York Times,* September 12, 1979; *Wall Street Journal,* September 12, 1979). The Cook County state's attorney disagreed with the possibility of strict gaming enforcement in Chicago and envisioned a casino attracting "more organized crime figures than we already have" (*Wall Street Journal*, September 12, 1979). The state attorney general also was prompt in expressing his opposition to the move. Quickly, the idea died. According to *Gaming Business Magazine*, it would remain dead unless New York legislated gaming casinos and Chicago felt strong competitive disadvantages for convention business (Klein and Selesner 1981:10), neither of which has happened in the intervening years.

Rhode Island

Like many other governors, the governor of Rhode Island was also opposed to casinos when legalization proponents in his state selected Newport as a likely site for legal casino gambling. Governor J. Joseph Garrahy was wise to be in opposition. In November 1980, 81% of the voters of Newport opposed a referendum on the question of casinos. The opposition group was organized as the Citizens Concerned about Casino Gambling. Their numbers included the governor, lieutenant governor, attorney general, all of Newport's legislators, and five of seven members of the city council.

Proponents remained optimistic. Leonard Souca, a Somerset, Massachusetts, businessman, announced plans to build a casino in Newport: "I think the chances are excellent" (Mello 1981:38). It was expected that the movement would resurface in 1982 or 1983; it did not (Davis 1983:16). Newport's loss of the America's Cup competition could cause some to take another look at gaming, but the 1980 experience indicates that Rhode Island's chances for casinos in the near future are slim, and the 1980 campaign stands alone as Rhode Island's foray into casino politics.

Conclusion

The states considered in this chapter are in the Northeast or Midwest. These states showed a propensity to turn toward gambling as a means to replace falling public revenues. The third wave of gaming legalizations originated with the New Hampshire lottery, spreading quickly to the other states discussed here. Each of the Frostbelt states examined had a lottery and other forms of legalized gambling. Yet, while the states were willing to turn to gaming in the 1960s and 1970s, their financial problems persisted into the 1980s. Their responses to continued fiscal crises often focused upon expanded gaming. Lotteries were modified with more frequent games and expanded prizes and more effective marketing efforts. And casinos were actively considered. In our veto model, we suggested that each of four major factors had to reflect positively on casino legalization for successful campaigns: political environment (the economy and experience with gaming);

political elites and active interests; campaign sponsorship (credibility and financial viability); and campaign issue dominance (economic or crime and morality issues). If one of these major factors was negative, the campaign would fail.

Under the alternative model—the gravity model—the four factors would be weighed and campaigns would be decided by the preponderance of factors on one side or the other. The gravity model was explicitly used to predict the coming of casinos to each of the Frostbelt states surveyed. Had the model been operative, that result naturally would have followed. The political environment was "right" for casinos in each of the states. Economies were weak and legalized gaming was accepted as a revenue generator for government. In some cases—for instance, in Massachusetts and Pennsylvania—scandals hurt the image of legal gaming. Campaign sponsors did enjoy some credibility and some financial backing, but overall the sponsorship factor was neutral to negative. The elite factor was also neutral to negative. Governors or attorneys general provided strong opposition in each jurisdiction, while business elites and other gaming interests were neutral or negative. Issue dominance was generally controlled by casino opponents, but the possibility of exploiting economic issues was certainly present in each state. The Atlantic City experience, however, was most often portrayed as a negative factor, with the emphasis upon crime and negative economic consequences of the casinos. Overall, an operative gravity model would have predicted casinos for several states. This did not happen. The results suggest that the negative factors identified were able as individual factors (that is, factor complexes) to veto entire efforts for casinos.

6 ❧ The Sunbelt States

The Major Efforts:
Florida (1984), Texas, Arkansas, Colorado

Florida, 1984: The More Things Change . . .

Introduction

Since 1978, the state of Florida has experienced major economic problems
along with the rest of the nation. The arrival of a new wave of Cuban
refugees in 1980 increased the state's financial burdens and added to an
already growing crime problem. Cocaine trafficking was becoming a major
concern of south Florida business and political leaders. Florida casino advocates forces seized upon the emerging fiscal strain to advance a proposal for
legal casinos in a political climate rendered more favorable with the exit from
office of vocal casino opponent Reubin Askew. A new legalization petition
drive was begun in May 1982 by Charles Rosen, president of the Florida
Casino Association. Rosen's proposition called for the legalization of casinos
throughout the state by local option as well as the creation of a state lottery
(*New York Times*, May 9, 1982). The premier strategy of proponents was
ostensibly to capitalize on widespread support for lotteries among senior
citizens and to neutralize casino opposition from resort areas outside of the
Miami area.

Political Environment

The Role of the Governor. While the Florida political situation had changed
with the exit of Askew, the primary actors concerned with the casino issue
were similar to 1978. Governor Robert Graham, the Democrat elected in
1978, remained prominent among the opposition, as he had been as attorney
general. Graham used an invitation to speak to greyhound track operators in
1982 as an occasion to attack casinos and solidify opposition forces. In his

speech he praised the pari-mutuel industries of the state and promised "to lend the weight of his office to again defeat casino legalization, and to protect existing 'legitimized' forms of gambling" (Selsner and Klein 1982: 56–57).

Governor Graham also attacked Atlantic City as a place that "sends out signals of a community that is not prepared to pay the price . . . that doesn't have the work ethic to achieve its goals. It wants to try to find an easy answer to the problems. That's not the kind of message . . . that brought Motorola, I.B.M., Pratt Whitney into this community. . . . Casino gambling would turn them off" (Selsner and Klein 1982:56–57). Graham formed an organization with former governor Askew to oppose the petition drive, which was also opposed by horse and dog tracks. According to Patrick McCann, the parimutuel industry "has a tremendous amount of influence on the legislature because parimutuels contribute a lot of revenue to the state and the legislators and local officials are very conscious of the fact." He continued: "The reason behind the parimutuel opposition to casino gambling is simple: If casino gambling is legalized in the state, parimutuel revenues will be diluted. . . . Instead of the state getting more revenues, it's simply going to be shifted . . . to an area that the state is not familiar in regulating. The regulation argument has been very effective" (McCann 1982:27).

The issue of organized crime remained an effective tool against casinos in 1982, as it had four years prior. In August, the *Miami Herald* printed an article that stated that relatives of mobster Meyer Lansky were behind proposals for gaming in Miami. An opinion poll taken during the summer indicated that only 37% of Florida residents would favor the casino proposition if it gained a spot on the ballot. It did not. The proponents dropped their drive in mid-July, saying that they had started too late to get enough signatures to get on the ballot in 1982. Rosen predicted correctly that casino proponents would regroup and try again.

Casino Proposals. In October 1983, while successfully campaigning for the mayor's seat in Miami Beach, Malcolm Frombers suggested that the beach city conduct a straw vote on the casino question. Miami Beach had held such an advisory election in April 1970, at which time voters rejected casinos by a 9,265 to 7,343 count (*New York Times*, April 26, 1970). Mayor Frombers was convinced that popular sentiment would be reversed in a new advisory referendum. However, the voters did not get to express their wishes. In January 1984, a majority of the city commission decided against holding an advisory referendum, perceiving such an exercise as futile. Commissioner William Shockett commented, "I feel like the issue is going to be on the November ballot. That's the vote that's going to have impact" (*Miami Herald*, January 12, 1984).

Shockett's expectations were not based upon unwise speculation. By January, casino proponents had begun in earnest, drafting a proposal and circulating petitions. John Brown, a former New Jersey legislator and key actor in the campaign for Atlantic City casinos, was named as the state referendum coordinator and director for the Florida Casino Associates. By February, the group claimed to have collected 100,000 signatures. Florida law mandated 298,743 signatures in nine congressional districts by August 6 in order to get the proposed constitutional amendment on the November 6 ballot. "I don't have to do any selling," one optimistic procasino spokesman claimed. "People have watched since 1978 and things didn't get any better" (*Miami Herald,* February 7, 1984). Indeed, the economic climate in the Miami area might have worsened. Some former opponents of casinos were coming to regard casinos as an attractive solution to their fiscal problems, aggravated by a drop in international tourism (*Variety,* January 11, 1984).

A statewide poll taken in March by the *St. Petersburg Times* found a considerable increase in support for both casino gambling and a statewide lottery. The lottery was favored by 62% of the respondents, while 46% favored casinos. The casino support figure, while less than the 49% opposing casinos, represented a 9% gain over earlier polls and a 17% gain over the election returns of 1978. In the Miami area, 55% favored casinos, while respondents split evenly in central Florida, and opposed casinos in northwest and southwest Florida (*St. Petersburg Times,* March 11, 1984).

The 1984 proposal separated the lottery question from the casino question. It provided that casinos could be licensed for operation on a small stretch of north Dade County beachfront called Sunny Isles. The area was north of Miami Beach, just south of the Broward County line. Other cities in the state with populations over 25,000 could authorize casinos in local option votes. Only hotels with 350 or more rooms would be permitted to have casinos. The gross revenues of casinos were to be taxed by the state at a rate of 7%, with one-half of the money being returned to the county or city in which the casino was located (*Fort Lauderdale News,* December 29, 1983). In their statements, casino proponents emphasized the economic benefits that would come from tourism attracted by casinos. They claimed that the casinos would attract an additional 15 to 20 million visitors to Florida in the first three to five years (*Miami Herald,* January 16, 1984). Opponents once again focused on the potential of an increase in organized crime, as well as a growth in street crime, and used Atlantic City as a negative example.

When the Governor's Council on Organized Crime invited Thomas O'Brien, director of the New Jersey Division of Gaming Enforcement, to speak to its members, he said what the opponents of casinos wanted to hear:

"As far as loansharking, obviously it follows casino gaming. Prostitution, the same thing. They are the stepchildren of casino gaming." O'Brien reported that even though New Jersey legislation had succeeded in keeping mobsters out of casino management, it had failed to keep them out of a number of allied industries: "From the leadership of the largest union in the area to the sale of hotdogs from pushcarts on the street, we have found evidence of the tentacles of organized crime" (*Miami Herald,* February 2, 1984).

A representative of the Florida Department of Law Enforcement reported to the Governor's Council that there were 438 members of organized crime families in Florida, primarily in Dade and Broward counties (*Miami Herald,* February 2, 1984). Evidence presented by FDLE suggested that organized criminal groups were attracted to Florida by the prospects of casino gambling. One real estate firm, allegedly tied to Canadian mobsters, was stockpiling property in Sunny Isles, as it had previously done in Atlantic City. Department of Law Enforcement officials spotted Canadian underworld members at one of BOP, Inc.'s Sunny Isles properties, the Desert Inn, a property that was designated as a potential casino (*Miami Herald,* February 20, 1984). Probes of Canadian organized criminals followed a marked increase in gangland slayings, firebombings, and arsons in south Florida.

Issue Dominance

The dominant issues in the 1984 Florida casino campaign resonated from campaigns elsewhere. The need for economic recovery in the face of declining tourism was set against a fear of attracting street crime and organized criminal activity. But the Florida campaign of 1984 was anything but a repeat of previous campaigns in Florida or elsewhere—it contained a structural aspect unique for casino campaigns. On April 29, 1983, Charles Rosen filed a stock sale plan with the Federal Securities and Exchange Commission. His proposal was refiled on December 13, 1983, when the details of the proposed constitutional amendment on casino gambling were finalized, and approved on January 13, 1984. Rosen sought to sell 5 million shares of stock in FCA. The shares would be sold for $1 each in lots of 300 or more. Purchasers had to be Florida residents. The proceeds of the stock sales would finance the 1984 campaign to get the proposed amendment on the ballot and then to win voter approval in November. All funds from stock sales would be held in escrow until February 28, 1984. If 1.5 million shares had not been sold by that date, all funds would be returned and the scheme would end. However, if the minimum 1.5 million shares were sold, money would then be drawn from the escrow account and utilized for the campaign, as would newly acquired funds from new sales.

According to the proposal, Rosen would draw a salary of $70,000 a year as president of FCA, and he would receive a $25,000 bonus if more than 2 million shares were sold. John Brown would receive a $50,000 a year fee as a consultant to the FCA. Up to $4 million from the sales would go to a political action committee called Citizens for Less Taxes. If the campaign for casinos in 1984 failed, the investors would be losers. They were told up front that this was a high-risk matter. Brokers were warned: "This offering involves a high degree of risk and shares should be purchased only by persons who can afford the complete loss of their investment" (*Barron's*, February 27, 1984; *Miami Herald*, January 22, 1984). However, unlike other political contributions, if this "contribution" resulted in a financial loss, it would be tax deductible in the same manner that other stock market losses were tax deductible. On the other hand, the investors were not faced with certain loss. If the proposition cleared all hurdles and casinos were legalized, there could be a sizable financial return. Seven potential casino properties, including the Desert Inn and three others in Sunny Isles, agreed to give the stock investors 1% of their gross winnings for ten years (*Miami Herald*, January 22, 1984). Based upon projections of a $1 billion annual gross win, comparable to that experienced by casinos in Atlantic City, the FCA could possibly collect $10 million a year to return to investors. Over the ten-year period, this could yield a potential $100 million, or 20 times an initial investment of $5 million. In the meantime, the stocks could be liquidated through trading (*Florida Trend Monthly*, January 1984).

To most responsible investment houses, the whole deal sounded rather questionable. *New Issues*, a publication of the Institute for Economic Research, reported in its January 27 issue, "The offering prospectus discloses what we believe to be a record 36 risk factors" (*Orlando Sentinel*, January 31, 1984). The FCA faced several refusals before it found an underwriter to sell the stock. Initial sales were brisk. Most buyers, however, were not the type who could afford to have a complete loss of their investment. According to the FCA, "a lot of these people have never bought stock before. The people who are calling are definitely underemployed. They're taxicab drivers, laborers, waitresses, bartenders. Their livelihood is related to tourism. They're not doing as well as they should be doing" (*Sun Sentinel* [Fort Lauderdale], February 6, 1984).

The Florida political establishment opposed the scheme and attacked it from several angles. Senator Lawton Chiles joined with Ohio's Senator Howard Metzenbaum and introduced federal legislation designed to plug the political contribution deduction loophole in the scheme (*Miami Herald*, February 28, 1984). A more crippling blow was delivered by state comptroller Gerald Lewis. On February 28, the deadline for accomplishing the 1.5 million minimum sales level, Lewis claimed that the stock sale was fraudulent. He suspended all sales immediately and did not allow sales to continue to the end of the day. He also suspended the registration of the underwriter's company and the licenses of all of its salesmen brokers. Lewis's main point of contention involved a mailgram that a casino supporter sent February 21 in a mass mailing throughout the state, claiming that "not only is this stock a tax-deductible expense, it is a sure bet." The mailgram further implied that the petition drive under way was "guaranteed" to get the question on the November ballot. Lewis claimed that the mailgram violated rules against mass merchandising of stocks and that it contained misleading information. FCA's John Brown called the mailgram a "juvenile goof" and said it had been sent without official approval (*Miami Herald,* February 29, 1984).

Lewis further maintained that the underwriter had fallen short of his binding 1.5 million sales goal, while an FCA spokesman asserted that they had not only met the goal, but exceeded it by $15,000. He claimed that the state had not counted sales made by brokers with firms other than the primary underwriter, which had not yet been placed in the special escrow fund. However, after an investigation, the state found that sales totalled only $1,422,000, $78,000 short of the goal (*St. Petersburg Times,* March 22, 1984). The state further found that $600,000 of the account was gained by last-day sales to one hotel owner with a vested interest in the project. Overall, 40% of the sales fell into this category—hotel owners with vested interests in casino legalization. The escrow account was frozen, the funds were ordered to be returned, and the scheme and petition drive were doomed.

However, FCA vowed to carry the fight. Following Lewis's final order, FCA spokesmen issued the following statement: "There seems to be a perception that the petition drive has reached an end. Nothing could be further from the truth. Our petition drive is alive and well" (*Miami Herald,* March 28, 1984). In April, FCA sued Lewis in federal district court. Judge James W. Kehoe ruled on April 23 that he had no jurisdiction, since it was a state matter. Two weeks later, a state circuit judge ruled he had no jurisdiction because it was an administrative matter and administrative remedies had not been pursued. FCA demanded that Lewis set a hearing. He set a date in November. FCA demanded an earlier time, and Lewis set August 1 for a hearing. However, in mid-July Rosen gave up (*Travel Weekly,* July 16, 1984). Rosen claimed that there was no way he could finish a petition drive between August 1 and August 6. Funds were returned to investors. Rosen revealed in

August that only 90,000 petition signatures had been gathered (*Miami Herald*, August 10, 1984).

While the 1984 effort was receiving its last rites, new advocates were appearing in the wings ready to carry on for the future. Stephen Muss, leading executive of the Fontainebleau Hotel in Miami Beach, had been a vocal opponent of casinos in 1978 and 1982 and an early opponent in 1984. When the FCA campaign appeared doomed, he spoke out in favor of casinos: "We need casino gambling to be competitive with places such as the Bahamas and even our own cruise ships. I recently returned from the south of France where the hotels are marvelous, the shopping experience is sensational and the restaurants are great. And to add salt and pepper, they have gambling. They have it all. Why shouldn't we?" (*Miami Herald*, July 16, 1984).

Business writer Dick Marlow of the *Orlando Sentinel* also caught the spirit but not until July. He wrote: "Everywhere you look these days, you can see a strong case building for casinos in Florida. The big sales pitch is that casino gambling is a painless tax—paid by the tourist. In view of what is happening in Florida, it is only a matter of time before casino gambling becomes a hot topic around the state. While opponents of casino gambling have always been able to rally Biblebelt voters . . . situations change with the times. And the times certainly are changing" (*Orlando Sentinel*, July 6, 1984).

As if to fulfill the old adage "The more things change, the more they remain the same," Florida was as unsuccessful in casino efforts during the early 1980s as it had been in 1978. The appeal of Florida had made it the primary focus soon after Atlantic City casinos opened in 1978. That appeal was based on the presence of an Atlantic City model, in Miami Beach, and the presence of a number of groups who were inclined toward gambling. With the second failure to promote casinos in Florida, it became apparent that another Sunbelt state might be more suited for legalization in the 1980s. Texas, which, like Florida, was expected to become one of the nation's three largest states by the end of the twentieth century, was not best suited for casinos in general, but Galveston was interested, as the following section shows.

Texas: Return of the Good Ole Boys

Political Environment

Prior Experience with Gambling. The American West and the river basins of the American heartland have traditions of gambling that extend well back into the nineteenth century. Casino gambling existed in mining towns and on riverboats, as an integral part of frontier life. A popular acceptance of illegal practices placed gamblers and politicians into the same camp—until scandals became so outrageous that reform elements gained momentum and temporarily closed down gambling activity. New Orleans, Nashville, Biloxi, Newport, and East St. Louis all thrived at one time as gambling capitals, as did Hot Springs, Arkansas, and Galveston, Texas. The cycle of public acceptance, public corruption, scandal, public outcry, and reform, followed again by business as usual and public acceptance, was broken, however, in the late 1950s and early 1960s.

Major criminal elements had shifted investment away from bootlegging and into these traditional gambling centers in the 1930s and 1940s. After operating with virtual immunity from the law for several decades, these criminal elements encountered a vigorous backlash from the American public as a result of Estes Kefauver's Senate investigations on crime in the early 1950s. When the national investigations generated "little Kefauver" inquiries in various states, the negative attention given to criminal activity was eventually translated into the election of state and local officials who saw the political wisdom of closing down illegal gambling operations.

State officials who experienced the wisdom of anticasino politics were attorneys general Will Wilson of Texas and Tom Gentry of Arkansas and governors Orval Faubus and Winthrop Rockefeller of Arkansas. In the 1940s and 1950s, Galveston was in its "glory days," known as "Pleasure Island" and "Sin City of the South" (*Houston Chronicle*, January 15, 1984). Just sixty miles from Houston, Galveston was well known for both its beaches and its casinos. Slot machines were in virtually every bar and a fair number of corner grocery stores. Band greats such as Guy Lombardo, Count Basie, and Duke Ellington played in fancy clubs like the Balinese Room. Not only were the gambling laws flaunted, but so were the liquor laws—the clubs stayed open twenty-four hours. Periodic raids by the Texas Rangers were usually unsuccessful because of advance warnings. Casino control was in the hands of two Sicilian-born brothers, Sam and Rose Maceo, both former bootleggers (*Fort Worth Star Telegram*, January 15, 1984). Illegal gambling brought millions of dollars into the local economy over the years, and Galveston thrived (*Austin American-Statesman*, June 26, 1983).

Reform candidates would occasionally seek office, prompting casino operators to close their doors, only to reopen after a favorable candidate won. In the 1954 elections, an ex-FBI agent ran for district attorney with the pledge that he would close the casinos, but was defeated by a four to one margin. He tried again in 1956 and lost again, but by a smaller margin. But, in 1956, a different antigambling candidate did win another "wrong" office. Will Wilson was elected Texas attorney general.

In the late 1940s, Wilson had cleaned gambling out of his jurisdiction while Dallas County district attorney. He was selected as president of the Texas District Attorneys' Association during that period and later served for six years on the Texas Supreme Court. As attorney general, Wilson pressed local officials to close down the Galveston casinos. The Galveston county sheriff said he couldn't raid the Balinese Room, because "I'm not a member. They won't let me in" (*Dallas Morning News*, July 3, 1983). Wilson was not so deferential. With 100 injunctions against the casino operations in hand, he made his raids one night in June 1957 (*Fort Worth Star Telegram*, January 15, 1984). About 60 clubs were padlocked, and more than 1,000 slot machines were thrown into Galveston Bay (*Dallas Morning News*, July 3, 1983). The affected clubs shut down and never reopened. Wilson stayed in office for six years, vigilant for any violations of the gambling laws. His crusading efforts won him the Wyman Award as the outstanding attorney general in the United States for 1960. However, he was not able to parlay his activity into a governorship, facing defeat in his try for the top state office at the hands of John Connally in 1962.

Economic Situation. Many local residents of Galveston have been dissatisfied since the night of Wilson's raid. The tourism business that used to run 365 days a year is now reduced to three or four months at the most (*Dallas Morning News*, July 3, 1983). Unemployment climbed to 13.6% in 1983. A local tax base was stretched to its limits. Governments owned 56% of local property and were exempt from taxation. The need for expanded local services was intensified after the area was hit by Hurricane Alicia in the summer of 1983, followed by record freezing weather in the fall (*Dallas Times Herald*, January 21, 1984). Nightclub business suffered. Buddy Kirk, a former trumpet player from the big band era who now runs the Balinese Club, described night life in Galveston: "If you walk around at 11 o'clock at night, you're walking by yourself. You can shoot a cannon down the street" (*Austin American-Statesman*, June 26, 1983).

Kirk and other businesspeople saw the answer to the city's economic problems in a proposition to legalize casinos. Early in 1983, state senator Tati Santiestaban of El Paso introduced a bill that would have permitted casinos in that border town (*El Paso Herald Post*, July 25, 1983). Legislative approval was all that was necessary to initiate casino development. However, after he was besieged with local opposition from business, civic, and church leaders, he decided not even to ask for committee hearings on his bill; it died a quiet death. Therefore, when state senator Chet Brooks of Pasadena, whose district includes Galveston, was approached by Kirk and the others, he was hesitant to offer support. Brooks saw some potential in casinos but withheld his endorsement until the proponents could demonstrate strong support in the area for it (*Houston Post*, March 25, 1983). The proponents immediately began to maneuver to show that support.

Casino Proposals. Galveston's mayor, Gus Manuel, said he could support the measure if it was approved in a local referendum vote. On May 25, the city council agreed to schedule a June 2 public hearing on whether to hold such an election. The hearing produced an animated debate in which seventy supporters and opponents vigorously presented their views. The city council voted six to one to put the question of casinos on the ballot sometime before April 1984. Senator Brooks responded by saying that he would introduce casino legislation in the 1985 session if an advisory vote in Galveston was approved by 60% of the voters. Kirk said he expected approval by a four to one margin. The Reverend Don Martin of the Bible Baptist Church promised Kirk a "rude awakening" (*Dallas Times Herald*, June 3, 1983).

The first "awakening" came when the thirty-member board of the Galveston Chamber of Commerce unanimously went on record in opposition to casinos and gathered 2,340 signatures on petitions urging the city council to reverse its action. While council members voted four to two against such a reversal, the city attorney voided the June 2 vote, because it was not given proper notice as an agenda item for the meeting. Under sustained pressure from opponents, the council gave in. On July 7, it decided to require casino advocates to submit petitions in order to get the question on the ballot. During the summer of 1983, Galveston suffered the attack from Hurricane Alicia, followed later by a severe freeze. The storms heavily taxed the public safety and public work services and left local roads in extremely poor shape. The extra financial burdens thus placed upon Galveston became added ammunition for the advocates of casinos. However, the calamities of weather also stole from their arguments—local employment soared during the cleanup and rebuilding period. Unemployment fell to 9% during the fall. Nonetheless, on November 4, supporters presented approximately 5,000 signatures to the council urging the election, well over the required 10% of the voters (3,128); a special election was set for January 21, 1984.

Issue Dominance: Disputing Atlantic City's Success

The casino proponents, under the name of Greater Galveston Beach Association (GGBA), were led by Kirk, Weinert, and developer Walter Teachworth, who was also a member of the county planning commission. Teachworth was very interested in developing his own casino. One newspaper called the proponents "a rather motley group of club owners and seawall property owners" (*Fort Worth Star*, January 15, 1984), while another called Kirk and Weinert "two bit players" (*Dallas Times Herald*, June 12, 1983). Doc Weinert dreamed of a "gambling strip along a two mile stretch east of the seawall and local clubs being able to have two or three slot machines to help pay their utilities . . . a town getting back on a 24-hour schedule with three work shifts, the cosmopolitan city I grew up in with fashionable stores and big name entertainment" (*Houston Chronicle,* January 15, 1984). Proponents claimed that the casinos would trigger a half-million dollars in development, provide as many as 45,000 new jobs, and reduce property taxes at least 55% (*Dallas Morning News,* July 3, 1983). Kirk and Weinert pointed with enthusiasm to economic reports from Atlantic City, where more than $150 million in tax revenues was generated by casinos in 1982 (*Houston Chronicle,* January 15, 1984).

The owner of one supper club felt that casinos were needed to attract "nice people" who would spend money. He lamented that the town of 60,000 residents had become just a dumping ground for Houston (*Fort Worth Star Telegram,* January 15, 1984), while another businessman said that Galveston had become a place where beach bums came with T-shirts and a five-dollar bill in their pocket, "and they never changed either" (*Austin American-Statesman,* June 26, 1983). A twelve-month tourist trade was seen as necessary to bring economic stability to the community, and a trade based upon casinos would be essentially a new and "nonpolluting" industry.

Teachworth asserted that casinos would save Galveston both from polluting industries and from a slow economic death. "We see this as an economic issue that can bring jobs, redevelopment, growth, lower taxes, and entertainment into Galveston," he claimed. "We think Galveston is a city that profited beautifully when it had illegal gambling. It seems natural to bring back gambling now that it is a legal and respected industry in the nation" (*Fort Worth Telegram,* January 15, 1984).

The opposition consisted of a coalition of the Chamber of Commerce, twenty-six ministers and clergy representing all Protestant, Catholic, and Jewish denominations, and the Galveston Historical Foundation. The coalition called itself Galvestonians against Casino Gambling (GACG). The chairman was Jim Mahan. Casino opponents refused to concede any of the economic arguments made by GGBA. They claimed that the Galveston economy was not in severe difficulties. A city councilman admitted the need for new tax revenues, but he claimed that Galveston was not a "dying town." The city manager said that $110 million in building permits had been issued in 1982 and 1983 (*Chieftain* [Pueblo, Colorado], December 12, 1983). Opponents of casinos also pointed to several high-rise condominiums and hotels that were under construction as evidence of future prosperity (*Houston Post,* January 15, 1984).

Casinos were portrayed by opponents as forces that would hurt the economy. George Mitchell, the island's biggest developer, said that casinos would drive out small business and "blemish the town's image as a family resort" (*Dallas Times Herald*, January 21, 1984). Roland Bassett, chairman of the Chamber of Commerce, said it would be an economic disaster to have gambling: "The mere threat of having it could hurt us," he said. "I think there are people who would come to town now who won't come if we have gambling" (*Dallas Morning News*, July 3, 1983).

The Atlantic City "success" story was disputed. The Reverend Don Martin said unemployment there was "12% before the legalized gambling and it's 12% now" (*Dallas Morning News*, July 3, 1983). Peter Brink of the Historical Foundation saw casinos as meaning an end to the historical renovation upon which much of the city's tourism was based: "We feel that gambling will have a devastating effect on the older neighborhoods," he argued (*Galveston Daily News*, November 23, 1983). The negative effect of casinos on Atlantic City housing was highlighted in the anticasino arguments.

The strongest arguments against casinos, however, involved crime and morality. Again, the case of Atlantic City was essential to the argument. It was pointed out that five years after casinos opened in Atlantic City, violent crime had risen 130% and nonviolent crime was up 178%. Casinos were also seen as a "magnet to organized crime" (*Dallas Times Herald*, January 21, 1984). Jim Mahan pointed his finger at Las Vegas, claiming "one in nine women between the ages of 15 and 39 in Las Vegas is a prostitute" (*Houston Chronicle*, January 15, 1984). Galveston district attorney Mike Gaurino asserted, "We'll get organized crime if casinos come to Galveston. Las Vegas, where they've had 50 years to learn to live with casino gambling, either leads the nation each year in the crime rate per capita or is very near the top" (*Galveston Daily News*, January 11, 1984). Former attorney general Will Wilson, now an Austin attorney, added that "gambling is so bad in corrupting local government. If it's legalized, I think it would be only a matter of time before you'd be indicting people for taking bribes and that type of thing" (*Houston Chronicle*, March 26, 1983).

The proponents of casinos countered the crime issue by suggesting that the streets of Galveston were much safer thirty years ago when casinos were open. One person noted that "the ladies of the night were confined to their own district and minded their own business" (*Houston Chronicle*, January 15, 1984). Walter Teachworth called organized crime "a totally phony issue." As for governmental corruption, he claimed, "We have corruption in Galveston right now. The casino industry will be the most tightly controlled industry in the state. It will probably be the cleanest industry in the state because of how it's controlled" (*Galveston Daily News*, January 11, 1984). He added that the casinos will have hundreds of millions of dollars invested, which they cannot afford to risk on corrupt practices: "They'll have the best law enforcement money can afford" (*Dallas Times Herald,* January 21, 1984). The city fire marshal, a "100% supporter" of casinos, also denied the crime issue. He asserted that he had been to Las Vegas and that the city "doesn't have an arson problem" (*Galveston Daily News,* January 11, 1984).

The *Galveston Daily News* accepted the arguments of the opponents and urged the city "not to give up its soul for pieces of silver" (January 20, 1984). At the same time, the proponents of gaming unleashed a barrage of newspaper and radio advertisements emphasizing the prosperity that would come with casinos. Their funding was minimal, most of it raised by a concert given by Pasadena, Texas, nightclub owner and entertainer Mickey Gilley. The supporters spent $9,362 in the campaign. In addition to the advertisements, funds were provided for free taxicab rides to the polls.

Opponents spent over four times as much—$40,943. Most of the money went for advertisements (*Galveston Daily News,* February 22, 1984). The GACG poll and newspaper polls showed that the vote would be extremely close. The press said it was "too close to call . . . a dead heat" (*Dallas Times Herald,* January 21, 1984).

The polls, it turned out, were wrong—it was not close at all. The voters were asked, "Do you favor government controlled legalized gambling on Galveston Island?" They answered with a resounding no. The margin of defeat was almost two to one, 7,992 against to 4,632 in favor (*Houston Post,* January 22, 1984). Bob Albright said the vote put the issue to rest: "Now Galveston can remain a tourist and family community" (*Reno Evening Gazette,* January 22, 1984). The opponents saw the margin of victory as a result of a huge organized effort that used over 500 volunteers (*Houston Post,* January 22, 1984). Casino proponents were quick to point out the funding discrepancy between the forces. "Elections are bought, and the other side just spent more money," Teachworth claimed. However, he agreed that the battle was over. "It came at the wrong time and it was all too sudden. I'm on the planning commission and this was my idea. I don't have any more ideas. . . . The voice of the people was too clear" (*Galveston Daily News,* January 22, 1984).

Arkansas: Burials, Long Sleeps, and Resurrections
Political Environment

Prior Experience with Gambling. Hot Springs, Arkansas, operated as a wide-open illegal gambling town for generations. Attempts by governors and attorneys general to close down casinos were made, but never had a lasting effect. When Orval Faubus was elected governor in 1954, he pledged to close them down again. But he soon witnessed the ineffective efforts of attorney general Tom Gentry and decided not to waste his energies. Gentry had closed the doors to the city's notorious gaming rooms and seized gambling equipment. The primary result of his activity was that the local Garland County circuit court issued orders stopping his actions. Faubus argued that gambling was an issue for local government to determine. That was a good political strategy until the Reverend Roy H. Galyean won election to the state House of Representatives. Taking his cues from his Hot Springs constituents, the Baptist minister demanded enforcement of the gaming laws. Faubus balked, but Galyean managed to maneuver a resolution to a vote. The House of Representatives found itself in a political bind. Given the religious nature of the state, they were compelled to back Galyean. By a vote of ninety-one to three they demanded that the governor enforce the law. On March 27, 1964, he ordered the casinos to close. After a peaceful police raid, they did. The governor put out the word: "No more gambling for the time being" (*New York Times*, November 8, 1984).

The gambling resorts, however, had represented a major share of the local economy. Hundreds of employees were put out of work, conventions canceled visits to Hot Springs, and the mayor wondered aloud if the city would be able to build a new city hall and police station as planned. The Hot Springs Chamber of Commerce asked its members what could be done, and they replied: "Legalize the casinos." The chamber sponsored a petition drive that gathered 74,645 signatures to put a constitutional question on the ballot (*Arkansas Gazette*, October 25, 1964). Only 30,810 were required. The proposed amendment, Proposal 55, provided for up to ten casinos in Garland County. Licenses would be granted by a five-member board. Gross revenues would be subject to a state tax ranging from 4% to 5½% and a 1% local tax, with additional fees based on numbers of tables and machines. Only ten-year residents of Arkansas could be licensees, and casinos would be completely separate from hotels and motels. Appeals on licensing questions would be taken to the Garland County circuit court (*Arkansas Gazette*, October 30, 1984).

The campaign for casinos was led by the Hot Springs Chamber of Commerce, while a ministerial group known as Churches United against Gambling (CUAG) opposed. State political leaders including Governor Orval Faubus and his 1964 opponent Winthrop Rockefeller opposed casinos. Only Garland County politicians supported the measure, which had been written by state senator Q. Byrum Hurst.

Proponents argued that casinos would bring $25 million a year in taxes to the state, with $5 million coming directly from the gambling taxes. Opponents said the figures were unrealistic—that to gain the numbers $1 billion would have to be played at the tables (*Arkansas Gazette*, September 10,

1984). Former attorney general Gentry endorsed the measure, saying that since casinos could not be effectively closed, they should be legalized, regulated, and taxed (*Arkansas Gazette,* October 1, 1984). This became a dominant theme of the supporters. However, Faubus and Rockefeller pledged casinos would stay closed if the measure failed, and CUAG indicated that it would remain organized to assure they stayed closed (*Arkansas Gazette,* September 9, 1984). Major newspapers opposed casino legalization, and in late October the *Arkansas Gazette* ran excerpts from the book *Greenfelt Jungle,* an exposé of mob crime in Las Vegas, on page one for seven days in a row (*Arkansas Gazette,* October 19–25, 1984). The *Gazette* emphasized the crime issue in a series of hard-hitting editorials opposing casinos.

Early in the campaign, CUAG challenged the wording of the proposition before the state supreme court. When the court refused to remove the question from the ballot, a CUAG spokesman said he was glad in a way: "This will give us a chance to defeat it resoundingly and put the issue to sleep for a long, long rest" (*Arkansas Gazette,* September 15, 1984). They did just that—the proposition was defeated by a decisive 318,000 to 215,000 vote (*New York Times,* December 24, 1964). Governor Faubus, who said that a defeat would sound the death knell for gambling in Arkansas, did let some gaming back into Hot Springs after the 1964 elections. However, after Faubus served out his final term in office, Winthrop Rockefeller was elected in 1966 and soon authorized the final raids. A bill to authorize Hot Springs casinos did pass the legislature, but was vetoed by the governor (*Arkansas Democrat,* July 5, 1984).

Casino Proposals. The doors of casinos were closed for good in 1967. Still, hotel owners and local civic leaders remember the "good ole days" of hot action and full rooms. In 1984, Q. Byrum Hurst, Jr., the son of Senator Hurst, authored a new ballot proposal for a constitutional amendment. He teamed up with Dane Harris, Jr., the son of the owner of a former illegal casino. Along with Leland Hillborn, manager of the Majestic Hotel, and Buddy McAfee, they led the Garland County Wagering Committee in a drive that gathered more than 155,000 signatures on petitions supporting Hot Springs casinos. The petitions easily met the state requirement of 10% of the voters, or 78,935 names. Half of the signatures were from Garland County (*Arkansas Gazette,* July 4, 1984).

There was some debate about whether a constitutional amendment was necessary in order to have casino gaming in Hot Springs. The state constitution prohibits lotteries, but it is silent about other types of gaming. It was, however, amended in order to permit horse race and dog race betting. The forces for casinos realized in 1984 that, unlike 1967, a bill could not make it through the Arkansas legislature and that the governor would have vetoed such a bill even if it passed. Also, proponents felt that constitutional status would give the casino interests necessary security for their operations (*Arkansas Democrat,* July 5, 1984).

The 1984 proposition was very similar to the 1964 question. A five-member gaming control board was to be appointed by the governor and secretary of state. The board would grant up to seven licenses to run major casinos and ten licenses for minor casinos with up to five tables and twenty slot machines. In addition to citizenship, licensees would be required to have been Arkansas residents for the ten consecutive years immediately prior to application for licensing. Corporations would be licensed only if they were Arkansas corporations with majority ownership meeting residency requirements.

There would be a 5% gross winnings tax—80% would be returned to cities and counties, while 20% was earmarked for reducing sales taxes and assisting senior citizens' purchase of medicine and burial supplies. Another 1% tax on gross winnings was targeted for Garland County and Hot Springs city governments. Licensees would pay fees up to $10,000 per year plus $250 per year for each slot machine. Unlike 1964, there was no provision for a local option vote by Garland County residents before licenses were granted.

The sponsors of the question did not claim that casinos were going to operate anyway so they might as well be legalized. That 1964 argument was defused by Winthrop Rockefeller's successful raids of 1967. Instead, proponents pointed to a different moral climate in 1984. Harris stated that Arkansas had become more liberal since the 1964 defeat. The wagering committee emphasized economic issues in its campaign, suggesting that casinos were needed to help a failing economy and to eradicate poverty and unemployment in Hot Springs. Thousands would be put to work in the casinos. A poll taken by the committee found that 62% of Hot Springs respondents rated their city's economy as poor or fair; 68% felt the city needed more funds for police and fire protection; while 61% felt casinos were a way to boost the economy (*Arkansas Democrat,* August 1, 1984).

The casino proponents gave generous assessments about the tax revenues that would come from Hot Springs casinos, predicting that the first year of operations would generate $36 million in taxes. Other expanded economic activity was also projected. Casino stock analyst Daniel Lee asserted that the city of Hot Springs would be turned into a boomtown. Land prices would soar, and there would be an immediate infusion of $100 million to $400 million into the city's economy. The new casinos would employ between 4,000 and 6,000 people. Another 13,000 would gain employment in industries generated by casinos. The casinos would attract between 10,000 and 15,000 people daily. They would come in 200 to 250 buses and 3,000 to 4,000 cars (*Arkansas Democrat,* September 8, 1984, October 8, 1984).

In mid-September, the Garland County Lawful Wagering Committee was dissolved and replaced by a new group, Arkansans for a Better Arkansas. Little Rock attorney Jack Files served as its executive director. The group appointed an advisory committee of thirty members from throughout Arkansas, including one of the state's leading black Republicans, Elijah Coleman of Pine Bluff (*Arkansas Democrat,* October 7, 1964). The place of black support in the campaign soon became a major issue. Little Rock civil rights activist Robert "Say" McIntosh, according to proponents, offered to support the amendment for a fee of $10,000. He was turned down. Soon McIntosh was at the state capitol checking petition names, charging the casino advocates with forgery and accusing the group of offering secretary of state Paul Riviere a $50,000 bribe to validate the petitions. All the charges were vigorously denied, and no investigations ensued (*Arkansas Democrat,* October 22, 1984).

Role of Political Elites

The opposition to casinos was once again led by CUAG. This time the initials stood for Citizens United against Casinos. The organizers of the group, Doug Dickins and Gary Thorson, saw their biggest challenge as convincing the voters that the proponents were playing fast and loose with their figures. They let it be known that they were willing to fight the battle on economic grounds as well as on moral issues. They pointed out that $36 million in revenue could be generated by a 6% tax only if the casinos had a gross win of $600 million a year. This, they asserted, would require 9 million bettors annually. New Jersey casinos took three years before they reached this level of activity. They pointed out that Hot Springs did not have a market of 50 million people within a day's drive as did Atlantic City (*Arkansas Gazette,* August 8, 1984; *Arkansas Democrat,* August 21, 1984).

To give emphasis to its economic arguments, on September 7, CUAG announced that Sheffield Nelson would serve as the general chairman of CUAG and its campaign. Nelson, the chairman of the board and chief executive officer of Arkla, Inc., was considered a prospective candidate for governor in 1986. However, he claimed that political aspirations played no part in his accepting the position—he believed that casinos were "absolutely not the thing to happen in Arkansas." At the time of the appointment, the *Arkansas Gazette* editorialized that the amendment "will probably be beaten overwhelmingly but the prospects for dispatching it are nonetheless strengthened by Sheffield Nelson's decision to lead the drive" (*Arkansas Gazette,* September 10, 1984).

In a series of debates with Jack Files, Nelson emphasized the theme that casinos would discourage business executives from locating in Arkansas

(*Arkansas Democrat,* September 24, 1984). "I think the insinuation that casino gambling would make this a Better Arkansas is totally obnoxious." The projections of gambling backers concerning added jobs are "hypothetical and problematical." He maintained that his own corporation, Arkla, Inc., would not have located two subsidiaries in Arkansas if the state had permitted casino gambling at the time. He added that Atlantic City had seen 90% of its industries leave, coupled with a 67% increase in the crime rate, because gambling was legalized there (*Arkansas Democrat,* September 24, 1984).

In addition to Nelson's support, CUAG drew together several other businesspeople under the name Businessmen United against Gambling. CUAG also drew support from the political leaders of the state. Heading the list of key political opponents were Governor Bill Clinton and his wife Hillary. Speaking to a rally on the capitol steps, she called casinos "a short term, quick fix solution" that would result in "damaging prospects." "We are on the move in Arkansas," she continued. "Why on earth would we want to give ourselves a burden we can't carry and an image we don't want?" Asa Hutchinson, U.S. attorney for Arkansas, addressed the same rally; his concern was crime. "Our hands are full with the drug problem. With casino gambling you can say we have just given up on the drug battle." He cited organized crime problems in Atlantic City in his plea against casinos (*Arkansas Democrat,* October 14, 1984).

Other top law enforcement officers formed an association called Peace Officers against Gambling. They promoted the theme that crime and casinos went together. The state police director Tommy Godwin said, "legalized gambling spawns illegal criminal activities and places additional burdens on law enforcement." In Garland County, Sheriff Clay White said he expected "major type crime" to increase in his county with casinos—"There is no way to keep organized crime out (White 1985). Lynn Davis was the director of the state police when raids were made on illegal casinos in 1967. He asserted that one unfortunate consequence of gambling was that law enforcement officers themselves were corrupted by it. During the 1967 raids, slot machines were taken, but twenty-three were "back in the gamblers' repair shop almost before we got home" because of corruption in the Hot Springs Police Department (*Arkansas Democrat,* September 28, 1984). Besides Clay White, other voices in Hot Springs opposed casinos. State land commissioner Bill McCuen was a Democratic candidate for secretary of state. Because he was from Hot Springs, he was forced to take a public position on the issue. He came out in opposition, claiming that the economy of Hot Springs was "healthier without gambling" (*Arkansas Gazette,* June 9, 1984).

In 1964, the mayor of Hot Springs lamented the ballot loss. A different mayor was in office in 1984, and he had different feelings. Mayor Jim Randall knew his opinion, but hesitated to go public until he knew what his citizens wanted. Therefore, he issued a plea for the citizens to write to him. He received over 1,400 letters. Opponents outnumbered supporters three to one. He announced his opposition.

Mayor Randall was especially concerned over the fact that the 1984 proposal did not provide for local option as did the one in 1964 (*Arkansas Gazette*, August 2, 1984). Randall reported that the response to his stand was supported by 98% of the people who called his office. "Their major concern is that they don't want Hot Springs to be changed from a family-type city, safe and comfortable, to a casino-type atmosphere that they feel would be unsafe and inconvenient and uncomfortable for them as family people" (*Arkansas Gazette*, August 3, 1984).

The Republican party convention passed a resolution opposing casinos and taunted the Democrats as "wimpy" for failing to take a stand on this issue. The Democrats took a position on only one of six ballot questions for 1984 (*Arkansas Democrat*, September 16, 1984). Such neutrality was about the best the proponents could hope for. Not one political leader on either the state or local level favored the casino proposition.

As expected, church groups opposed casinos. When the proponents announced their petition drive in May, twelve Garland County Baptist ministers immediately announced opposition (*Arkansas Democrat*, May 22, 1984). The United Methodist Church soon joined in the cause by passing a resolution at its Little Rock annual conference urging all Methodists not to sign petitions (*Arkansas Gazette*, May 23, 1984). A Religious Council was formed as a part of CUAG. Its director, the Reverend Erwin L. McDonald, said that casinos would "enslave" state government with additional duties and have a "destructive influence on society" (*Arkansas Democrat*, September 11, 1984).

In a letter to the *Arkansas Democrat*, Bishop Richard B. Wilke of the United Methodist Church lamented that the church had to spend energies on the casino question: "Other issues confront a caring and compassionate people: the threat of nuclear war, racial justice, fair treatment of women, public education and child abuse, just to name a few. For the moment the spotlight is on highpowered gambling. Let's bury it deep so we can get on with other critical matters. The case against casino gambling is strong. I not only hope that we will defeat it at the polls, I plead that we will bury it deep" (*Arkansas Democrat*, October 26, 1984).

A sidelight of the campaign involved several squabbles between casino supporters and churches. Many churches in Arkansas serve as polling places. The petition drive began on May 22, and primary elections were held on May 29 and June 12. Polling places are very good spots for circulating petitions, because the circulator can have good assurances that a signer is a registered voter. On May 29, casino workers went into the churches seeking signatures. So did other petitioners. However, the casino petitioners were harassed and in at least ten cases asked to leave. They were evicted by ministers and other church people. CUAG acknowledged that the incidents had taken place, but maintained that the churches had the right to ask casino advocates to leave their property even when it was serving as a polling place. Harris and McAfee protested. They pointed out that the churches received money to serve as polling places. Harris suggested that they might take legal action if the incidents were repeated on June 12. However, his committee rethought the position and decided not to use churches for the petition drive on June 12. McAfee suggested that the churches not be used as polling places (*Arkansas Gazette*, June 5, 1984, June 6, 1984). Several churches agreed that they did not want their properties compromised for political reasons and a $25 fee. They withdrew permission to be used as polling places (*Arkansas Democrat*, September 12, 1984).

The casino advocates scored few points in their campaign. They did hold opponents relatively even in financing. Files claimed that they raised $250,000. Nelson estimated that CUAG would spend between $250,000 and $300,000. Both sides had to answer charges that out-of-state casino interests were injecting money into their campaigns. Both sides made complete denials (*Arkansas Democrat*, October 27, 1984, October 31, 1984).

Early in September, the Arkansas Radio Network authorized Area Market Research to conduct a random sample survey of 400 registered voters throughout the state. It found that 57.8% were opposed to casinos. Opinion against the proposition ranged from a low of 51% in the third congressional district to 70% in the first district (*Arkansas Democrat*, September 11, 1984). If the poll was anywhere near accurate, the casino campaign must have been all downhill the rest of the way. On November 6, the voters gave more than 70% of the state's votes to the opponents—552,585 (70.5%) said no to casinos; only 231,831 (29.5%) said yes. The proposal did not win in a single county. In Hot Springs it was defeated by a 10,165 to 7,433 margin.

Sheffield Nelson said he wasn't surprised by the results. "I think this is exactly what the state of Arkansas wanted to do to casino gambling. I think it would have been so horrible to see the outside interests come in and take this state over. I think the voters realized what was happening, and I am pleased." Jack Files said, "No question about it. It failed better than 2 to 1 around the state and it failed in Garland County by 18,000 votes. It's dead and buried" (*Arkansas Democrat*, November 8, 1984).

Colorado: "A Nice Man Pushing a Bad Issue"

Political Environment

Experience with Legalized Gambling. A history of mining and frontier life has left a mark on present-day living in the Centennial State. Coloradans love the freedom that can be felt in the mountain air; they like to be left alone. "Rocky Mountain Gambling Fever" has never been totally suppressed, although the state has not recently suffered wide-open illegal casinos such as were found in Hot Springs and Galveston. The voters of Colorado were quite ready to join in the swim when the third wave of gambling legalization hit America. They had supported race tracks for dogs and horses, endorsed bingo, created a state lottery, and for a time approved of charity poker games. Several serious efforts have been made to gain popular approval for legalized casino gaming. But in Colorado the wave has been turned back: casinos have not been embraced by the voters.

Colorado has a history of controversial petition drives for casinos. A 1960 effort sought to win a vote for casinos throughout the state. Petition circulators were required to gain a number of signatures exceeding 8% of the voters in a previous state election. Their proposition was a 3,000-word constitutional amendment whose wording was drawn largely from Nevada's gaming statutes. The amendment would have created a state gaming commission to license private casinos and a gaming control board to oversee their operations and collect gaming taxes—from 2 to 5% of gross win. The tax, minus regulatory costs, was to be divided into four equal shares going to the general fund, schools, veterans, and old age assistance. Petition sponsors were based in southern Colorado, with offices in Pueblo and Walsenburg. On July 8, 1960, they submitted 45,131 signatures to secretary of state George Baker, over 3,000 more than the required 41,960. A battle was on. The Young Democrats called the proposition "morally offensive," leading to the control of state politics by "underworld elements" (*Denver Post*, July 9, 1960). The Republican state convention strongly opposed it. The Democratic governor and his party's candidate for the United States Senate immediately opposed casinos. An antigambling organization was formed under the name Colorado Citizens Committee to Oppose Open Gambling. Their numbers included business, political, and religious leaders. They planned to organize in each of the state's sixty-three counties, and their efforts were given strong editorial support by the *Denver Post* (August 16, 1960).

However, the opposition campaign in 1960 really fell on the shoulders of an attorney and former legislator, Hubert Henry of Denver (*Denver Post*, July 20, 1960). He challenged the validity of the wording of the proposition and the validity and legality of the petition signatures. Working with *Denver Post* reporters, Henry found forged signatures, signatures from ineligible voters—specifically, military personnel—and illegal circulation practices. Henry demanded a hearing in front of the secretary of state and presented his evidence on August 11. It was revealed that petition supporters and circulators had ties to certain unsavory characters—including illegal gamblers—and it was charged that the petition drive was financed by Las Vegas interests. The secretary of state first threw out 11,455 signatures for forgery, and later an additional 15,000 for improper notarization. Petition backers sought judicial relief, but Baker's actions were upheld by the Denver district court and the Colorado supreme court (*Denver Post*, August 26, 1960, September 20, 1960).

Casino Proposals. Twenty-two years later, Colorado experienced another casino campaign. Pueblo restaurant owner Robert Klausing seized on the fact that unemployment in his city exceeded 12%. The solution he suggested for a failing economy centered around a steel industry was casino gambling. A proposition was promoted in the legislature by a Pueblo representative, but failed for the lack of other support. Klausing then created the Committee for Economic Development and Tax Reform, and, with 700 volunteers, circulated petitions for casinos. His proposal would have allowed local option votes for private casinos in nineteen low-employment counties of southern Colorado as well as at ski resorts. A five-member state gambling commission would control licenses and collect a 12% tax on gross winnings, with 4% going to the local government hosting the casino and 8% to the state. The state share was to be equally divided among water projects, highways, education, and social services. Proponents projected tax revenues of $250 million a year coming from the casinos. Klausing predicted an additional 20,000 to 30,000 jobs in the newly created casinos of Colorado.

Democratic governor Richard Lamm did not read the proposition in the same light as did Klausing. He formed a committee with the state attorney general, J. D. McFarland, and county district attorneys in opposition. "Casino gambling," Lamm said, "would create economic and social leprosy" in the state. The attorney general pointed a finger at Nevada, saying the gaming state had "the highest per capita crime rate" in the nation (Freed, 1983:41). Denver district attorney Dale Tooley quoted a New Jersey official as saying "keeping organized crime out of a state with casinos is like keeping ants away from a blanket at a picnic" (*Colorado Springs Sun*, March 20, 1982). Another district attorney said, the "quality of life for the people, when this kind of an operation comes in, substantially declines." The Pueblo district attorney, Gus Sandstrom, described the people behind the casino push as "honest businessmen no way involved with organized crime, but they just don't see what the problems are. This would allow the professionals to take over and destroy everything we have in Pueblo" (*Colorado Springs Sun*, March 20, 1982). The Pueblo city council and county commission passed resolutions against the measure, as did the Democratic party of Denver (*Chieftain* [Pueblo], April 27, 1982; *Denver Post*, April 21, 1982).

Despite this opposition, the casino backers submitted petitions with over 42,000 signatures to secretary of state Mary Buchannan. Only 38,896 names were necessary to win a ballot spot. Governor Lamm, however, was not prepared to concede a ballot position to the measure. He organized a coalition of district attorneys, clergy, business leaders, lawyers, and politicians to fight ballot certification. Operating as No Casino Gambling, Inc., they challenged the petitions. As in 1960, the opponents found flagrant evidence of forgeries, improper addresses, and illegal petition circulation practices. In a hearing before the secretary of state, they argued that 25,000 signatures were invalid. In September, Buchannan agreed and rejected every petition signature and removed the question from the ballot. Klausing was later charged with both felony and misdemeanor charges of filing fraudulent petitions. In a plea bargaining arrangement, he accepted a guilty verdict on the misdemeanor charge, paid a $700 fine, agreed not to participate in any more petition drives, and then moved out of state. He indicated that he intended to enter law school (Davis 1983:23; Freed 1983:40).

Undaunted by this failure, Pueblo business supporters vowed to try again. Even Louis Giovanetti, the chairman of No Casino Gambling, Inc., saw casinos in the Colorado future, saying that "some form of casino gambling will come to the state within five years" (*Chieftain* [Pueblo], November 18, 1982). Perhaps 1984 would be the year. That certainly was the hope of Pueblo West businessman John A. Verna.

Proponent Activism. John Verna was drawn into the casino issue during the summer of 1982. He is a lifetime resident of Pueblo and a leader of business and civic organizations. According to Verna, an acquaintance approached him one day and said, "John, what are we going to do about this casino thing?" (Verna 1982). In the course of the conversation, John and his friend agreed on several basic points. One was that gambling fever was sweeping the nation, and with it was coming an expansion of casino gambling. They agreed that casinos would be coming to Colorado, but that the Klausing proposal was wrong. They felt that Klausing had not been totally proper in the manner in which he was promoting the issue and agreed that it would be wrong to have casinos operating openly throughout a large area of Colorado. Most importantly, they agreed that Pueblo was in poor economic shape and needed the help that casino gaming could bring to the community.

John Verna concluded that casino gambling should come to just one controlled area in Colorado. He knew about a 4,000-acre parcel of unused state land above the bluffs of the Arkansas River seven miles west of the city of Pueblo. The land was a former honor farm. It was a perfect location for three to five casino hotels and a large recreational area. He studied the parcel and went into action, not even waiting for the secretary of state to sound the death knell on Klausing's plan. He found that the land would be available for his plan. It was suitable for building. Architects helped him draw plans that set aside 2,000 acres for casinos and 2,000 acres for a family-style entertainment area. In this area was located an existing motor-sport track that could be expanded. He also saw a future coliseum, three golf courses, a western theme park, and a horseman's park. The state gaming and lottery commission would have its headquarters on the land. Currently, the lottery headquarters are in Pueblo.

In March 1983, Verna formed a corporation called Rocky Mountain Resorts and Recreation, Inc. He contacted a local legislator who had expressed some interest in casinos, and together they ironed out wording for a constitutional initiative proposal. The next goal was to gather petition signatures. Verna indicated that it would take $500,000 in order to carry the petition campaign and subsequent election. The Pueblo proposition asked voters if the Colorado Constitution should be amended "to provide for the appointment of a [five-member] commission to regulate and license gaming . . . and to control an adjacent recreation area," to collect "up to 10% of the gross proceeds from casino gaming," and to provide that, after deducting administrative costs, 70% would go to public schools and 30% to a medically indigent program. If the 4,000-acre site designated by Verna would not be available, the Gaming Commission could select other Pueblo County land and acquire it by eminent domain. The Colorado general assembly would be empowered to pass enabling laws and to determine the powers and duties of the commission.

Signatures were gained mostly as a result of a last-minute blitz. Verna and other businesspeople from Pueblo loaded their cars and vans with supporters and drove to Denver for weekend canvasses of large shopping areas. Verna himself stayed in Denver the last week of the drive and personally collected over 1,000 names (Verna 1984). On July 31, 1984, Rocky Mountain Resorts submitted petitions with over 53,000 signatures to the secretary of state, Natalie Meyer. Only 46,737 valid signatures were required to win a ballot position.

Opponents, led by Dale Tooley, the former district attorney of Denver, started making spot checks of the signatures. His opposition group, Casino-Free Future, had until August 31 to challenge the petitions. But in a strange turnabout, Verna issued his own plea for an attorney general's investigation of the petitioning process. Along with 53,000 signatures on 2,536 "good" petitions, Verna turned in 8,000 additional names on 353 petitions that he claimed were "tainted." "I have been informed that there is a likelihood that an organized and concentrated effort has been made by parties unknown to illegally interfere with the initiative process," he told a press conference (*Denver Post*, August 1, 1984). The matter was turned over to the state attorney general's office for investigation. No results of the investigation were released before the November election.

Role of Political Elites

Opponents of casinos were led by Governor Lamm, Tooley, and Gus Sandstrom, still the Pueblo district attorney. They again emphasized crime as an issue in the campaign. However, the proponents did have some new faces this time. The Pueblo county commission passed a resolution of support. Local legislators and some members of the Pueblo city council first endorsed casinos. Some changed their minds later. Their line of argument, as before, was an economic one. Verna claimed that his plan would provide 6,000 to 8,000 direct jobs with an additional 20,000 "spin-off" jobs (Verna 1984; *Rocky Mountain News*, April 14, 1983). Congressman Ray Kogovsek from Pueblo commented that the city "is going to have to take care of itself. The federal government is not going to be providing many new jobs. Pueblo has just about everything we need to make something like this go" (*Chieftain* [Pueblo], December 18, 1983).

In 1983, a poll showed that Pueblo residents supported casinos by a fifty-three to thirty-five margin. A large majority saw casinos helping the economy, while the survey respondents were evenly divided on the question of whether the casinos would improve the "quality of life" (*Chieftain* [Pueblo], June 19, 1983).

The economic argument lost some of its steam with the decision of the Sperry Corporation to build a $10-million-dollar defense computer systems plant in Pueblo. The announcement that 1,000 Sperry jobs were coming to Pueblo was made early in 1984. Local morale was said to have increased at once. Enthusiasm for casinos cooled. Tooley expressed doubt about whether the new plant would have come to a casino city. He also pointed out that Colorado had developed more than twice as many jobs as Nevada during the past decade.

The opponents drew support from a rival resort, the Broadmoor Hotel in Colorado Springs. Hotel head William J. Hybl felt that casino gaming would not enhance the attractiveness of southern Colorado to the space-oriented industries that were already beginning to arrive. "I can understand why Pueblo is seeking a variety of avenues to produce economic growth, but legalized gambling is a short-term resolution." There was also a moral stance against casinos. Most churches restated their opposition. The Catholic bishop of the Pueblo Diocese summarized the position of many, saying that we couldn't condone what comes with gambling: crime, detrimental effects on children, drugs, and abuse of women. The hopes of winning the support of educators by earmarking taxes for schools were dashed when the Colorado Board of Education voted eight to zero to oppose casinos. One board member commented that "education should have a broad-based financial support, because it is worthwhile to all of us (*Chieftain* [Pueblo], June 16, 1984).

The credibility factor was greatly enhanced by Verna's presence in the campaign. He was a responsible citizen who had not been involved in politics previous to the casino campaign. He had no political ambitions. He had no ties to any gaming interests. Indeed, until October 1984, he had not visited Las Vegas in over ten years. He had no business interests that would directly benefit from casinos in Pueblo. His housing stone supply business would certainly be helped if the entire surrounding economy was growing, but it was not tied to tourism or gambling. Verna's campaign was driven by what political scientists call "public regardingness." The campaign was certifiably clean. Doubts that surrounded the Colorado campaigns of 1960 and 1982 as well as many other campaigns for casinos did not surround Verna.

Verna's efforts to gain $500,000 in funding were not successful. His campaign did receive a respectable level of funding during the petitioning stages. He raised $106,000 and spent $105,000. The funds, however, represented his strength. They came almost exclusively from fellow business-people in Pueblo. However, when they were used up, more money did not follow. He had to run his campaign for votes on the limited budget; much of the money came out of his own pocket. Verna's lack of ties to gaming interests certainly aided in his quest to make a credible case for casinos, but it had drawbacks as well. During the campaign, Verna indicated that some businesses were very interested in locating in the family recreation portion of the 4,000-acre parcel. However, no corporate casino interests came forth to say that they wished to build a casino. No such interest advanced funds to the campaign.

Verna had no money for extensive media campaigns. Therefore, he sought to generate publicity as best he could. His group held many meetings that received attention in the press. He gained the governor's cooperation for participation in a series of debates. The debates were well reported and Verna was given credit for holding his own. The citizen-turned-politician was quite proud of the fact that with his eighth-grade education he was able to stand on the stage with equal stature beside the law-school-educated and very popular chief executive of his state. It was almost a Cinderella story, but no glass slipper was to be found. Verna was up against too much.

Governor Lamm assigned his top research staff member to the casino campaign. Casino-Free Future, Inc., engaged Galloway Associates, a professional campaign consultant group, to manage the campaign, at a fee of $20,000. They sought to raise $200,000. Funds came from the top business leaders of the state. Lamm campaigned tirelessly. His first efforts took him right into Pueblo, where he won the support of key community leaders against casinos. The *Chieftain*, the Pueblo newspaper, took a lead in educating the public. Its reporters traveled to Reno, Las Vegas, Laughlin, and Atlantic City to gain material. They presented a detailed series of stories that collectively gave a very balanced point of view. The paper conducted a poll of Pueblo County residents in October 1984. The results showed that local opinion had turned against the idea of casinos. Only 36% approved of the measure. Editorially, the *Chieftain* opposed the proposal, as did the other major papers in Denver. So did the voters, 816,816 to 406,637; only 33.2% favored the proposal. Verna could take a measure of satisfaction from the fact that he did better than the pollsters figured in his home county. In Pueblo, he just barely lost, receiving over 49% of the votes.

Governor Richard Lamm said he was pleased with the outcome: "But I think it's one of those races I take very little joy in winning. I've gotten very fond of John Verna. I think he's a nice man pushing a bad issue. Now I hope we can all do something effective to create jobs in Pueblo" (*Chieftain* [Pueblo], November 7, 1984).

Other Campaigns:
Arizona, Washington, Hawaii, and California

This chapter has focused its attention on four Sunbelt states. Each of these states witnessed actual election campaigns on the casino issue and efforts to revive a previously illegal gaming industry through legalization. Efforts that have not yet resulted in electoral campaigns have occurred in other Sunbelt states as well. The campaigns have not always been treated seriously. Nonetheless, they indicate that the issue of casinos has been pervasive in the Sunbelt and that it will probably remain on the horizon as a potential issue for future political agendas. For one of these states, Louisiana, the item has been elevated to a central spot on the political agenda by none other than the governor, a unique factor among all the campaigns for casinos. It is appropriate that some attention be given to the efforts of Governor Edwards, and also the efforts of casino proponents in Arizona, Washington, Hawaii, and California.

Arizona

Gambling is no stranger to Arizona. Pari-mutuel horse- and dog-race betting has existed for years. A lottery was established in 1980. The past is dotted with episodes of frontier gambling houses. And, as recently as 1948, a state attorney general of Arizona, John L. Sullivan, was removed from office following his conviction for accepting bribes from people operating gaming "traps" for tourists along old Route 66. Most of today's residents of Arizona have roots outside of the state. They do not recall the days of John L. Sullivan. Rather, they see that gambling in many forms, including casino gambling, can be a legitimate way to enhance economic growth. Some important people, however, disagree.

In the spring of 1983, the *Arizona Republic* conducted a random survey of residents in Phoenix, Bullhead City, Lake Havasu City, and Parker, Arizona, and found that 56% of the residents responding to the poll favored casinos (*Las Vegas Review Journal*, July 24, 1983). A subsequent attitude survey was directed solely at the resort retirement community of Lake Havasu. Of 1,005 respondents, 52% favored casinos for their city, 35% were opposed, and others had no opinion. However, of seventy-five selected community leaders surveyed, only 26% favored casinos, while 60% were opposed.

These surveys sparked rumors that there would be an initiative drive to place a casino question on the 1984 state ballot. Lake Havasu residents were generally positive toward the idea. The president of the Chamber of Commerce there said, "I think the main feeling in the community is that if casino gambling is brought in, it would certainly be a boon to the economy, so to speak." A resident replied, "If it's controlled, I think it would be the best thing for the state." Government officials strongly disagreed. The governor and attorney general vowed to fight any attempt at legalization. Mohave County supervisor Jim Schultz questioned the state's ability to administer gaming activities: "I don't think Arizona is prepared to handle gambling per se. The proof is in their handling of horseracing, dogracing. . . . The lottery is a typical example of a horror story. It's been a disaster, lawsuit after lawsuit. We just don't have the ability to police gambling." While Schultz denied the credibility of the "real" forces favoring casinos, attorney general Robert Corbin said, "There are indications people who are allegedly connected to organized crime are interested in legalized casino type gambling in Arizona" (*Las Vegas Review Journal*, July 24, 1983). A federal organized crime strike force operating out of Los Angeles agreed, reporting that known organized crime figures appeared to be making efforts to attract legalized gaming to Arizona. These reports indicated that meetings of known organized criminals had been held to discuss prospects of Arizona casinos. Governor Bruce Babbitt said he would do everything in his power to stop casinos from entering Arizona. In the end, the 1984 petition drive did not materialize.

In 1985, the Arizona attorney general was just as adamant in his opposition to casinos. Corbin's attentions had shifted from the fleeting noncampaign for casinos to the very real problem of Indian reservation gambling. As in other states, Indian tribes in Arizona have established high-stakes bingo operations. Corbin is convinced that organized crime elements have been able to penetrate some of the Indian operations. Unlike other states, tribes in Arizona have increased their interest in gaming beyond the bingo operations that have been established as legally permissible by federal courts. Arizona tribes are attempting to establish a jai alai fronton in the Phoenix area, but jai alai is not permitted in Arizona. The attorney general has vowed that he will use all legal resources to stop the establishment of jai alai in Arizona. Corbin has expressed a fear that if such an operation is permitted and upheld by federal courts, the door will be wide open for the Indians to establish casino gambling in Arizona (Corbin, *Arizona Republic,* February 20, 1984).

Not only will any prospective Arizona casino proponents have to fight established political opposition and the credibility issue, but they will also have to conduct their fight against an economically strong Nevada casino industry. Nevada casinos are expanding southward to the banks of the Colorado River across from Bullhead City, Arizona, and Mohave County and will certainly not sit idly by and allow Arizona casinos to threaten their new investments. The chairman of Del Webb Corporation, one of these investors, expressed his views: "It is our position Arizona shouldn't jump into something it knows nothing about" (*Wall Street Journal,* July 20, 1983). Based on all these factors, there is little likelihood that Arizona will allow casinos in the near future, at least not state-authorized casinos (*Arizona Republic,* July 19, 1983).

Yet based on this political background, another campaign for casinos in Arizona was launched in 1988. Opposition to casinos appeared to soften somewhat. Attorney General Corbin reiterated his negative stand, however he also indicated that there would be economic advantages with casinos. In fact, he stated that the political climate might be right this time. He said in early 1989, "If there was a referendum on the ballot to legalize gambling right now, I'm pretty sure that it would pass" (*Gambler's World* 1989). A changed atmosphere came about with local economic problems. Resort hotels in Scottsdale were suffering from high vacancy rates. The state faced a taxation crisis. And certainly the impeachment of a governor left many in the state questioning the government's capacity to deal with the crises on a business-as-usual basis (Reiterman 1989).

Gambler's World, Inc., a Tempe-based bookstore and gambling supply house, seized the initiative. Led by company executives Robert and Jim Reiterman, Gambler's World circulated petitions seeking 86,659 signatures from Arizona voters in order to force a November 1990 vote on the legalization of casino gaming. The proposal creates a gaming commission and authorizes large-scale casinos (*Gambler's World* 1989). While there are ma-

jor doubts remaining about whether the Reitermans have the financial connections to coordinate a winning campaign for casino gaming, it does appear
that they have a good chance of having their proposition on the ballot in
1990. Now, in contrast with the early eighties, Arizonans do know more than
a little about gaming. In 1987 the legislature permitted private card games to
be played for money stakes in taverns. Obvious abuses provide a rationale for
the Reitermans' proposal. They wish to regulate gaming to make it more
honest. And Indian reservations in Arizona offer high-stakes bingo and card
games. A gaming commission could negotiate with the Indians to have their
casino-type games regulated in a rational manner. Moreover, Arizona fur-
nished 1.15 million gamblers (visits) for Nevada casinos in 1988. This repre-
sents 6.7% of the Nevada gaming market (*Las Vegas Sun*, February 28,
1989). Arizona gamblers spent over 500 million dollars in southern Nevada
in one year. While Nevada draws annual convention attendance of
1,677,716, Arizona drew only 87,200 conventioneers. Gaming could help
bring a balance between the two areas. The proponents of gaming suggested
that between 30,000 and 100,000 jobs could be created with casinos, and
that gaming would generate direct and indirect taxation revenues of $300
million a year. The arguments appear strong enough to force the question.
We will have to await an active campaign to determine whether a veto factor
will surface to stop the movement toward casino legalization (*Gambler's
World* 1989).

Washington and Hawaii

In Ocean Shores, a beach town halfway between Seattle and Portland, an
initiative to bring casinos to the tourist town on a local option basis began in
1984. The issue of gambling appeared on a list made by the Ocean Shores
Chamber of Commerce of efforts the area could make to attract industry or
otherwise improve the seasonal status of its mainly tourist economy. A group
called LOG—Local Option Gambling—ran full-page advertisements in
several newspapers throughout the state. The ads, with room for 25 signatures each, were responsible for amassing approximately 100,000 signatures to place a gambling initiative on the state ballot. A number of stories
regarding casinos in Washington were published by the *Seattle Times*,
emphasizing the taxation potential of casino legalization. Washington, which
currently permits charity gambling and three legal lottery games, had been
mentioned as a possibility for legal casinos since the late 1970s. With other
areas besides Ocean Shores said to be favorable toward local option gambling, Washington remains a state where the interest in casinos might be
rekindled. Ocean Shores had its best year in its fourteen-year history in
1984, and the desire for casinos may remain in the minds of many.

A casino movement in Hawaii rested on the weak political shoulders of state legislator Ollie Lunasco. The "maverick" house member introduced a casino bill in 1980 and did get it past the first reading stage, but that was about all. The governor's office indicated total opposition. In response to opponents' claims that gaming would "bring in a very undesirable element," Lunasco replied, "Hell, take a look around. We've got organized crime here already; they've been into everything for years" (Hill 1980:46). This is certainly not the political style that wins support for casinos. The movement has gone nowhere in Hawaii.

California

If one state ever had the capacity to destroy the economy of another state, it would be California. The victim would be Nevada. The weapon would be legalized casino gambling. Nevada's economy is essentially a one-product economy. Tourism and gambling account for approximately one-half of the income of the people and one-half of the revenues of the governments of the state. Californians provide a substantial share of the dollars that flow into the Nevada economy. Estimates have suggested that as many as 82% of the Nevada tourists are from California (Pinney 1975:4). Even the lower estimates show the majority of the tourists are from California. These tourists come for one main purpose—to gamble in the legal casinos of Nevada (McQuade 1981:135–137).

The legalization of casino gambling by the state of California could doom Nevada to economic oblivion comparable to that faced by the state in the 1880s and 1890s when silver mining died out. At that earlier time, there were serious debates in Congress about whether Nevada should continue to exist as a state governmental entity. One major church organization—the Methodists—abolished the state as a church district and made it a "mission" during this period. With casinos in California, the state of Nevada would be ripe for "mission" or "colony" status once again.

California is a state familiar with legalized gambling within its borders. The unique feature of California gaming is the poker parlor. Established by local option and regulated by the state, over 400 such parlors are in operation. One—the Bicycle Club of Bell Gardens—rivals almost any Las Vegas casino in its action and the size of its table area. These legal poker parlors have been in existence since the 1870s. Pari-mutuel betting on horse races has been authorized since 1933 (McQuade 1981:116–131). The state also has widespread bingo operations, both for charity and on Indian reservations. In 1984, the voters of California promised to become the biggest government lottery in the world. Gambling revenues in California are second only to the gambling revenues of New York.

There are those who have desired to add casinos to the list of California gaming attractions. The environmental protection of the beautiful shores of Lake Tahoe (lands in both California and Nevada) motivated the late California assemblyman Edwin L. Z'Berg to promote casinos for Placer and El Dorado counties. Z'Berg felt that the casinos would induce Nevadans to limit casino growth at Lake Tahoe. Supervisors from both counties supported the 1975 bill, which would have authorized one casino in each of the two counties for each new casino Nevada authorized at Lake Tahoe (Mc-Quade 1981:166).

Environmental protection and economic retaliation were the motives of state senator John Holmdahl's 1977 proposal. He wished to amend the state constitution in order to permit casinos in a twenty-mile corridor along three major highways coming out of Nevada (McQuade 1981:167). While Z'Berg's and Holmdahl's efforts failed, they did serve notice on the state of Nevada that the former "colony" had better cooperate in protecting natural resources common to both states. A bistate regional compact to regulate growth in the Tahoe area had been created, and casino efforts activated its operations.

Others have been motivated by fiscal concerns to develop California casinos. The passage of the landmark tax revolt initiative Proposition 13 in 1978 has caused more than a few to think about the option of "painless taxes." That tax-cutting measure certainly had an impact on the creation of the large majority vote for the lottery in 1984. Earlier efforts saw an unsuccessful petition drive for casinos in Riverside County in 1974. A 1976 effort targeted the town of Adelanto in San Bernardino County for casinos. A 1978 drive added Lakeport in northern California to Adelanto. However, the residents of Lakeport led a charge against the petition drive. In 1979, citizens also killed a drive for casinos in Jackson, in northern California's Amador County. When the state government "dragged its feet" in funding a local sewer project that the state had mandated, the city council of Jackson endorsed casino gambling. The council submitted a resolution to the state legislature and sought out the sponsor of the Adelanto petition drive, asking that Jackson be added to the petition. When this happened, a group of town residents quickly organized against the casino move. What some had seen as a political joke was taken quite seriously by this group. The residents forced the council to call a local referendum election on the casino question. When the votes were counted, it was found that 511 citizens wanted the city council to rescind its actions. Only 177 supported casinos (McQuade 1981:167–172).

The sponsor the city council sought out for an alliance was Robert Wilson. The May 1981 issue of *Gaming Business Magazine* reported that Wilson "was at it again." In 1981, he again promoted gaming for San Bernardino County in a petition drive that also sought to establish off-track betting statewide through 500 proposed offices (Klein and Selesner 1981:10). The *Los Angeles Times* (February 19, 1982) reported that Wilson's petition drive included two casino sites at Adelanto and Clear Lake in northern California's Lake County. In his efforts to get financial support for his drive, Wilson conducted bingo games. However, he was arrested when authorities decided that his games did not meet the criteria for charity bingo. Once again, his drive failed (*Los Angeles Times*, February 19, 1982).

Wilson's bingo operations were not the only ones to raise the ire of authorities. Like other states, California has had its share of problems with Indian gaming operations, and a series of articles in the *Los Angeles Times* focused on deficiencies in the management of charity bingo. Local regulation of poker parlors was also found to be wanting; at the urging of the state attorney general, the state government instituted regulation of the poker parlors in 1983. In this period, both Democratic attorney general John Van de Kamp and Republican governor George Deukmejian became leading spokesmen against legalized gaming in all forms. The two executives provided a focal point of opposition on the lottery question in 1984. However, the lottery petition drive was successful—59% of the voters responded to pleas for more state funding within the boundaries of Proposition 13 tax limits. A measure of success for the drive was provided by Scientific Games, a division of Bally Gaming Company and a provider of lottery ticket supplies. Scientific Games "invested" a reported $2 million in the referendum election. Subsequently, it won the contract to supply tickets to the lottery. The type of support Scientific Games threw into the 1984 contest was never duplicated in any of the California campaigns for casinos, all of which appeared to be one-man efforts. Scientific Games was credited with writing the ballot proposal for the lottery, making sure that the California lottery would never have to face the competition of local casinos. The lottery amendment to the state constitution provided that casinos could not be established in California. Perhaps it was this vested interest in lotteries that led to this provision in the amendment—or maybe the company was concerned about the livelihood of the Nevada economy. In 1986, the parent company purchased the MGM Grand, the largest casino hotel complex in Las Vegas and Reno.

Conclusion:
Florida and Louisiana, Two 1986 Failures

In most of the Sunbelt states' casino campaigns, negative conditions prevailed for several veto factors. Still, the gravity model advanced by the Public Gaming Research Institute predicted casinos for Florida, Colorado, Arkansas, and Louisiana in the 1980s. Campaigns in the Sunbelt region continued in 1986, but our analysis suggests that casinos were once again vetoed by critical factors in Florida and Louisiana.

The 1986 Louisiana effort stands out from all the other casino campaigns examined. Since Brendan Byrne in New Jersey, only in the Bayou State has a governor been willing to be the outspoken leader in the fight for casinos. Even in New Jersey, the governor was more of a team player, and his failure to take a lead contributed to the 1974 defeat. Other governors in the Sunbelt region have been the central opponents of casinos: Lamm in Colorado, Graham in Florida, and Clinton in Arkansas. Proponents of casinos in these states had to face hostile political atmospheres. While they could assert that specific locations for casinos such as Hot Springs, Pueblo, and Miami Beach were economically deprived, they had to convince voters in other regions of the respective states that casinos were needed. These other regions—Little Rock, Colorado Springs, Denver, and Orlando—did not share the economic distress of the selected casino cities. The Louisiana campaign again can be distinguished—economic conditions were at low ebb throughout the state, and the public fiscal crisis was focused upon the state political leadership.

The sponsorship factor had negative aspects in most of the campaigns. In Florida and Louisiana there was respected business and political leadership for casinos, but that was balanced by similar opposition. The governor of Louisiana was vulnerable as a leader because of his personal relationships with casinos. Other casino efforts were almost Quixotic tilts at windmills. Efforts were often started by individuals who were out of the mainstream of state political power. Some, such as John Verna óf Colorado, had the credibility of respected businessmen, while others such as Colorado's Klausing and California's Wilson lacked credibility. Leaders in Texas and Arkansas had family ties back to the days when their towns had wide-open illegal casinos. The Arizona effort suffered from suggestions that organized crime interests desired a casino foothold in Phoenix. None of the states outside of Florida found established casinos indicating firm support for the propositions. The lack of a felt statewide economic crisis in most of the states allowed opponents to focus public attention on the negative aspects of casinos—crime and quality of life—hence dooming campaigns.

In examining the factors, we would envision a narrow preponderance of support in only Florida and Louisiana. Yet when Florida voters cast ballots, their favorable response of less than 30% confirms that the veto factors were effective. If future proponents are going to turn things around, a strong effort will be required. The Florida voters again cast ballots in 1986. However, the question was on the ballot only because petition circulators were paid 60¢ for each name gathered. The petition names, while over 340,000 in number, did not indicate true support. A vote against casinos provided a second resounding failure for Florida casinos, eight years after the 1978 defeat.

Florida, 1986

From 1978 through 1986, there seemed to be a continuity of forces for and against casinos in Florida. But there were some changes in 1986. South Florida hotels were more united than in the past. The hotels funded the petition drive and were expected to fund most of the election costs as well. Stephen Muss, operator of the Fountainebleau-Hilton came out for casinos for the first time. He donated $95,000 to the cause. Religious opposition was no longer solid. Miami Beach Rabbi Pinchas Weberman, a vehement opponent in the past, was a supporter in 1986. The Miami Chamber of Commerce, an opponent group in the past, was neutral and split in 1986. Governor Bob Graham, busy running for a United States Senate seat, was not active in opposition as he had been in the past. Some suggested that he feared that an opposition stance would cost him votes in his own election. The *Miami Herald* decided that it was improper to try to cover the news and be an active campaign participant at the same time and stayed out of the campaign as an opponent, as did some other major newspapers.

The tourism industry of south Florida continues to falter, and the proponents of casinos have kept this economic fact in front of the voters. These factors gave the supporters a ray of hope for November, but the opposition camp was active and well financed. Jack Eckerd, a prominent businessman and former candidate for governor, headed the No Casinos, Inc., group that had been started by Governor Askew in 1978. The opponents felt that they could get their act together without the leadership of Askew or Graham. In 1978, the casino question was certified for the ballot in August. With only three months for campaigning, it was essential to utilize a formal political and business elite leader for the contest. In 1986, there was much more time for organization and fund raising. Religious leaders joined with attorney general Jim Smith in a group called FACT—Floridians against Casino Takeover, Inc. The jai alai fontons and racetracks formed Floridians against Casinos and Crime.

The casino supporters strengthened their south Florida base somewhat in 1986, in comparison to 1978, but in the rest of the state they were still weak. The Disney-based Orlando tourism industry was economically healthy and strongly against casinos. The 1986 proposal raised the possibilities of casinos in north Florida. This situation made the religious opposition, which is concentrated in the north of the state, even more vocal.

One of the major weaknesses in the 1986 campaign was the language of the ballot proposal. Even if the measure had won voter approval, Florida might never have seen casinos. A hostile legislature might have balked at passing implementing legislation, or a governor might have vetoed such legislation. More than one state has passed a constitutional provision for a lottery only to see the legislature fail to provide for one. On the other hand, the Florida legislature could have passed an extremely restrictive law regulating and taxing casinos beyond what any casino organization would desire. Nevada casinos complained loudly when a recent legislative session sought modest increases in a 5¾% tax on gross profits. Casinos would predictably respond to a 10% or 20% tax. But then, even with acceptable legislation, the local voters have had an opportunity for "second thoughts." They would have to approve casinos a second time. For these reasons, it is not surprising that no casino corporation came forth and endorsed the November measure. But some casino organizations, notably Resorts International, joined a silent opposition. These opponents feared that Florida competition would have been especially damaging to their casinos in New Jersey, the Bahamas, and the Caribbean.

The dominant issue in the 1986 campaign was crime. The proponents' hopes of concentrating on the economic benefits of casinos were dashed as more reports—such as articles appearing in the *Wall Street Journal*—focused on the negative economic impact of casinos on the Atlantic City community. A mid-campaign poll in the *Miami Herald* revealed that the number one concern of Florida citizens was crime, not surprising, considering the enormous drug traffic there. Opponents of casinos used this concern to their advantage. The issue of crime vetoed Florida casinos again in 1986.

Louisiana, 1986

The economic picture in Louisiana had kept the dismal crime statistics for New Orleans on the back pages of the press in 1986. For instance, the following headlines appeared in the *New Orleans Times Picayune* in the first three months of 1986: "Budget cuts may kill adult learning center" (February 27, 1986), "State district offices of conservation closed" and "Oil price may fall to $10" (March 4, 1986), "Miserly budget pinches tourism" (March 16, 1986), "300 city employees to lose jobs" (March 20, 1986), "S.E. La. drops football—raises fees" (March 20, 1986), "Hotel tax revenues drop sharply" (April 4, 1986). And if these items did not offer enough bad news, the space shuttle explosion caused the Martin Marietta plant in New Orleans to lay off 600 workers, depriving the local economy of a $21 million payroll (*New Orleans Times Picayune*, March 18, 1986). Years of fiscal irresponsibility, high spending and low taxes, a mismanaged world's fair, and a drastic fall in oil prices have all added up to fiscal disaster. Maintenance of current levels in state spending would require additional revenues of between $500 million and $1 billion. Otherwise, budget cuts of at least 22% (accepting the $500 million figure) would be required. Louisiana certainly had an economic disaster that even surpassed the one felt by the voters of New Jersey in 1976. The need was obvious. Governor Edwin Edwards offered a plan in 1986: a lottery and wide-open casino gambling.

Louisiana has had a scarlet history of illegal gaming operations. But it was the "legal" lottery of the late nineteenth century that made the state's name synonymous with public corruption. This notorious lottery was authorized by the state legislature, promoted by bribery, and run by a New York syndicate. As the only public lottery in the nation, the sweepstakes gained revenues from ticket sales across the country. Federal pressures were exerted to end the lottery. In 1890, Congress gave the postmaster general the authority to refuse the delivery of mail to lottery agents; in 1895, a bill was passed prohibiting the use of all forms of interstate commerce by lottery companies. This action effectively cut the Louisiana lottery off from its markets and spelled its doom (Weinstein and Deitch 1974:11–12). Illegal gaming continued. Governor Huey Long purportedly helped Meyer Lansky's effort to divest New York of gaming paraphernalia in the face of Governor Thomas Dewey's crime-busting campaign of the 1930s. Long purchased Lansky's stock of slot machines and moved them south. The two shared in revenues produced by the one-armed bandits of the Bayou (Messick 1971).

The latest drive for legal gambling was initiated by Governor Edwards. Lotteries are prohibited by the state constitution. Therefore, if Louisiana is to have a lottery, the measure must first be proposed by two-thirds of the membership of each house of the legislature and then ratified by a statewide election. Casino gambling may be authorized by a simple act of the legislature passed by majority votes in each house. In 1984, Edwards reluctantly endorsed the lottery even though he felt that it was unfair to the poor. In 1985, Edwards proposed that one casino be established in the Old Fisheries Building in the French Quarter. The operator of the establishment was to pay an annual licensing fee equaling 12% of the gross revenues (*New Orleans Times Picayune* February 26, 1985). There was to be a dress code and a $25 door charge that would be refunded in chips that had to be played. The casino would have neither a bar nor a restaurant, and it would not be connected to any hotel. Legislative sponsors of the bill suggested that the New Orleans casino would not be "gaudy" like casinos in Atlantic City or Las Vegas. "We are looking for a high-class, high-roller facility that would not serve as a place for local people to participate in gambling," remarked state senator Ben Bagert (*Baton Rouge Morning Advocate*, May 22, 1985). One study saw the casino drawing $15 million to the state treasury. The bill died on the Senate floor.

In the meantime, Governor Edwards was indicted and put on trial in federal district court for allegedly accepting bribes to issue permits to build hospitals in his state. Testimony exposed Edwards's personal gaming behavior. Evidence was presented indicating he had lost over $2 million gambling in Las Vegas. The prosecution suggested these losses provided the motive for accepting bribes. The Edwards trial coincided with the sharp drop in oil prices that turned the state's depressed economy into a disaster (*New Orleans Times Picayune*, March 12, 1986).

In December, a mistrial was declared. Edwards accepted the jury's eleven to one vote in his favor as a sort of vindication. He came out swinging. He quickly revealed his plans for a lottery and wide-open casino gambling as a needed tool to eliminate the $500 million shortfall facing the state. He also advocated an increase in property taxes. His plan provided for ten to twenty casinos in New Orleans, with additional casinos in two adjacent parishes. He also wanted casinos on riverboats. The governor indicated that he would call a special legislative session for February to deal with his proposals. The month of December 1985 was kind to the governor; January 1986 was not. First, Edwards found that he could not line up simple majorities for casinos or the needed two-thirds majorities for a lottery. He called off the special session. Second, the federal government indicated that Edwards would be put on trial a second time. The new trial would take place in late spring during the regular session of the legislature.

Edwards readjusted quickly and came up with a new strategy. He decided that the casino question should be resolved with a constitutional amendment. He then went to reluctant legislators and tried to persuade them to "let the people decide." He presented a budget that could not be balanced without his gambling proposals and an increased state property tax. Edwards angered the members of the legislature when he suggested that he would veto any budget passed that did not follow his guidelines. If this occurred, he would call a special session for the summer after his second trial was over, assuming an innocent verdict.

New Orleans has a very high crime rate. Crime would be an issue in any casino campaign, but Edwards downplayed the notion that casinos would bring extra crime. He admitted that an extra 400 police officers would be necessary to watch over the casino areas, but he felt that the extra 100,000 jobs he foresaw would improve poverty conditions that breed crime. Others disagreed. Warren de Brueys, director of the Metropolitan Crime Commission of New Orleans, saw an increase of 20% in crime rates—an additional 10,000 crimes per year. This would lead to the need for one additional prison (*New Orleans Times Picayune*, February 22, 1986).

While Governor Edwards was the first governor since Brendan Byrne of

New Jersey actively to endorse casinos, his participation in the drive presented some problems for casino advocates. The major problem was credibility.
His personal problems did not bring a favorable response to the casino
industry. And his statistical projections raised many doubts about his budget
plans. At first, he said casinos would bring in $350 million a year to the state,
then he revised the estimates down to $250 million. Somehow he expected
casinos to be in place in early 1987 shortly after a November election and a
special legislative session that would pass legislation for licensing, regulating,
and setting tax structures for gaming. Then he expected that within a year
more than ten casinos would be producing the same kinds of revenues as
produced in Atlantic City. Edwards also expected the economy to add
100,000 new jobs, more than were created in New Jersey. Yet opponents
pointed out that New Orleans does not have 53 million people within a day's
drive like Atlantic City. But even if Edwards's projections for revenue were
correct ($250 million from casinos, $150 million from a lottery), the amounts
would still be far short of funds needed. His plan was based on a shortfall of
$500 million, projecting oil prices of about $19 a barrel. While the legislature was meeting in the spring, prices were near $14.

Edwards also had opponents. The Greater New Orleans Federation of
Churches sponsored a letter-writing campaign that headed off the special
session in February. Major newspapers were opposed to casinos, as were
economic elites. An economic task force meeting under the leadership of
Tulane University president Eamon Kelly drew up alternative plans for
economic recovery (*New Orleans Times Picayune,* March 25, 1986). The
legislative budget office was working on nongambling state budgets that the
legislators could pass. Most of these legislators knew two things: their constituents really liked Edwards and they really disliked casinos. This provided
the final veto to casinos in Louisiana.

7 ∾ Obstacles to Casinos

When the governors of the fifty states met amidst the opulence of the Atlantic City casinos in 1981, a wave of gambling fever was cresting in America. Considered the third wave of legalized gambling to hit the nation (Rose 1979), it had already seen the establishment of legal bingo games and horse race betting in a majority of the states and lotteries in nearly twenty. The third wave brought legalized casino gaming to the state of New Jersey and campaigns for casinos in more than a dozen other jurisdictions.

The first major casino campaign after the successful New Jersey vote for casinos in 1976 saw a similar measure fail in Florida in 1978. Nevertheless, as the governors met by the Boardwalk in the summer of 1981, there were predictions that casino gaming could come to as many as twenty states during the 1980s. It is apparent now that the predictions were either flatly wrong or misjudged the timing. The purpose of this study has been to explain why the casino campaign succeeded in New Jersey but failed in every other jurisdiction where it was considered by policymakers or voters.

In chapter 1, we began the task by examining the politics of the third wave. We looked at the forces that propelled states to consider legalized casino gaming as a viable policy option. We also looked at the strongest issue presented as a breakwater to blunt the force of the wave—the relationship between organized crime and legal gambling activity. In chapter 2, we presented a detailed commentary on the New Jersey casino campaigns as they proceeded from the proposal stage to an unsuccessful vote in 1974 to fruition in the election of 1976.

In chapter 3, we presented an analysis of the 1978 Florida campaign. The elements of the Florida and New Jersey campaigns provided stark contrast with one another and stood out from the campaigns experienced in other states. In chapter 4, therefore, we posed the question: were the New Jersey and Florida campaigns, either one or both, unique events in the politics of gambling legalization or did they fit a discernible pattern? We proposed that there was a pattern to the events. The prognosticators who had suggested that casino gaming was going to spread across the land had used a predictive rhetoric we called the gravity model. Basically, those who suggested that we would see casinos in many more states counted reasons why there would be legalizations and reasons why there would not be legalizations in each state. Where the reasons supporting legalization outweighed the negative factors, they concluded that legalization was likely. We found their predictions to be in error. Therefore, we rejected their model. We suggested that another model, the veto model, explains the results of the campaigns. We speculated that there may be a series of critical factors, any one of which would cause the failure of a casino campaign. Opponents of casino legalizations are not, in terms of the veto model, required to manifest a sufficient number of negative factors in order to outweigh the positive factors. They can achieve their desired result if one critical negative factor appears in the campaign.

In chapters 5 and 6, we examined casino campaigns in sixteen other states as well as the subsequent effort to bring casinos to Florida. We sought evidence that would confirm our rejection of the gravity model and sustain the proposed veto model. Our test was based upon the histories of campaigns in eight Frostbelt states. These states had shown a willingness to legalize gambling, participating heavily in the other forms of gambling that came with the third wave. Chapter 5 looked at campaigns in the states of New York, Massachusetts, Michigan, Pennsylvania, New Hampshire, Connecticut, Illinois, and Rhode Island. In chapter 6, we focused upon campaigns in four Sunbelt states: Florida, Texas, Arkansas, and Colorado. Additionally, we gave superficial attention to some other campaigns that really did not emerge much beyond the stage of suggested proposals.

The Structure of a Veto Model

We conclude that a veto model explains the results of the casino legalization campaigns. Moreover, we suggest that the veto model can be used to predict the results of future casino campaigns. Later in this chapter, we discuss how these factors apply to contemporary campaigns and other legalization efforts. In sustaining the veto model, we consider it axiomatic that casino legalization campaigns are political campaigns and exercises in the mobilization of resources. Campaigns focus upon ideas, to be sure; but ideas are translated into actual public policy only if several factors occur. Whether the campaign is for a candidate or a ballot proposal—conducted in a legislative body or in an electoral contest—many hurdles must be overcome before success is realized. The campaign must encompass an idea that responds to a perceived societal need. A political environment offers conditions that foster perceived needs and consequently demands for solutions. The environment also sets boundaries around proposals that may be advanced to meet the needs.

The proposals that are within the range of the boundaries are not automatically adopted. Rather, they must compete with other feasible proposals. Society can turn in many different directions in order to meet its needs and can also defer meeting those needs. Decision makers, whether individual voters marking ballots or public officials in legislative chambers, are regularly confronted with proposals that are designed to meet society's needs— as the proposers see them. Decision makers do not quest to find the ideal solution. They gravitate toward accepting proposals that meet the tests of adequacy better than other proposals put before them. Much maneuvering takes place just to get proposals before the decision makers in formats that can be accepted or rejected. Ideas for policy decisions must gather support from individuals as they are articulated into proposals. Individuals must reach out to organized groups and key political actors if the proposals are to receive serious consideration.

Our heterogeneous political system features dominance by prominent elites and activated interest groups. Sometimes the elites and groups act in concert with one another; most often there are divisions. The elites and activated groups rarely act without a cognizance of underlying public opinion. However, their activity just as rarely offers a mirror image of that opinion, at least as it may be measured in survey opinion polls. The elites and activated interest groups are magnets for attracting financial resources for campaigns. And they are critical in translating the messages of campaigns to the voters. They set the tone for the campaigns.

The veto model suggests that successful casino proponents must clear several hurdles in order to accomplish their goals. Failure to clear any major hurdle will result in campaign failure. Casino issues are unlike many other policy issues. In other campaigns, hurdles may be dodged or sidestepped. Success may be achieved if more hurdles are crossed than not crossed. It is not so with casino propositions. In our veto model, we identify four major hurdles or veto factors: political environment factors; political elites and active interests; campaign sponsorship; and campaign issue dominance.

Political Environmental Factors

Two Existing Forces

Before a casino campaign begins, there are already forces at work in a political environment that have a profound effect on the campaigns. The forces include an economic and a moral climate in the community. One such force is an underlying opinion about gambling. Two givens existed in the environment of each of the campaigns studied.

First, in every jurisdiction religious groups opposed casinos. The groups command the support of a block of organized moral opinion that always stands ready to oppose casinos and to activate resources and mobilize voters to cast ballots against casinos. However, the environments show variations in the strength of these groups. Factors affecting such group strength include the prominence of churches in the ongoing process of politics in a state and the number of people who will readily be mobilized on the basis of appeals from a "political pulpit." Church activity as such is not a veto factor. It alone will not defeat a campaign for casinos. But churches are a force that can trigger other veto factors. In New Jersey in 1976, churches were almost the only force that was mobilized against casinos. They lost, but in defeat they still demonstrated a certain viability—almost 44% of the voters cast ballots against Atlantic City casinos.

The opponents of legalization in Florida in 1978 recognized the limitations of church opposition even though churches were a power in state politics. Consequently, they managed to have church opposition operate separately from the central forces of the campaign. In Arkansas, the 1964 opposition effort saw churches take the lead. But they did so by enticing the governor to enter the campaign on their side. Churches were also leaders in the 1984 Arkansas campaign, as they were in Detroit. In the 1981 Motor City campaign, churches joined with horse race interests in an "unholy alliance" against casinos.

Second, the negative environmental factor of church opposition is generally balanced by a positive factor. There is an underlying positive public opinion supporting legalized gambling. National opinion polls taken in 1975, 1982, and 1984 demonstrate that a majority of the American public participates in gambling and favors the legalization of many types of gambling, and that majorities often support the legalization of casino gambling. The polls show that most support levels have been increasing.

The 1975 poll was conducted by the University of Michigan for the Commission on the Review of the National Policy toward Gambling. The survey found that 68% approved of legalized bingo, 61% approved of lotteries, and 62% approved of horse race betting; 40% approved of casinos, while 52% opposed. Support for bingo and lotteries went over the 70% level in a 1982 Gallup poll sponsored by *Gaming Business Magazine*. The 1982 survey found that 51% of the respondents supported legalization of casinos. Casino support fell to 44% in the 1984 survey, which was again conducted by the Gallup poll for *Gaming Business Magazine*, but majority sentiments for

Table 1. Political Environmental Factors

Campaign	Economy Local	Economy State	Gaming Legalizations*	Gaming Experience**
New Jersey 1974	Weak	Weak	Several	Positive
New Jersey 1976	Weak	Weak	Several	Positive
Florida 1978	Mixed/Weak	Mixed/Strong	Some	Mixed
Florida 1982–1984	Mixed	Mixed/Strong	Some	Mixed
Florida 1986	Mixed	Mixed/Strong	Several	Mixed/Pos.
Massachusetts 1978–1982	Weak	Strong	Several	Mixed/Neg.
Connecticut 1979–1983	Weak	Mixed	Several	Negative
New York 1977–1984	Mixed	Mixed	Several	Mixed/Pos.
New Hampshire 1979–1980	—	Mixed	Lottery	Positive
Pennsylvania 1977–1984	Strong	Weak	Some	Mixed/Neg.
Michigan 1976–1981	Weak	Weak	Several	Positive
Michigan 1988	Weak	Weak	Several	Mixed/Pos.
Texas 1984	Mixed	Strong	None	Neg./History
Arkansas 1964	Mixed	Good	Some	Neg./History
Arkansas 1984	Mixed/Strong	Good	Some	Neg./History
Colorado 1960	Mixed	Good	None	None
Colorado 1982	Weak	Mixed	Some	Positive
Colorado 1984	Weak	Strong	Some	Positive
Louisiana 1986–1988	Weak	Weak	Some	Mixed/Neg.
Iowa 1986–1989	Weak	Weak	Several	Positive
South Dakota 1988–1989	Weak	Weak	Several	Positive
Ohio 1988–1989	Weak	Mixed	Some	Positive

*Several = three or more forms.
**In terms of scandals and corruption.

175

casinos were expressed in the East (56%) and West (51%) and among males (50%) and college-educated respondents (51%). In the three surveys the respondents were asked if they had participated in casino gambling during the previous year. In 1975, 9% had participated; in 1982, the figure was 13%; and in 1984, 18%. In 1982, the poll found 68% agreeing or strongly agreeing with the statement that they would rather see legalized gambling than a rise in state taxes; 66% agreed with the same statement in 1984. While one can argue with *Gaming Business Magazine*'s 1982 proclamation that there was a "landslide for gambling" (Klein and Selesner 1982), the statistics offered some hope for casino proponents. Proponents could advance the alternative of casino gambling as a means of solving economic problems with the knowledge that the public would give the idea serious consideration. The wave of gambling legalizations is not a wave that is going against the wishes of the public.

Nevertheless, public sentiment only offers casino proponents a resource that can be converted into actual electoral public support. The possibilities of conversions are difficult, as the results of the campaigns we have examined indicate. Proponents cannot count on the sentiments to carry the issues. The polls probably do not capture more than a superficial notion of support for casinos, which can be reversed when the respondent is presented with the experience of a real political campaign. Saturated with campaign messages, information, and themes, the voter is asked to make a real choice about placing casinos in communities near his or her home.

The Economy

The environmental factors that keep positive sentiments from being translated into favorable votes for casino legalization include the condition of the economy in the state and local casino area, the willingness of the state to legalize other gaming forms, and the general state experience with gambling activity.

The primary justification for the legalization of gaming in the third wave era has been economic. At other times in American history, other reasons for legalizing vice have focused on issues such as personal liberty or the inability of the state to enforce the vice laws adequately. Most illegal casino operations, such as those in Hot Springs or Galveston, had been elminated or strongly controlled by the time the third wave era was well under way. The appeal of legalization because "they'll be operating anyway" was made in only one campaign studied, the Arkansas campaign of 1964. The personal liberty issue has been used to support charity gaming, but it was not used in any overt way by the casino proponents studied. Rather, proponents concentrated their energies on demonstrating that economic good would result from the legalization of casinos. Direct and indirect jobs, money for a local economy, revitalization of blighted areas, new and renewed tourist trade, and lower taxes: these were the themes of the campaigns for casinos.

A veto factor may be established if the public is unable to accept the proposition that there is an economic need that requires major policy changes. During most of the period studied, 1976–1989, the national economy fluctuated from periods of high to severe inflation and moderate to severe unemployment. These were years of fiscal crises for state governments. Yet the economic picture has varied considerably across the nation. Some states have gone through years of national recession with little indication that there was an unemployment problem. Other states have suffered severely. The Atlantic City economic story was not a happy one during the mid-1970s. Levels of unemployment exceeded 12%, while national levels held at 8% or below. New Jersey also exceeded the national rates. While not as severe, the economic picture in Florida was not without problems. Unemployment rates were in excess of national levels. The picture in the Miami area was bleaker than in other parts of the state. Florida did have growth areas—Orlando was establishing itself as a major national resort. Overall, however, the economic situation was not a veto factor against the efforts of casino proponents in the Sunshine State.

The economic situation was not a veto factor in several other states. Michigan saw unemployment levels near the national average in the mid-1970s, but as the 1980s approached, the state levels exceeded national rates by over 5%, climbing to over 15% in 1982 and 1983. The Pennsylvania rate was considerably higher than the national level. However, signs of strength in the Pocono area may have presented a veto situation for voters in advisory campaigns there. The relatively strong state economies of Arkansas, Texas, Massachusetts, Connecticut, and Colorado in the early 1980s presented major hurdles to those desiring legalization of casino gambling. Yet within these states local economies were not uniformly strong. Still, the overall political environment of the states was not conducive to legalization efforts.

Prior Gaming Legalizations

The political environment for legalization also includes the state's experience with gambling. First, if the voters or legislators have never participated in legalizing other gambling forms, the likelihood that casinos will be legalized is quite remote. Chances of passage are enhanced if there are several legalized forms of gaming. Second, if gambling has caused scandals in the past, legalization efforts may be subject to veto forces.

All of the states studied permitted some form of legalized gambling. Texas, however, allowed only charity bingo games. For many sessions the Texas legislature has refused to approve horse race betting. The voters have also rejected pari-mutuel betting. Arkansas permitted pari-mutuel betting on dog and horse racing, but allowed no other forms of legalized gambling. At the time of the 1960 Colorado campaign, there were no other forms of gaming there. By 1984, horse and dog racing, bingo, and a lottery were established. Florida had no lottery, but pari-mutuel betting for horse racing and dog racing as well as jai alai was allowed.

The Frostbelt states examined in chapter 5 were very much caught up in the third wave. All had legalized lotteries, charity bingo, and horse race betting, as did New Jersey. Connecticut, Massachusetts, and New Hampshire had dog racing. Connecticut and New York had off-track betting for horse races, and Connecticut had jai alai betting. This receptivity to gambling in the Frostbelt states assured that casino gambling would be considered as a possible policy option. However, another facet of the veto factor is the particular experiences states had with their gaming activity, legal and illegal.

Experience with Gaming Activity

Several of the states examined had been the location of illegal casinos in the past. Casinos in Hot Springs, Galveston, and Miami had operated with some connection to organized crime elements. This past experience caused contemporary campaigns to start with a disadvantage. So did experiences of minor scandals surrounding charity gambling in Massachusetts and New York and the lottery in Pennsylvania. A jai alai scandal in Connecticut discredited the casino campaign there. To some extent, these negative experiences were outweighed by favorable revenue gains from legalized gambling.

We conclude that the combined factors in the political environment of several jurisdictions precluded opportunities for successful casino campaigns. This veto factor was probably operative in Massachusetts, Connecticut, Pennsylvania, Texas, Arkansas, and Colorado.

Political Elites and Active Interests

Political elites and interest groups are critical in the mobilization of resources for political campaigns. The importance of these elements to any successful drive for casinos is suggested by the New Jersey experience. The 1974 proposal in the Garden State was placed on the ballot by the legislature. The governor was a major sponsor of the bill passed by the legislature. However, after passage, the governor reduced his role in the casino campaign. By contrast, the attorney general entered the fray as an active opponent. So did the horse racing interests of the state. In 1976, a new formula of forces brought success. The governor became very active in the campaign. He solicited business support for the casino question. The attorney general and horse racing interests retreated to positions of silent neutrality.

Table 2. Political Elites and Active Interests

Campaign	Public Officials		Business Interests	Other Gaming Interests
	Governor	Other		
New Jersey 1974	Neutral	Neut./Neg.	Neutral	Negative
New Jersey 1976	Positive	Positive	Positive	Neutral
Florida 1978	Strong/Neg.	Strong/Neg.	Negative	Negative
Florida 1982–1984	Strong/Neg.	Negative	Negative	Negative
Florida 1986	Negative	Negative	Negative	Negative
Massachusetts 1978–1982	Neut./Neg.	Neut./Neg.	Neutral	Neutral
Connecticut 1979–1983	Neut./Neg.	Negative	Neutral	Neutral
New York 1977–1984	Neutral	Negative	Neutral	Neutral
New Hampshire 1979–1980	Strong Neg.	Negative	—	—
Pennsylvania 1977	Negative	Negative	Negative	Neutral
Michigan 1976–1981	Strong Neg.	Negative	Neut./Neg.	Negative
Michigan 1988	Neutral	Mixed	Neut./Neg.	Negative
Texas 1984	Neutral	Negative	Neut./Neg.	Negative
Arkansas 1964	Negative	Negative	Negative	Neutral
Arkansas 1984	Strong Neg.	Strong Neg.	Negative	Neutral
Colorado 1960	Negative	Negative	Negative	—
Colorado 1982	Strong Neg.	Strong Neg.	Negative	Neutral
Colorado 1984	Strong Neg.	Strong Neg.	Negative	Neutral
Louisiana 1986–1988	Positive	Mixed	Positive	Neutral
Iowa 1986–1989	Positive	Positive	Mixed	Positive
South Dakota 1988–1989	Positive	Positive	Positive	Neutral
Ohio 1988–1989	Neutral	Mixed	Negative	Negative

A governor is undoubtedly the most important actor in a casino campaign. His or her incumbency is evidence that he or she has experience in building coalitions of group support with financial resources and translating the resources into electoral success. Also, as state governments have become professionalized, the governorship of the states has become a professional top management post. Governors have political credibility because they possess political and managerial talents and because their offices have political power. Where they choose to be active supporters of issues, they can be more effective than anyone else in achieving the results they desire. Some governors did not enter into the battle over the casino issues. In the early stages of the New York, Massachusetts, and Connecticut campaigns, governors were neutral, although in the latter two cases they later adopted a public stance against casinos. The Texas governor did not involve himself in the Galveston campaign. Pennsylvania's chief executive was consistently negative toward casinos, although he indicated at one point that he might consider changing that position. Eventually, he remained opposed. In other jurisdictions the governors were vigorous and adamant opponents of casinos. The militancy of their stands often suggested a willingness to risk their political credibility over the issue. Reubin Askew and Robert Graham of Florida fit this mold, as did William Milliken of Michigan, Richard Lamm of Colorado, and Hugh Gallen of New Hampshire. In Massachusetts, Governor Edward King finally proclaimed his position against casinos with his "over my dead body" statement.

State attorneys general were once considered to be minor officials in most places. However, as more and more issues facing state governments became mired in the judicial process, this office has emerged as a major policy position. Attorneys general are now key actors in such areas as consumer protection, the environment, and control of organized crime. The offices are staffed with large numbers of attorneys and investigators, as befits the chief law enforcement office of a state. Increasingly, state attorneys general have taken advantage of their heightened responsibilities and expanded visibility by seeking to win election to higher offices—the governorship and seats in the United States Senate. In these quests they are mindful of a need to win popular favor and to build effective coalitions. The presence of an attorney general in a casino campaign does many things. First, it sends a message to political and financial supporters. Next, because their duties are closely related to issues of crime and law enforcement, attorneys general give credibility to campaign themes that emphasize crime. If they side against casinos, they can do great harm to the campaigns. The attorney general of New York spoke where the governor had been silent and his actions of 1981 effectively vetoed the campaign in that state. The attorneys general of Massachusetts,

Michigan, Colorado, and Florida caused great disadvantage to casino advocates.

Where local officials of communities selected for proposed casinos voice opposition, considerable damage was done to campaigns as well. Mayors opposed casinos in Miami, and county and city boards did the same in the Poconos, Pueblo, Hot Springs, and Galveston. The reluctance of the mayor of Detroit actively to endorse and work for casino campaigns after he had favored legalization was certainly a signal that major interests in Detroit either did not or should not support casinos.

Business interests can be the ostensible beneficiaries of casino campaigns. The general economic improvements that proponents project for communities with casinos should be welcomed by Chambers of Commerce and other business organizations. These business groups have the power to give legitimacy to the economic claims of the proponents in much the same way that attorneys general can give credibility to the crime issue. Prominent business groups supported proponents' economic projections in New Jersey. They did so in other local areas. The Hot Springs Chamber of Commerce led the 1964 campaign effort (but not the 1984 campaign), and Pueblo businesspeople promoted the Colorado initiative in 1984. Some Hartford and Bridgeport businesses did the same in Connecticut. In most states, sizable business community support was not forthcoming for casino proponents. In Arkansas, Florida, and Colorado, governors turned to prominent state business leaders to lead opposition forces. The business opposition was translated into campaign revenues that sealed the doom of the propositions. One effective source of activated business opposition in several jurisdictions came from rival gaming interests—specifically, horse racing interests. This was true in New Jersey (1974), Michigan, and Florida.

The preceding examination of political elites and interests suggests that a veto was activated in many of the states studied. The strength of the veto had its greatest impact in Florida (1978), New York, New Hampshire, and Michigan.

Campaign Sponsorship

Casino campaigns in our study had a greater chance of success when they were led by people who have credible standing in the community and where they enjoy greater financial resources than those possessed by their opponents. Sponsors' presence introduced problems of credibility in several casino campaigns. Some sponsors had questionable pasts, while others used dubious methods in their campaigns. These sponsors thus managed to become issues in the campaigns and in all cases detracted from opportunities to build positive cases for casino legalization. One Michigan sponsor was convicted of taking a bribe, and another was a former adult bookstore owner who fraudulently claimed the support of businesspeople during the campaign. Prominent Texas and Arkansas sponsors had ties to former illegal casinos, as did the sponsors of a Miami Beach campaign in 1971. In both Colorado campaigns (1960 and 1982), sponsors used fraudulent methods to collect initiative petition signatures. The Florida sponsors of a 1984 petition drive promoted a stock sale scheme of questionable legality. In several of these cases, the questionable campaign methods directly resulted in legal actions that removed the casino proposals from further consideration by the voters.

In New Jersey, neither the 1974 nor the 1976 procasino campaigns suffered from these credibility problems. Nor did the two proponent campaigns suffer from a lack of funding. In 1976, casino proponents outspent opponents by a ratio of seventy-five to one. A considerable boost to the campaign treasury was provided by one casino corporation, Resorts International. Hotel and casino interests were effective in raising money for the Florida campaign in 1978, but they did not succeed in outspending their opposition. In most other jurisdictions, casino interests were reluctant to come forth to

Table 3. Campaign Sponsorship

Campaign	Credibility of Sponsors	Campaign Financing (*Elections*)
New Jersey 1974	Positive	Positive
New Jersey 1976	Positive	Positive
Florida 1978	Mixed/Negative	Neutral
Florida 1982–1984	Negative	——
Florida 1986	Positive	Neutral/Negative
Massachusetts 1978–1982	Mixed/Negative	——
Connecticut 1979–1983	Mixed/Negative	——
New York 1977–1984	Positive	——
New Hampshire 1979–1980	Neutral	——
Pennsylvania 1977–1984	Mixed/Negative	Negative
Michigan 1976–1981	Negative	Negative
Michigan 1988	Mixed	Mixed
Texas 1984	Negative	Negative
Arkansas 1964	Negative	Negative
Arkansas 1984	Mixed/Negative	Negative
Colorado 1960	Negative	——
Colorado 1982	Negative	——
Colorado 1984	Positive	Negative
Louisiana 1986–1988	Negative	——
Iowa 1986–1989	Positive	——
South Dakota 1988–1989	Positive	Positive
Ohio 1988–1989	Mixed	Mixed

endorse the legalization effort. In Massachusetts and Connecticut, casinos' sponsorship of casino propositions was so obvious that it led to charges of self-interest. In other states' campaigns, the refusal of casino interests to become involved led opponents to suggest that legalization would not work, because no casino would wish to locate in that particular market.

With the exception of New Jersey and Florida, procasino campaigns were underfunded. In most jurisdictions, legalization proponent groups spent the bulk of their resources just trying to get a proposition on the ballot. Pro-casino campaigns need money to be successful, since they represent major changes in state policy. To prevail they must possess major funding advantages over opponents.

Campaign Issue Dominance

The establishment of campaign themes is related to sponsorship. It naturally takes adequate funding and credible sponsors to establish each side's message. Still, even with money and credibility, conveying that message is not easy to accomplish. In 1974, New Jersey opponents, led by churches and law enforcement interests, used a budget of $30,000 to establish a dominant campaign message linking casinos to crime and the deterioration of the quality of life in communities across that state. Those themes were lacking in the 1976 campaign, as the proponents were able to establish the agenda for debate. Instead, the dominant campaign theme was economic development. The Florida campaigns were vetoed as opponents were able to focus campaign attention on the issue of organized crime. This was also the theme of the Michigan campaigns, as it was a major issue in Arkansas and Colorado.

When campaign proponents were unable to establish the primacy of the issue of economic development, and campaigns turned to debates on other issues—especially the relationship between crime and gambling—legalization campaigns were doomed to failure.

The Atlantic City campaign of 1976 had a major advantage not shared by campaigns that took place after casinos came to the Boardwalk. The New Jersey campaign could focus on casinos as an abstract phenomenon. The unsavory experiences of Las Vegas casinos were easily cast aside and considered the unique problems of the deviant state of Nevada. Since publicly traded corporations had operated the casinos increasingly since 1969, the role of organized crime was presumed to have been reduced. Other Las Vegas horrors were attributed to the inability of a small, rural, and relatively unsophisticated state to exercise proper controls over business enterprises. By comparison, New Jersey was urban, eastern, and sophisticated. New Jersey officials would know how to control casinos even if it meant paying top salaries to attract qualified gaming control personnel. Even though New Jersey has strict controls over gaming activity, unsavory elements of orga-

Table 4. **Campaign Issue Dominance**

Campaign	Issues
New Jersey 1974	Crime, morality, threat to local communities
New Jersey 1976	Economic development, employment, tax relief
Florida 1978	Quality of life, crime, preserving economic growth
Florida 1982–1984	Quality of life, crime
Florida 1986	Crime, quality of life
Massachusetts 1978–1982	Quality of life, Atlantic City experience
Connecticut 1979–1983	Quality of life, crime, Atlantic City experience
New York 1977–1984	Atlantic City experience, local political divisions
New Hampshire 1979–1980	Quality of life
Pennsylvania 1977–1984	Quality of life
Michigan 1976–1981	Crime, quality of life, Atlantic City experience
Michigan 1988	Crime, quality of life
Texas 1984	Crime, quality of life
Arkansas 1964	Morality, crime
Arkansas 1984	Quality of life, crime, preserving economic growth
Colorado 1960	Petition techniques, corruption
Colorado 1982	Petition techniques, corruption
Colorado 1984	Quality of life, crime, Atlantic City experience, Las Vegas image
Louisiana 1986–1988	Crime, quality of life
Iowa 1986–1989	Economic development
South Dakota 1988–1989	Economic development
Ohio 1988–1989	Crime, quality of life

nized and unorganized crime have penetrated the ambience of the new casino city. Street crime is a major problem surpassing levels found in Las Vegas and the cities in America with the highest crime rates. The predicted economic impacts of casinos have missed their marks in many respects. As of 1989, Atlantic City has not been totally revitalized. Slums persist and in many ways are worse now than before casinos. The unemployment rate has not been dramatically improved by casinos, since many of the casino jobs went to people from outside Atlantic City.

The Atlantic City experience has become a part of the campaign rhetoric in all subsequent contests. More often than not, the emphasis is on the negative experiences of Atlantic City, cited frequently by opponents of legalization efforts.

The Veto Model: Casinos Are Different

Two questions remain for the conclusion of our study. First, why are casino campaigns subject to the veto model, while other gambling campaigns are not? Second, can any future casino legalizations be predicted from the model?

Table 5. Veto Factors

Campaign	Environmental Factors	Political Factors	Issues	Campaign Sponsorship
New Jersey 1974		veto	veto	
New Jersey 1976				
Florida 1978		veto	veto	
Florida 1982–1984		veto	veto	veto
Florida 1986	veto	veto	veto	
Massachusetts 1978–1982	veto	veto		
Connecticut 1979–1983	veto	veto		
New York 1977–1984		veto		
New Hampshire 1979–1980		veto		
Pennsylvania 1977–1984	veto	veto		veto
Michigan 1976–1981		veto	veto	
Michigan 1988		veto	veto	
Texas 1984	veto	veto		veto
Arkansas 1964		veto	veto	veto
Arkansas 1984	veto	veto	veto	veto
Colorado 1960	veto	veto		veto
Colorado 1982		veto		veto
Colorado 1984	veto	veto		
Louisiana 1986–1988			veto	veto
Iowa 1986–1989				
South Dakota 1988–1989				
Ohio 1988–1989	veto	veto	veto	

The answer to the first question is simple: casinos are different. A wave of gambling legalizations has swept the nation, but casinos have been excluded. The veto model is apparently not an effective tool for explaining the results of campaigns for other forms of gambling. Table 6 presents the results of several recent campaigns for lotteries and pari-mutuel betting. Where the lottery question reaches the ballot by itself rather than combined with other forms of gambling, the question succeeds. Vote percentages of popular approval for lotteries range from 53% to more than 80%. Prolottery campaigns are apparently stopped only if they can be kept off the ballot. Once on the ballot, they have not been stopped by denials of economic need. States well into economic recovery as well as states suffering from high unemployment and budgetary crises approved lotteries in the past decade. Lotteries cannot be thwarted solely by the opposition of key political leaders. Governors opposed lottery questions in Washington and California, but lotteries still passed. In a twist on other events, North Dakota voters rejected the legalization of a lottery, apparently in an effort to protect their legal blackjack operations. In California, the attorney general and horse race interests also opposed the lottery. Lottery campaign sponsorship has not been entirely free

Table 6. Campaign Predictions and Results

Campaign	Gravity Model Prediction	Campaign Results
New Jersey 1974	——	election defeat; 40% support
New Jersey 1976	——	election victory; 56% support
Florida 1978	late 1980s	election defeat; 27% support
Florida 1982–1984	late 1980s	petition drives fail
Florida 1986	late 1980s	election defeat; 32% support
Massachusetts 1978–1982	1981	legislative defeat
Connecticut 1979–1983	1981	legislative defeat
New York 1977–1984	1981	legislative defeat
New Hampshire 1979–1980	1983	legislative defeat
Pennsylvania 1977–1984	1982	legislative defeat; advisory votes defeat; 20% support
Michigan 1976–1981	1983	legislative defeat; advisory votes defeat; 40% support
Michigan 1988	1983	advisory vote, defeat; 41% support
Texas 1984	no casinos	advisory vote defeat; 42% support
Arkansas 1964	——	election defeat; 39% support
Arkansas 1984	late 1980s	election defeat; 29.5% support
Colorado 1960	——	petition drive disqualified
Colorado 1982	late 1980s	petition drive disqualified
Colorado 1984	late 1980s	election defeat; 33% support
Louisiana 1986–1988	1985	legislative defeats
Iowa 1986–1989	no casinos	legislative victory
South Dakota 1988–1989	no casinos	consitutional victory (64%); legislative success; local election victory (65%)
Ohio 1988–1989	no casinos	legislative defeat

from suspicion. Companies that wished to win business contracts from a lottery have carried most of the financial burdens of some campaigns. The veto formula has simply not been in force. The same finding applies to horse race betting campaigns, although success in these campaigns has not been uniform. Nonetheless, the opposition of key actors, negative environmental factors, and negative sponsorship factors have not in and of themselves prevented success.

We can advance several reasons why most gambling propositions can be analyzed by the gravity model while we must use the veto model for casino propositions. One reason is that legalization of other forms of gambling is usually approved by a majority of citizens at the outset of campaigns, while casinos begin either disapproved or only even. Voting trends indicate that most lottery propositions win majorities that approach or even exceed polling levels. Horse race betting results are mixed, with some votes surpassing nationwide polling levels and others not doing so.

A second reason that lotteries and horse race betting propositions enjoy victories in the face of veto factors is that they have a position of familiarity and acceptance in our national culture. Lotteries helped pay for colonization efforts, Revolutionary War expenses, and the development of internal improvements and social institutions in our early history. The lottery was eliminated as a national phenomenon because of the abuses of the private managers of the Louisiana lottery. The sixty-year period between the demise of that lottery and the establishment of the New Hampshire lottery in 1963 removed from our public consciousness the notion of corruption in lotteries. Since 1964, there have been problems with state lotteries, but scandals have been minor and few in number. A drawing was rigged in Pennsylvania, and the perpetrators were caught. Bidding procedures for state lottery contract work have been challenged in some jurisdictions. However, overall, the lottery enterprises have been clean and in most cases have produced anticipated revenues. The emerging picture of state-owned, state-run, efficient, honest lotteries is a welcome one for proponents of new state lotteries.

Horse racing has also been a prominent social institution throughout American history. The horse was the primary means of transportation in America into the twentieth century. Many people engaged in matching the speed of their horses against those of their neighbors. Commercial racing was an activity to which they could personally relate. Commercial racing was first sanctioned in 1664 in New York. As the commercial enterprise flourished, a horse-breeding industry developed. Since the entire population needed horses, the industry became a favored one. The nation was soon accepting the belief that horse race betting was an activity that protected and promoted the breeding industry. The notion persists and gives a special legitimacy to horse racing that other forms of gambling do not have. In addition, the idea persists that horse racing is a sport and that betting on races is not gambling but a reasoned exercise in applying certain skills. Certainly there are many horse races where there is no organized betting. The terminology of horse race betting is indicative of this view: betting is "handicapping," and horse racing forms and charts are detailed, complex, and confusing to the novice or outsider.

As the racing industry developed, there were problems and there have been scandals. But efforts to implement control systems have lessened public concern to a degree. Horse race betting changed radically with the development of the totalizator in the late 1800s. This machine and its computerized offspring allowed the pari-mutuel system to come into being and grow. Bettors now create a pool among themselves with their bets. The track operators and the state take a share (usually under 15%) and return the remaining funds to the winning bettors (85%). The house (track), therefore, is not a bettor. As with the lottery, the house only holds the money for a fee. With this system operators of the betting system have no incentive to rig races. This incentive is not entirely removed for bettors, however.

The state has taken over many operational facets of horse racing and betting. In some places they actually run the betting system. In others they always have officials at the betting scene. The state also performs functions in the management of racing events. Additionally, the industry has created associations that operate nationwide to assure the public that horse racing is legitimate. Horse registers are kept and racing matches are developed that will be competitive contests. The racing associations have existed for nearly a century and are respected as appropriate controlling agencies.

The historical situations surrounding lotteries, horse racing, and casinos are easily contrasted. Casino owners have rarely been accepted as benefactors of society, at least outside of Nevada. Casinos, too, have existed during most of our national history. But their operations more often than not have been illegal, and the operators have often been associated with organized crime. Questions remain about the effectiveness of government controls over privately owned and operated casinos.

The three institutions—lottery, horse racing, and casinos—vary in several other ways. The state may expect to gain revenues from each form, but must incur risks with legalization. States must control and administer the gaming activities. Controls are costly and must be in place before gaming begins. The burden of lottery regulation is less than that for the other forms, while horse racing regulation is not as costly as casino regulation. Some private companies currently offer to start and operate state lotteries for a small percentage of the lottery revenues. The state has to advance no money. In contrast, before casinos start operating, dozens of state employees must be hired to investigate the backgrounds of potential casino operators. Once operating, casinos require regulation that costs millions of dollars—$42 million annually in New Jersey, $12 million a year in Nevada.

The risks of the casino games are even greater for the establishment. Lotteries may be established at no cost to the state. Horse tracks and betting operations may cost millions of dollars to build. A recently constructed Colorado track cost about $30 million. Casinos, by comparison, have astronomical costs. Resorts International invested $77 million to open its Atlantic City operations. Bally's Park Place cost over $300 million. Other New Jersey casinos ranged between these extremes. Nevada permits the operation of smaller casinos, so opening costs range from a few million dollars to the higher range of figures in New Jersey. While the state does not incur direct

Table 7. Results of Recent Lottery and Horse Racing Betting Campaigns

Lotteries	Percentage in Favor	Horse Racing	Percentage in Favor
Indiana 1988	62	Virginia 1988	56
Kentucky 1988	61	Nebraska 1988	62
Minnesota 1988	59	Kansas 1986	58
Idaho 1988	52	Texas 1987	56
Wisconsin 1987	***	Missouri 1984	60
Virginia 1987	57	Minnesota 1982	58
Florida 1986	64	Oklahoma 1982	58
Kansas 1986	64	Virginia 1978	48
Idaho 1986	60*	Texas 1974	45
Montana 1986	69	Oklahoma 1974	46
South Dakota 1986	60	Missouri 1971	46
North Dakota 1986	44	Indiana 1968	47
Missouri 1984	68	New York (OTB) 1963	76
California 1984	58	Arkansas 1956	53
Oregon 1984	53/66		
West Virginia 1984	66		
Arizona 1980–1981	***		
Colorado 1976	***		
Vermont 1976	***		
Illinois 1974	***		
Rhode Island 1973	76		
Ohio 1973	64		
Maine 1973	72		
North Dakota 1972	58		
Maryland 1972	77		
Michigan 1972	73		
Iowa 1972	67*		
Washington 1972	62**		
Pennsylvania 1972	***		
Connecticut 1972	***		
Virginia 1970	63*		
New Jersey 1976	81		

*Not implemented.
**Not implemented until 1982.
***By legislative action.

risks with these investments, it does have other risks. The casinos must take all reasonable means to make sure their large investments are safe. This usually means that the gaming establishments have a strong incentive to develop good relationships with politicians—or better yet, to gain a controlling interest over the politicians. States have to consider the possible loss of some control over their policy processes when casinos come into their midst.

While horse tracks are also concerned about state policy, the investments they have at risk are minor in comparison to casinos.

With their expensive plants, casino operations hire large numbers of people. This is generally presented as a major positive factor for legalization. Horse tracks also create many jobs. However, a large number of these jobs are seasonal. Lotteries have small employment needs, although ticket agents may receive good commissions for their activity. The positive impact of employment can be reversed for casino states. The state has to be reluctant to interfere with facilities that have such large-scale employment, fearing it might be threatened. The control of casinos is hampered by a bias to keep them open at all costs.

The concentration of "action" in one location also sets casinos apart from lotteries and horse race betting. Casinos are a powerful force in the communities of the two states where they are legal, often dominating decision making on economic development, zoning, and other key areas. Horse racing tracks are few in number and are distant from most residential areas. The lottery is a diffuse operation that penetrates the community but has minimal effect on the flow of community life. Horse racing and lotteries are also time-bounded activities. Races are held during a season and there are a limited number of races each day. Lotteries, except for the instant format, are daily or weekly, or hold occasional special drawings. Casinos offer constant gaming activity, twenty-four hours a day in Nevada, eighteen hours a day in Atlantic City. The heavy action in one location causes a concentration of people, a number of whom present social problems to the community. Thieves, prostitutes, and drug merchants are drawn to casino centers. So are compulsive gamblers. These elements are not drawn to lotteries; where they are drawn to horse tracks, they disperse when the event is completed. They persist around the casinos. To be sure, their antisocial activity can be controlled. But their presence and their activity cannot be stopped. Casinos are different. People like them and people want to go to them, but proximity may be less important.

New Casino Jurisdictions—View from 1989

The efficacy of the veto model as a tool for explaining the results of campaigns for casino legalization is implied in the fact that prior to 1989 only one casino campaign—New Jersey, 1976—was successful. However, the movement for more and more legal channels for gambling activity proceeds as if I. Nelson Rose's "Third Wave" has yet to crest. As the wave continues to gain strength, casino gaming activities may also be propelled into more states. Perhaps the factors that vetoed casinos in the past will not reappear. Governors, attorneys general, and economic elites may come to accept all forms of gambling as inevitable and cease their active opposition to casinos. Perhaps the widespread popularity of lotteries will drive the issue of gaming and crime out of the public psyche, allowing the economic issues to dominate casino campaigns. In such cases, the veto model may still be controlling, but its application in defeats of casino propositions is less likely.

On the other hand, there is a possibility that casino gaming can be drawn away from Las Vegas and Atlantic City images and instead be presented as merely an incremental extension of existing acceptable legal gaming forms. In such a case, a gravity model could supplant the veto model as an explanatory tool for campaign results.

The year 1989 deserves a postscript commentary because the year finds campaigns for casinos continuing in Arizona, Ohio, and Indiana. But more importantly because this year also witnessed the first legalizations of commercial casino gaming since 1976. In November 1988 South Dakota voters authorized their legislature to enact local-option casino gaming for the historical town of Deadwood. In April 1989 the voters of Deadwood gave final approval to casinos, and their opening is imminent. During the same month, the Iowa legislature gave its approval to a plan for casino gaming aboard riverboats beginning in 1991.

Before we attempt to analyze the events of 1989 and seek to interpret whether they represent applications of the veto model or deviations from the model, the events deserve further exposure. The Arizona case was discussed above in chapter 7. The Indiana legislature has responded to the continuing economic decay in the Lake Michigan city of Gary. Local voters have been authorized to take an advisory vote on the question of having wide-open casino gaming. At the same time, the legislature has established a study commission to examine the social and economic impacts casinos would have on the city of Gary. No final decisions will be made on the issue in 1989.

A potential influence over the Indiana decision to pursue casinos may have come from Ohio, where in March 1989, the lower house of the state legislature approved a bill to set up one casino in the city of Lorain. The Ohio plan was to have been a five-year pilot project. Local voters would have had to consent to the plan before it began, and also five years later if it continued. The single casino was to be part of a theme park which would be developed with a major hotel on land adjacent to the Lake Erie waterfront. The gaming opportunities would be somewhat restricted as crowds entering the casino would be limited in size, and patrons might have been required to provide identification and pay entrance fees, as is almost a universal practice in continental European casinos. While the Ohio effort may have propelled Indiana into thinking about casinos, it will not force Indiana to choose casinos for competitive reasons. On May 23, 1989, the Finance Committee of the Ohio State Senate decisively rejected the casino plan for Lorain (Cleveland *Plain Dealer*, May 24, 1989). Observers indicated that the successful house vote had merely resulted from clever politics as the casino proponents were able to get a quick vote without serious debate. By the time the bill went to the senate, the opponents were ready. Catholic Church interests against casinos found alliances with officials of the Cleveland city government. Horse tracks also had their lobbyists lined up in opposition as they felt that the competition of casinos would not be healthy for their enterprise. No major politicians lined up in support of casinos. Those on the scene suggest that the issue is dead until at least the 1991 legislative session.

While Iowa and South Dakota have suffered tremendous economic setbacks in recent years, the casino propositions in the two states were not advanced as "last resorts." The casino gaming which was approved in both was quite limited in scope and was advanced as a means of aiding the economy, not turning it around.

Iowa

Traditional images fall with difficulty, but they can fall quickly. The Iowa of "American Gothic" and the River City of "The Music Man" were well represented by Attorney General Richard Turner in the 1970s. Turner advocated the values of the prosperous farm state as he led a "war on gambling" with raids on charity carnivals and church bingo games. "If it was against the law, it was against the law." But those were days of prosperity. Then came the drought and the farm depression. In the 1980s conservative Iowans saw banks fail, farms sold at sheriffs' auctions, and local factories close. Gambling took on other meanings. Moral questions could be set aside, especially since the neighboring states were attracting the scarce Iowa dollars with their lotteries and pari-mutuel gaming. Quite willingly, the voters of the Tall Corn State removed a constitutional prohibition against lotteries. The legislature passed bills to create a state lottery. However, in 1983 and 1984 Governor Branstad vetoed the legislation. But he tired of receiving boos and catcalls as he rode in parades, and in 1985, with the state economy sinking even lower, he signed a lottery bill which dedicated funds for development grants and loans to Iowa businesses. Soon he permitted bills for pari-mutuel gaming to pass into law. Now the pool halls of River City have given way to widespread legalized gaming. Indeed, Iowa has more forms of legalized gaming than any other state—lottery, dogs, horses, bingo, and Indian gaming. Over $400 million is being wagered legally each year, with $50 million going into the state treasury. The Iowa state government has even taken a leadership role in sponsoring programs for people with gambling problems. Nonetheless, gaming is seen by most Iowans as making a very positive contribution to the state. In 1989 the state was ripe for gaming expansion.

The idea of riverboat gaming was generated during a local political race in Davenport in 1985. The next year the first bill for the gaming was introduced into the state legislature for consideration. It failed to win passage, but the lawmakers in Des Moines did establish a special committee to study the question. In December 1986 they gave the idea a favorable recommendation. Serious consideration followed in the next three legislative sessions. In 1987 the house passed a bill by a 52 to 48 vote; however, the senate postponed action until 1988. In 1988 debate focused on questions of where the boats would be docked and how many boats there would be. A fight ensued between the east and the west in the state, and between river communities and inland areas. Suggestions were advanced that boats be allowed on small lakes, and also in areas without waters. Amidst the confusion over details, the bill's passage was impossible. In 1989 a new strategy was followed. The questions of 1988 were set aside. A new bill provided that the Iowa Racing Commission would settle such matters as the number of boats, locations, and licensing provisions. In early March the bill sailed through the state senate. The real clash of proponents and opponents was saved for the house.

The opposition to riverboats came from religious groups, Republican legislators, and areas of the state that lacked facilities for riverboat gaming (*Cedar Rapids Gazette*, April 20 1989). The Farm Bureau opposed the idea. However, there was no opposition from other gaming interests, and most economic elites supported the proposition. The main sources of support came out of the Quad Cities (Davenport) area on the Mississippi River in eastern Iowa (*Des Moines Register*, April 22, 1989). Davenport had lost six factories and 20,000 jobs in the 1980s. The Davenport Chamber of Commerce had a full-time lobbyist working for the bill. So did the operators of the riverboats such as the *Delta Queen*. These lobbyists held regular strategy sessions with key legislators. They constantly stressed the need to describe riverboat gaming as a "mere adjunct" to the noncontroversial activities on the boats—"classy entertainment and fine dining." They specifically avoided using the term "casino gambling" in promoting the legislation. On April 11, the house vote down the bill by a 53 to 47 margin. The lobbyists turned up the heat. After what one legislator called "the toughest fight I've ever seen," four votes were changed. On April 20, the bill was passed by a 51 to 47 vote, as 5 Republicans joined 46 Democrats for the majority. There were no votes to spare since legislation requires a constitutional majority of 51 for passage. The governor, who had vetoed lottery bills before, signed SB124 into law on April 27.

As mentioned, the Iowa Racing Commission will determine the number of boats and their location. However, voters of counties where the boats will dock must also approve of the gaming in special elections. The boats will have designated gaming areas that may not exceed 30% of deck space. All persons in the gaming areas must be at least 21 years old. The law limits wagers to $5 per game. All betting will be done with chips, and a player may purchase no more than $200 in chips on any excursion. Excursions will be for a limited time each day, and will be made only between April and October beginning in 1991.

The opponents of riverboat gaming saw the passage as yet another case of gambling spreading across their state. And the question arose again, "what will be next?" Almost immediately, attention was directed at the Indian reservations of the state. Under federal legislation passed in 1988 (Public Law 100–497), reservations may offer games that are legalized in any form within a state. The question of the hour has become "what will the Indians do?" Will they want to offer casino games? Will they do so with the same low stakes as games on the riverboats, or will they try to develop high stakes Las Vegas–style casinos?

South Dakota

The state of South Dakota tolerated many illegal gaming activities well into the twentieth century. Old mining communities permitted taverns and saloons to have slot machines and table games operating in open fashion. But, as in other parts of the country, reformers gradually saw to it that the law was enforced. Gaming in the historical community of Deadwood came to a halt in the late 1940s. This community, located in the Black Hills a little more than an hour from Mount Rushmore, has an illustrious past. Deadwood was the home of Calamity Jane, and it was the place where "Wild Bill" Hickok was shot in the back during a poker game. His two-pairs hand of "aces and eights" has affectionally become known as the "dead man's hand" (*Rapids City Journal*, October 3, 1988). In the mid-1980s the city suffered a major fire in its central historical block. Community leaders sensed that much history could be lost if an effort for preservation and restoration was not undertaken. Situated as the town is, near Rushmore and the major westward highway leading to Yellowstone Park, city fathers envisioned a restored wild-west town setting as being a major tourist attraction. In 1987 they came up with a plan to secure the $20 million needed to fulfill their restoration dreams. The plan called for limited-stakes casino gambling in Deadwood.

While South Dakota had previously tolerated illegal gambling, forces attempting to win legalization of gaming had not enjoyed great success. In

1970 the voters changed the state constitution to permit bingo and charity lotteries, but a state lottery was not authorized until after the 1986 election. In 1982, voters rejected local-option gaming by a large (58% to 42%) margin (Sioux Falls *Argus Leader*, September 25, 1988). Nonetheless, the town of 2,000 residents decided that gaming would be their tool for historical preservation. The Deadwood You Bet Committee was established by the Deadwood-Lead Chamber of Commerce to conduct a statewide petition drive. The effort was successful and a proposition for casino gaming in Deadwood was placed on the 1988 South Dakota ballot as a constitutional amendment (*Rapid City Journal*, March 15, 1988).

The Deadwood You Bet Committee then persuaded the town council to appropriate $10,000 for the campaign for casinos (*Rapid City Journal*, October 2, 1988). The funds came from a hotel-restaurant tax dedicated to the promotion of tourism activities. While the opposition—led by local ministers—objected to this public funding of the gaming campaign, they hesitated to launch a campaign against passage of the amendment. One church leader indicated in October 1988 that their campaign would begin "in the closing days" before the election (*Rapid City Journal*, October 3, 1988). It was too little, too late. The voters of South Dakota said *yes* to Deadwood casinos by a 65% to 35% margin. The proponents of casinos, however, maintained that the voters were really saying *yes* to historic preservation. They had deemphasized the gaming nature of their plan throughout the campaign (*Rapid City Journal*, November 9, 1988).

Actually, the vote in November only opened the door for consideration of casinos by others. The amendment authorized the legislature to set up a regulatory and licensing mechanism for casinos with no more than fifteen games (tables or machines) each and with wagers of no more than $5. The amendment also provided that Deadwood could have casinos only if 60% or more of its voters approved of the casinos. After expressing some concern over the effect of Deadwood gaming on Indian-reservation gaming in the state, the legislature authorized the casinos and set April 11, 1989 as the date for a local vote on the question (*Rapid City Journal*, March 16, 1989). Deadwood residents responded by giving overwhelming approval to the plan. By a vote of 690 to 230, a 75% to 25% margin, they met the constitutional requirements (*Las Vegas Review-Journal*, April 12, 1989). In late 1989, casinos with blackjack, poker, and slot machines will open in Deadwood. However, with their betting limits they are unlikely to rival the action in Las Vegas or Atlantic City gaming halls. Nonetheless, with licensing fees of $2,000 per game each year and a share of win taxes, it is expected that the historical preservation fund for Deadwood can gather in over $500,000 a year (*Rapid City Journal*, November 9, 1988).

No other state might vote to permit casinos in this century—or several could vote casinos in. In either case, the experience of the past decade indicates that campaigns for casinos will be complex and expensive enterprises in which key political and business leaders are influential in the struggle by supporters and opponents for issue dominance. The sudden emergence of legal gambling as "America's newest growth industry" in 1978 has given way to a more sober consideration of costs and benefits. The rush to embrace casino legalization as a fiscal panacea and magical economic development mechanism has been replaced by a cautious appraisal of this form of legal gambling as a social good.

Epilogue

In the thirteen years since New Jersey voted to permit casinos in Atlantic City, much has transpired in American politics. The transition from the Ford administration to the Carter administration coincided with the 1976 vote favoring Atlantic City casinos, and the Iranian hostage situation was still some years off. The "Reagan Revolution" had not yet come center stage, and even the property tax revolts (like California's Proposition 13) were in their infancy. Several Soviet leaders would come and go before 1989 would become a landmark year with regard to the cold war and Eastern European governance.

More women would join the work force during those thirteen years, affecting American family life and male-female relations. And a whole retinue of blue-collar jobs would shift abroad, as deindustrialization affected many of America's older, Frostbelt states. America's cities felt fiscal crises, racial antagonisms, and infrastructural deterioration. In short, the world of 1989 seemed far different than the one of 1976.

When we try to explain why casino legalization is excluded from other forms of gambling legalization, we adopt a model which emphasizes the power of any significant segment of a state's business or political elite to scuttle such a measure. The events of the last thirteen years did indeed disprove the optimistic predictions of gambling experts about the spread of legal casino gambling, in some ways because they ignored what is now commonsense knowledge about the ability to salient "negatives" to influence a political campaign. The fears of crime and corruption that accompanied casino issues did not accompany other gambling matters and have played on an apparent ambivalence that exists in American culture and political values: we think casinos are fine for Las Vegas and Atlantic City but not for our own backyards.

As we come to the close of the 1980s, we can say with certainty that this was not, as was predicted, the decade of widespread casino legalization. Still, events of 1989, as discussed at the end of the last chapter, mandate that we keep an open eye. (Even some Eastern European countries are permitting the existence of casinos.)

The examples of Iowa and South Dakota are curious, to be sure. When New York, Florida, Massachusetts, Louisiana, and other states considered casino legalization over the past decade, they did so with the understanding that wide-open, full-scale casino gambling in the spirit, if not the image, of Las Vegas, was contemplated. The recent legalization successes do not cast doubt on our veto model—indeed, all forces supported these cases much as New Jersey did in 1976—but they are of a scope and scale altogether unique. In Iowa, the remote location, unique gambling limits, and seasonality may combine to make the impact of legalization a minor event compared to that in New Jersey and Nevada. Still, other midwestern states, such as Illinois, are considering competing with Iowa in this regard, and before long we may see as much competition there as presently exists between the lotteries in the Northeast. The casinos of Deadwood, South Dakota, which opened on November 1, 1989, are no less anomalous. It is unlikely that the significant capital of the legal casino business, and the leisure industry that has taken such notice of legal gambling since 1978, are readying a move based on Deadwood's performance.

Still, the 1990s may see a renewed effort to bring casinos to the major industrial states that take advantage of the small openings provided by the riverboats and Deadwood experiences. Already, voters in Gary, Indiana, have approved a measure permitting casinos in that industrial city, but observers of the governor and state legislature there do not see state movement on this issue forthcoming.

The increasingly complex issues surrounding control of Native American lands offer their own complications. Because of sovereignty, state legalization, and recent court rulings, there remains the possibility that Indian gaming might play an important role in removing barriers to states' entries into the legal casino business.

It is even possible that some state may launch a state-owned casino drive, or more states may arrive at slot machine gambling through lottery venues and video outlets. Other states may pursue efforts which include strict controls on the nature of the games, such as limiting the number of hours played, table limits, use of alcohol, use of credit, registration, and so on. Other countries do this, but it is unclear whether American voters would believe such good intentions would ultimately waver in the face of economic development concerns and competition among states, and see even a modified or limited gaming referendum as the harbinger of more wide-open gaming.

While we are confident that we have explained the phenomenon of casino legalization over the past fifteen years, we have not presented our findings as a prediction of the next fifteen. There have been some consistencies in the gaming area over this period of time, but there have been some surprises as well. Americans' consideration of the virtues of vice have shifted over the past fifteen years, but scandals or conflicts of interest in government have often jaundiced the American perception of any activity to which organized crime can be even remotely connected. Even the actions of one person like Pete Rose may have far-reaching effects.

In completing this epilogue, we came across a 1955 issue of *Life* magazine that featured some of the showrooms of Las Vegas and asked the question, "Has Las Vegas expanded to its limits?" People are asking similar questions now as Steve Wynn's bold and beautiful Mirage casino defines a new era for Las Vegas Strip hotels, which will be followed by theme hotels and resorts on a large scale. Certainly the fate of one city, or even a number of its major investors, does not tell the story of gambling or casinos nationwide. But the suspicion remains that we understand much more about how to run a profitable gambling operation—even one surrounded by several thousand hotel rooms—than how to decipher and disentangle some of the deep-seated American ambivalence toward this topic.

References

Abrams, Robert. 1981. Report of Attorney General Robert Abrams in Opposition to Legalized Casino Gambling in New York State. Albany, May 20.

Abt, Vicki, James F. Smith, and Eugene Martin Christiansen. 1985. *The Business of Risk: Commercial Gambling in Mainstream America.* Lawrence: University Press of Kansas.

Ackerman, Marsha. 1981. Why Casino Gaming Died Again: Little Interest, Lots of Hostility. *Buffalo Courier Express,* July 10.

Albini, Joseph L. 1971. *The American Mafia: Genesis of a Legend.* New York: Appleton-Century-Crofts.

Alcaly, Roger, and David Mermelstein (eds.). 1977. *The Fiscal Crisis of American Cities.* New York: Vintage.

Allen, Francis. 1964. *The Borderland of Criminal Justice: Essays in Law and Criminology.* Chicago: University of Chicago Press.

Alvarez, Albert. 1983. *The Biggest Game in Town.* Boston: Houghton Mifflin.

Anderson, Eddie. 1981. *Las Vegas: An Insider's Guide.* Las Vegas: Oracle Publishers.

Anderson, Geoffrey (attorney, United States Department of Justice, Organized Crime Strike Force, Las Vegas). 1979. Interview, August.

Aranson, Peter H., and Roger LeRoy Miller. 1980. Economic Aspects of Public Gaming. *Connecticut Law Review,* 12/4 (Summer):822–853.

Asbury, Herbert. 1938. *Sucker's Progress.* New York: Dodd, Mead.

Askew, Reubin. 1978a. Anti-casino gambling luncheon meeting transcript, February 3.

———. 1978b. Casinos in Florida: A Bad Gamble. *Presbyterian Survey* (October):22–23.

Auletta, Ken. 1980. *The Streets Were Paved with Gold.* New York: Vintage Books.

Bearak, Barry. 1978. The Man in the Hot Slot. Tropic Magazine, *Miami Herald,* June 4.

Becker, Howard. 1963. *Outsiders.* New York: Free Press.

Bell, Daniel. 1962. Crime as an American Way of Life: A Queer Ladder of Social Mobility. In *The End of Ideology.* New York: Collier Books.

Belloti, Francis X. (attorney general for Massachusetts). 1982. Letter to Daniel M. O'Sullivan, director, Legislative Research Bureau. November 9.

Berger, A. J., and Nancy Bruning. 1979. *Lady Luck's Companion.* New York: Harper and Row.

Bergler, Edmund. 1957. *The Psychology of Gambling.* New York: Hill and Wang.

Bergman, Lowell, and Jeff Gerth. 1975. La Costa: The Hundred-Million-Dollar Resort with Criminal Clientele. *Penthouse,* 6/7 (March):47–48, 110–112.

Blakey, G. Robert. 1979. State Conducted lotteries: History, Problems, and Promises. *Journal of Social Issues,* 35/3 (Summer):62–86.

Blanche, Ernest E. 1950. Lotteries, Yesterday and Tomorrow. *Annals of the American Academy of Political and Social Science,* 269 (May 1950):72.

Bloch, Herbert A. 1951. The Sociology of Gambling. *American Journal of Sociology,* 57 (November):215–221.

———. 1962. The Gambling Business: An American Paradox. *Crime and Delinquency,* 8/4 (October):355–364.

Bomar, Thomas (president, First Federal Savings and Loan Association). 1979. Interview, January.

Bonnie, Richard J., and Charles H. Whitebread II. 1974. *The Marihuana Conviction.* Charlottesville: University Press of Virginia.

Brown, B. Mahlon, III (former United States attorney for Nevada). 1979. Interview, August.

Brown, Mary (state representative). 1984. Interview, August, Lansing, Michigan.

Burke, Duane. 1977. A Forecast of the Legalization of Gambling. *Public Gaming Magazine* (Spring):4–5.

Burnham, J. C. 1968. New Perspectives on the Prohibition "Experiment" of the 1920s. *Journal of Social History,* 2/1 (Fall):51–68.

Business Week. 1978. Special Report: Gambling: The Newest Growth Industry. June 26:110–129.

Caesars World, Inc. 1975. Letter of Justification for the Paradise Stream-Cove Haven Transaction, July 3.

Cahill, Robbins. 1976. Recollections of Work in State Politics, Government, Taxation, Gaming Control, Clark County Administration, and the Nevada Resort Association. Reno, University of Nevada Oral History Project.

Caillois, Roger. 1962. *Man, Play and Games.* London: Thomas and Hudson.

Casino Control Act, New Jersey, P.L. 1977. C. 110, Article 1, Section 9.

Casino Control Commission. 1988. *Casino Chronicle* (Trenton, N.J.), 5/32 (January 18):1–2.

Casino Gambling Task Force. 1981. Final report, South Shore Chamber of Commerce, Quincy, Mass., December.

Casino Study Committee of the Berkshire Hills Conference Report. 1978. Pittsfield, Mass., October.

Casinos Are Bad Business. 1978a. Gambling Casinos: The Single Worst Thing That Could Happen to Florida.

———. 1978b. Memo.

———. 1978c. Bomar letter.

———. 1978d. Radio spot, October 27.

———. 1978e. Seven Reasons Why Casinos Are Bad Business.

———. 1978f. Memo (long-time resident).

———. 1978g. Memo (look who supports casinos).

———. 1978h. Letter from Carol Bellamy.

Chafetz, Henry. 1960. *Play the Devil.* New York: C. N. Potter.

Chambliss, William J. 1978. *On the Take: From Petty Crooks to Presidents.* Bloomington: Indiana University Press.

Chapman, Alvah H., Jr. 1978. *Herald* Executive Explains Rationale for Contribution. *Miami Herald,* November 26.

———. (publisher, *Miami Herald*) 1979. Interview, January.

Christiansen, Eugene Martin. 1985a. The Gross Annual Wager of the United States (Calendar 1984), Part I: Handle. *Gaming & Wagering Business* (July):24–26, 46.

———. 1985b. The Gross Annual Wager of the United States (Calendar 1984), Part II: Revenues. *Gaming & Wagering Business* (August):1, 8–9, 42–43.

Christiansen, Eugene Martin, and Michael D. Shagan. 1980. The New York Off-track Betting Law: An Exercise in Selective Decriminalization. *Connecticut Law Review,* 12/4 (Summer):854–869.

Cialella, Edward C. 1975. A Study of the Relationship between Leisure Gambling and Job Satisfaction. Master's thesis, Education, Temple University.

Coggins, Russ (ed.). 1966. *The Gambling Menace.* Nashville: Broadman Press.

Cohen, Albert K. 1965. The Sociology of the Deviant Act. *American Sociological Review*, 30/1 (February):5–14.

Cohen, Barbara, and David M. Rubin. 1977. Rancho La Costa: A Story the Press Can't Touch. *MORE* (November):30–34.

Colson, William (partner, Colson and Hicks). 1979. Interview, January.

Commission on Gambling. 1983. Report. Concord, N.H., January 5.

Commission on the Review of the National Policy toward Gambling. 1976. *Gambling in America*. Washington, D.C.: GPO.

Committee to Rebuild Atlantic City. 1976. Help Yourself: Help Atlantic City: Help New Jersey.

Cook, Fred J. 1970. The People v. the Mob, or, Who Rules New Jersey? *New York Times Magazine*, February 1.

Corbin, Robert (attorney general). 1985. Interview, August, Phoenix, Ariz.

Cornell Law Project. 1977. *The Development of the Law of Gambling: 1776–1976*. Washington, D.C.: National Institute of Law Enforcement and Criminal Justice.

Cressey, Donald R. 1969. *Theft of the Nation: The Structure and Operations of Organized Crime in America*. New York: Harper Colophon Books.

Curtis, Stuart. 1981. Silver Turns to Gold. *Public Gaming Magazine* (August):19.

———. 1986. Telephone interview with Nevada Gaming Control Board official, April.

Davenport, Elaine, and Paul Eddy. 1976. *The Hughes Papers*. New York: Ballantine Books.

Davis, Fred. 1961. Deviance Disavowal: The Management of Strained Interaction by the Visibly Handicapped. *Social Problems*, 9/2 (Fall):120–132.

Davis, Michael P. 1983. U.S. and Canadian Gaming at a Glance. *Gaming Business Magazine* (July):16–17, 56–58.

DeFeo, Mike (attorney, United States Department of Justice, Organized Crime Strike Force, Los Angeles, Kansas City) 1977. Interview, June.

Demaris, Ovid. 1986. *The Boardwalk Jungle*. New York: Bantam Books.

Department of Law and Public Safety, Division of Gaming Enforcement. 1978. Report to the Casino Control Commission with Reference to the Casino License Application of Resorts International Hotel, Inc., December 4.

Dermer, Jay (chairman, Floridians against Casino Takeover). 1979. Interview, January.

Devereux, Edward C., Jr. 1949/1980. *Gambling and the Social Structure: A Sociological Study of Lotteries and Horse Racing in Contemporary America*. Doctoral dissertation, Harvard University. New York: Arno Press.

Dielman, T. E. 1979. Gambling: A Social Problem? *Journal of Social Issues*, 35/3:36–42.

Dinitz, Simon, Russell R. Dynes, and Alfred C. Clarke. 1969. *Deviance: Studies in the Process of Stigmatization and Societal Reaction*. New York: Oxford University Press.

Donohue, Michael. 1977. What's Ahead in the Legalization of Gambling. *Public Gaming* (Spring):8, 27.

Dorman, Michael. 1972. *Payoff: The Role of Organized Crime in American Politics*. New York: David McKay.

Douglas, Geoffrey. 1977. The Selling of Casino Gambling. *New Jersey Monthly*, 1/3 (January):21–25.

Douthat, Bill. 1978. Pari-mutuels Fear Casinos Will Rake in All Bets. *Miami News*, June 15.

Downes, D. M., Bleddyn P. Davies, Miriam E. David, and Peter Stone. 1976.

Gambling, Work and Leisure: A Study across Three Areas. London: Routledge and Kegan Paul.

Dulles, Foster R. 1965. *A History of Recreation.* New York: Appleton-Century-Crofts.

Duncan, Carol H. 1976. Gambling-related Corruption. Report prepared for the Commission on the Review of the National Policy toward Gambling, Washington, D.C., pp. 574–599.

Dunne, John Gregory. 1974. *Vegas: Memoirs of a Dark Season.* New York: Random House.

Eadington, William R. 1973. *The Economics of Gambling Behavior: A Qualitative Study of Nevada's Gambling Industry.* Research Report Number 11, Bureau of Business and Economic Research. Reno: College of Business Administration, University of Nevada, Reno.

———. (ed.). 1976. *Gambling and Society: Interdisciplinary Studies on the Subject of Gambling.* Springfield, Ill.: Charles C. Thomas.

———. 1982a. The Evolution of Corporate Gambling in Nevada. *Nevada Review of Business and Economics,* 6/1 (Summer):13–22.

———. (ed.). 1982b. *The Gambling Papers: Proceedings of the Fifth National Conference on Gambling and Risk Taking.* Reno: Bureau of Business and Economic Research, College of Business Administration, University of Nevada, Reno.

———. 1984. The Casino Gaming Industry: A Study of Political Economy. *Annals,* 474 (July):23–35.

Eadington, William R., and James S. Hattori. 1978. A Legislative History of Gambling in Nevada. *Nevada Review of Business and Economics,* 2/1 (Spring):13–17.

Economics Research Associates. 1976. Impact of Casino Gambling on the Redevelopment Potential of the Uptown Urban Renewal Site and on the Economy of Atlantic City. Washington, D.C., June.

———. 1978a. Backgrounds and Trends of the Miami Beach Economy. Interim Report #1 prepared for the Let's Help Florida Committee, April.

———. 1978b. Projections of the Economic Impact of Legalized Casino Gambling for the Period 1990–1995. Interim Report #2 prepared for the Let's Help Florida Committee, April.

———. 1978c. Projections of the Economic Impact of Legalized Casino Gambling for the Period 1985–1986. Interim Report #3 prepared for the Let's Help Florida Committee, April.

———. 1978d. Projections of the Economic Impact of Miami Beach Casino Gambling Program upon the Florida Economy and Its Impact upon Pari-mutuel Wagering in Southeastern Florida. Interim Report #4 prepared for the Let's Help Florida Committee, April.

———. 1983. *The Role of Gaming in the Nevada Economy: An Update.* Prepared for the Gaming Industry Association of Nevada and Nevada Resort Association. San Francisco: Economics Research Associates.

Edmondson, Brad. 1986. The Demographics of Gambling. *American Demographics,* July:38–41, 50.

Edwards, Jerome E. 1982. *Pat McCarran: Political Boss of Nevada.* Reno: University of Nevada Press.

Eisenberg, Dennis, Uri Dan, and Eli Landau. 1978. *Meyer Lansky: Mogul of the Mob.* New York: Paddington Press.

Elfman, Linda (press secretary, Let's Help Florida Committee). 1978. Interview, June.

Engelmann, Larry. 1979. *Intemperance: The Lost War against Liquor.* New York: Free Press.

Ezell, John Samuel. 1960. *Fortune's Merry Wheel: The Lottery in America.* Cambridge, Mass.: Harvard University Press.

Fact Research, Inc. 1974. *Gambling in Perspective.* Washington, D.C.: Commission on the Review of the National Policy toward Gambling.
Findlay, John M. 1986. *People of Chance.* New York: Oxford University Press.
First Pennsylvania Bank. 1984. Regional report, first quarter.
Florida, Division of Elections, Department of State. 1978. Campaign Treasurer's Reports for Let's Help Florida Committee, No Casinos, Inc., People against Casinos, Floridians against Casino Gambling, and Casinos Are Bad Business.
Florida International University. 1975. Survey of Characteristics of Guests of Miami Beach.
Floridians against Casino Takeover. 1978. The FACTs: 50-plus Good Reasons Why Casinos Are Bad for Florida. Pamphlet.
Fosdick, Raymond B. 1920. *American Police Systems.* New York: Century.
Fowler, Floyd J., Thomas W. Mangione, and Frederick E. Pratter. 1978. *Gambling Enforcement in Major American Cities.* Washington, D.C.: GPO.
Freed, David. 1983. Legalized Gambling for Colorado. *Gambling Times* (January):40.
Freud, Sigmund. 1953. Dostoevsky and Parricide. In James Strachey (trans. and ed.), *The Standard Edition of the Complete Psychological Works of Sigmund Freud.* London: Hogarth Press.
Frey, James H. 1984. Gambling: A Sociological Review. *Annals,* 474 (July):107–121.
Friedman, Bill. 1974. *Casino Management.* Secaucus, N.J.: Lyle Stuart.
Fuller, Peter. 1974. Gambling: A Secular "Religion" for the Obsessional Neurotic. Introduction to Jon Halliday and Peter Fuller (eds.), *The Psychology of Gambling.* New York: Harper and Row.
Fuller, Richard C., and Richard R. Myers. 1941. The Natural History of a Social Problem. *American Sociological Review,* 6/3 (June):320–329.
Fund for the City of New York. 1972. *Legal Gambling in New York: A Discussion of Numbers and Sports Betting.* New York: Fund for the City of New York.
Funnell, Charles E. 1975. *By the Beautiful Sea.* New York: Alfred A. Knopf.
Galliher, John F., and Linda Basilick. 1979. Utah's Liberal Drug Law: Structural Foundations and Triggering Events. *Social Problems,* 26/3 (February):284–297.
Galliher, John F., and John R. Cross. 1983. *Morals Legislation without Morality.* New Brunswick, N.J.: Rutgers University Press.
Galliher, John F., James L. McCartney, and Barbara E. Baum. 1974. Nebraska's Marijuana Law: A Case of Unexpected Legislative Innovation. *Law and Society Review,* 8 (Spring):441–455.
Gamblers' World. 1989. For Legal and Honest Gambling. February.
Gaming & Wagering Business. 1988. U.S. and Canadian Gaming at a Glance. July 15:22.
Gaming Business Magazine. 1980. Gaming in the 80's. February:24–29.
Garzia, Ralph A. 1977. Letter from Pennsylvania State Representative to I. Nelson Rose.
Gastel, Raymond D. 1975. *The Cultural Regions of the United States.* Seattle: University of Washington Press.
Geertz, Clifford. 1973. Deep Play: Notes on the Balinese Cockfight. In *The Interpretation of Cultures.* New York: Basic Books.
Geis, Gilbert. 1972. *Not the Law's Business?* Washington, D.C.: GPO.
Ginsburg, Gerald P., James J. Blascovich, and René C. Howe. 1976. Risk-taking in the Presence of Others: Blackjack in the Laboratory and in the Field. In William R. Eadington (ed.), *Gambling and Society.* Springfield, Ill.: Charles C. Thomas, Publisher.
Glass, Mary Ellen. 1981. *Nevada's Turbulent '50s.* Reno: University of Nevada Press.

Goffman, Erving. 1963. *Stigma: Notes on the Management of Spoiled Identity.* Englewood Cliffs, N.J.: Prentice-Hall.

———. 1967. Where the Action Is. In *Interaction Ritual.* Garden City, N.Y.: Anchor Books.

Goldman, Marion S. 1981. *Gold Diggers and Silver Miners: Prostitution and Social Life on the Comstock Lode.* Ann Arbor: University of Michigan Press.

Gomes, Dennis. 1979. Interview with New Jersey Gaming Control official, August, Trenton, N.J.

Gottlieb, Bob, and Peter Wiley. 1980. Don't Touch the Dice: The Las Vegas/Utah Connection. *Utah Holiday,* 9/12 (September):22–32.

Greater Miami Chamber of Commerce. 1978. Analysis of State and Local Expenditures.

Green, Jonathon H. 1857. *Gambling Exposed.* Philadelphia: Peterson.

Grinspoon, Lester. 1977. *Marihuana Reconsidered.* Cambridge, Mass.: Harvard University Press.

Grinspoon, Lester, and James B. Bakalar. 1976. *Cocaine: A Drug and Its Social Evolution.* New York: Basic Books.

Gusfield, Joseph. 1967. Moral Passage: The Symbolic Process in Public Designations of Deviance. *Social Problems,* 15/5 (Fall):175–188.

Hall Graphics. 1978. Miami Muscle. Campaign literature prepared for Casinos Are Bad Business.

Haller, Mark H. 1976. Bootleggers and American Gambling 1920–1950. In *Gambling in America: Final Report of the Commission on the Review of the National Policy toward Gambling,* Appendix 1. Washington, D.C.: GPO.

———. 1979. The Changing Structure of American Gambling in the Twentieth Century. *Journal of Social Issues,* 35/3:87–114.

Hamill, Pete. 1975. Can Casino Gambling Save New York: *Village Voice,* October 13.

Hamilton, William R., and Staff. 1978a. Florida Voters' Attitudes toward Casino Gambling, August.

———. 1978b. Memo to Floridians against Casino Gambling regarding Florida Voters' Attitudes toward Casino Gambling, August.

Hayano, David M. 1982. *Poker Faces.* Berkeley: University of California Press.

Helsing, Patricia. 1976. Gambling—The Issues and Policy Decisions Involved in the Trend toward Legalization—A Statement of the Current Anachronism of Benign Prohibition. In *Gambling in America: Final Report of the Commission on the Review of the National Policy toward Gambling.* Washington, D.C.: GPO.

Herman, Robert D. 1967. Gambling as Work: A Sociological Study of the Race Track. In Herman (ed.), *Gambling.* New York: Harper and Row.

Hicks, William (partner, Colson and Hicks, Speakers Bureau chairman, Casinos Are Bad Business Committee). 1979. Interview, January.

Hill, John, G. 1980. Gambling on Paradise—The Future of Casino Gaming in Hawaii. *Gambling Times* (May):46–47.

Hudson Institute. 1973. Increased Legal Gambling in New York: A Policy Analysis. Croton-on-Hudson, January.

Huizinga, Johan. 1955. *Homo Ludens: A Study of the Play-element in Culture.* Leyden: 1938; reprint, Boston: Beacon Press.

Hulse, James W. 1986. *Forty Years in the Wilderness.* Reno: University of Nevada Press.

Hunterton, C. Stanley (attorney, United States Department of Justice, Organized Crime Strike Force, Las Vegas). 1979. Interview, August.

Ianni, Francis A. J. 1974. *Black Mafia: Ethnic Succession in Organized Crime.* New York: Simon and Schuster.

Ianni, Francis A. J., and Elizabeth Reuss-Ianni. 1972. *A Family Business: Kinship and*

Social Control in Organized Crime. New York: Russell Sage Foundation.
Israel, Stuart M., and Kenneth M. Mogill. 1975. Decriminalizing Heroin. *Michigan State Bar Journal* (May):283–290.
Jennings, Dean. 1967. *We Only Kill Each Other: The Life and Bad Times of Bugsy Siegel*. Greenwich, Conn.: Fawcett Crest.
Jennings, M. Anne. 1976. The Victim as Criminal: A Consideration of California's Prostitution Law. *California Law Review*, 64:1235–1284.
Johnson, David R. 1977. A Sinful Business: Origins of Gambling Syndicates in the United States, 1840–1887. In David Bayley (ed.), *Police and Society*. Beverly Hills, Cal.: Sage.
Johnson, Earl (former United States Department of Justice, Organized Crime Strike Force attorney, Las Vegas). 1977. Interview, June.
Joyce, Kathleen M. 1979. Public Opinion and the Politics of Gambling. *Journal of Social Issues*, 35/3 (Summer):144–165.
Kadish, Sanford. 1967. The Crisis of Overcriminalization. *Annals*, 157 (November):374.
Kallick, Maureen, Daniel Suits, Ted Dielman, and Judith Hybels. 1976. *Survey of American Gambling Attitudes and Behavior*. Commission on the Review of the National Policy toward Gambling. *Gambling in America*. Washington, D.C.: GPO.
Kallick-Kaufman, Maureen. 1979. The Micro and Macro Dimensions of Gambling in the United States. *Journal of Social Issues*, 35/24:7–26.
Kaplan, H. Roy. 1978. *Lottery Winners*. New York: Harper and Row.
———. 1979. The Convergence of Work, Sport and Gambling in America. *Annals of the American Academy of Political and Social Science*, 445 (September):24–38.
———. 1984. The Social and Economic Impact of State Lotteries. *Annals* 474 (July):91–106.
Kaplan, John. 1971. *Marijuana: The New Prohibition*. New York: Meridian.
———. 1975. A Primer on Heroin. *Stanford Law Review*, 27:801.
Kefauver, Estes. 1951. *Crime in America*. Garden City, N.Y.: Doubleday.
Kennedy, Robert F. 1967. The Baleful Influence of Gambling. In Robert D. Herman (ed.), *Gambling*. New York: Harper and Row.
King, Rufus. 1969. *Gambling and Organized Crime*. Washington, D.C.: Public Affairs Press.
Kitsuse, John I. 1979. Coming Out All Over: Deviants and Social Problems. Presidential address presented at the meetings of the Society for the Study of Social Problems, August 15.
Kitsuse, John I., and Malcolm Spector. 1973. Toward a Sociology of Social Problems. *Social Problems*, 20:407–419.
———. 1975. Social Problems and Deviance: Some Parallel Issues. *Social Problems*, 22:584–594.
Klein, Howard, and Gary Selesner. 1981. Legalization Drives Reach Crossroads. *Gaming Business Magazine* (May):6–9, 12–15.
———. 1982. Gallup Poll: A Landslide for Gaming. *Gaming Business Magazine* (November):5–7, 48–49.
———. 1983. Results of the First Gallup Organization Study of Public Attitudes toward Legalized Gambling. *Gaming Business Magazine* (July):19–21, 52–53.
Klein, Howard J., Gary Selesner, and Michael P. Davis. 1983. Gaming Industry Report, 1982: A Revolution at the Starting Gate. *Gaming Business Magazine* (February):5–8, 11–15, 43–56.
Knapp Commission. 1973. *Report of Commission to Investigate Allegations of Police Corruption and the City's Anti-Corruption Procedures*. New York: George Braziller.
Knowles, Eric S. 1976. Searching for the Motivations in Risk Taking and Gambling.

In William R. Eadington (ed.), *Gambling and Society*. Springfield, Ill.: Charles C. Thomas, Publisher.

Koten, John. 1978. Another Resort Area Is Seeking Salvation via Gambling Tables. *Wall Street Journal*, August 14.

Kristol, Irving. 1973. Editorial. *Wall Street Journal*, September 13.

Krog, Jim (campaign coordinator, No Casinos Committee). 1979. Interview, January.

Kusyszyn, Igor. 1972. *Studies in the Psychology of Gambling*. New York: Simon and Schuster.

LaBrecque, Ron. 1978. Casino Drive Opens With a Pair of Aces. *Miami Herald*, February 5.

Lasch, Christopher. 1978. *The Culture of Narcissism*. New York: W. W. Norton.

Laxalt, Robert. 1977. *Nevada, A History*. New York: W. W. Norton.

Legislative Research Bureau, Commonwealth of Massachusetts. 1983. Report Relative to Casino Gambling, Boston, April 13.

Lehne, Richard. 1986. *Casino Policy*. New Brunswick, N.J.: Rutgers University Press.

Lempert, Richard. 1974. Toward a Theory of Decriminalization. *Et Al.*, 3/3:1–8.

Let's Help Florida Committee. 1978a. A Brighter Economic Future for Florida? Yes!. Brochure.

———. 1978b. Campaign Treasurer's Report: Report of Contribution Receipts and Expenditures for a Candidate for Committee.

———. 1978c. Miami Beach Resort Hotel Association Says We Can All Be Part of Florida's Brighter Economic Future. Paid political advertisement, *Sun Reporter*, June 22.

———. 1978d. Press release, September 18.

———. 1978e. Casino Gambling Means $147,734,000 Increase in Tax Revenue to Dade County. Paid political advertisement, *Miami Herald*, November 2.

Levi, Edward H. 1973. The Collective Morality of a Maturing Society. *Washington and Lee Law Review*, 30:399.

Levin, Richard. 1976. Testimony before the Assembly State Government, Federal and Interstate Relations Committee on Assembly Bill 2366 (Casino Control Act), December 15.

Mahon, Gigi. 1978. Landing on the Boardwalk: Will Resorts International Have Trouble Passing Go? *Barron's*, November 20, 4–5, 22–23.

———. 1980. *The Company That Bought the Boardwalk*. New York: Random House.

Mangione, Thomas W., and Floyd J. Fowler, Jr. 1979. Enforcing the Gambling Laws. *Journal of Social Issues*, 35/3:115–128.

Mangione, Thomas W., Floyd J. Fowler, Jr., Frederick E. Pratter, and Cynthia L. Martin. 1976. Citizen Views of Gambling Enforcement. In *Gambling in America: Final Report of the Commission on the Review of the National Policy toward Gambling*, Appendix 1. Washington, D.C.: GPO.

Marcum, Jess, and Henry Rowen. 1974. How Many Games in Town?—The Pros and Cons of Legalized Gambling. *Public Interest*, 36 (Summer):25–52.

Markel, Ed (consultant, Allem and Associates). 1979. Interview, January.

Martinez, Robert (director, Division of Gaming Enforcement, Department of Law and Public Safety, State of New Jersey). 1978. Interview, June.

Martinez, Tomas M. 1972. Deviance and Shift: A Sociological Study of Gamblers and Gambling. Master's thesis, University of California.

———. 1983. *The Gambling Scene: Why People Gamble*. Springfield, Ill.: Charles C. Thomas.

Matza, David. 1969. *Becoming Deviant*. New York: Prentice-Hall.

McCann, Patrick. 1982. Prospects for Legalization of Casinos and Lotteries in Florida. *Public Gaming* (September):27–28, 34.

McMahon, Patrick. 1978. Newspapers Defend Gifts to Anti-Casino Campaign.

Miami Herald, September 4.

McMaster, John B. 1914. *The History of the People of the United States, from the Revolution to the Civil War.* New York: D. Appleton and Company.

McQuade, Stuart. 1981. An Economic Analysis of the Casino Gaming Industry and Its Implications for California. Master's thesis, California State University at Stanislaus.

McWilliams, Carey. 1979. Second Thoughts. *Nation* 228/15:36–39, 79.

Mello, John P. 1981. New Casino State. *Gambling Times,* 228/15 (April):422.

Messerschmidt, Al. 1978. Drug Figure Links Lansky, '74 Casino Effort. *Miami Herald,* October 24.

Messick, Hank. 1971. *Lansky.* New York: Berkeley Medallion.

Miami-Metro Department of Publicity and Tourism. 1977. Latin American Visitors to Miami by Country.

Michigan House of Representatives. 1976. Interim and Final Report of the 1975–1976 Special Casino Gambling Study Committee (State of Michigan, Lansing).

Mollenkopf, Clark R. 1972. *Strike Force: Organized Crime and the Government.* Englewood Cliffs, N.J.: Prentice-Hall.

Moody, Gordon E. 1965. *Gambling.* London: SPCK.

Moore, William Howard. 1974. *The Kefauver Committee and the Politics of Crime, 1950–1952.* Columbia: University of Missouri Press.

Morin, Richard. 1978. Casino Forces Eye Bankroll, Start Picking the Next Race. *Miami Herald,* November 9.

Musto, David F. 1973. *The American Disease: Origin of Narcotic Control.* New Haven, Conn.: Yale University Press.

National Advisory Committee on Criminal Justice Standards and Goals. 1976. *Organized Crime.* Report of the Task Force on Organized Crime. Washington, D.C.: Fact Research, Inc.

Nevada Report. 1969. Hughes Mysteries Fewer in Number. July 15:2.

Nevada State Gaming Control Board. 1975. Investigative Hearing, Bally Manufacturing Corporation, Transcript of proceedings, January 31.

———. 1976. Hearing on Argent Corporation and Frank L. Rosenthal, Transcript of proceedings, January.

Nevada State Gaming Control Board, Audit Division. 1976. Investigation of the Background of Alvin Malnik and His Financial and Social Relationships with Caesars World and/or Its Stockholders and Executives, March 5.

Nevada State Gaming Control Board, Securities Division. 1974. Draft report on Bally Manufacturing Corporation, June 5.

New Jersey Election Law Enforcement Commission. 1977. Special Report of Contributions and Expenditures re Public Question #1, 1976 N.J. General Election—Authorizing Casino Gambling in Atlantic City, N.J.

New Jersey Statutes, Chapter 47. 1976.

Newman, Otto. 1972. *Gambling: Hazard and Reward.* London: Athlone Press of the University of London.

No Casinos, Inc. 1978. Are You Ready to Gamble with Florida's Future? Pamphlet.

Oakland Tribune. 1978. No-dice Campaign in Florida, May 25.

O'Connor, John J. 1976. Consultant Seeks Shop for New Ad Campaign to Push Gambling for N.J. *Advertising Age* (August 23):3, 181.

Olsen, Edward A. 1970. My Careers as a Journalist in Oregon, Idaho, and Nevada; in Nevada Gaming Control; and at the University of Nevada. Reno, University of Nevada Oral History Project.

———. 1973. The Black Book Episode—An Exercise in Muscle. In Eleanore Bushnell (ed.), *Sagebrush and Neon.* Reno: Bureau of Governmental Research, University of Nevada.

————. (former chairman, Nevada State Gaming Control Board). 1976. Interview, March.

O'Neill, Sandy (Greater Miami Chamber of Commerce). 1979. Interview, January.

Packer, Herbert. 1968. *The Limits of the Criminal Sanction.* Stanford: Stanford University Press.

People against Casinos. 1978. Nine Reasons to Vote against Proposition 9. Brochure.

Peterson, Bill. 1978. Miami—The New "Capital" of Latin America. *San Francisco Sunday Examiner and Chronicle,* December 17.

Peterson, Virgil W. 1951. *Gambling: Should It Be Legalized?* Springfield, Ill.: Charles C. Thomas, Publisher.

Pinney, J. Kent. 1975. Gambling as a Heterogeneous Set of Goods and Services for a Heterogeneous Marketplace. Paper presented to the Second National Conference on Gambling, June.

Program Planners. 1981. The Economic Impact of N.Y. State Gaming Industry. New York, March.

Prugh, Jeff. 1978. Improbable Allies Oppose Casinos in Florida Vote. *Los Angeles Times,* September 25.

Public Gaming Research Institute. 1980. Further Legalization of Gambling in the United States in the Decade of the Eighties. Rockville, April.

Puzo, Mario. 1977. *Inside Las Vegas.* New York: Grosset and Dunlap.

Ralenkotter, Rossi (marketing director, Las Vegas Convention and Visitors Authority). 1976. Interview, July.

Ranulf, Svend. 1964. *Moral Indignation and Middle Class Psychology.* New York: Schocken Books.

Reid, Ed, and Ovid Demaris. 1964. *The Green Felt Jungle.* New York: Pocket Books.

Reiterman, Robert (company executive for Gamblers' World, Inc.). Interview in Las Vegas. August.

Reuter, Peter. 1976. Enforceability of Gambling Laws. In *Gambling in America: Final Report of the Commission on the Review of the National Policy toward Gambling,* Appendix 1. Washington, D.C.: GPO.

————. 1983. *Disorganized Crime: The Economics of the Visible Hand.* Cambridge, Mass.: MIT Press.

————. 1984. Police Regulation of Illegal Gambling: Frustrations of Symbolic Enforcement. *Annals,* 474 (July):36–47.

Reuter, Peter, and Jonathan Rubinstein. 1982. *Illegal Gambling in New York.* Washington, D.C.: National Institute of Justice.

Rock, Paul. 1973. *Deviant Behavior.* London: Hutchinson University Library.

Rose, I. Nelson. 1980. The Legalization and Control of Casino Gambling. *VIII Fordham Law Review,* (1980):245–300.

————. 1986. *Gambling and the Law.* Los Angeles: Gambling Times.

Rothman, David J. 1978. The State as Parent: Social Policy in the Progressive Era. In Willard Gaylin, et al. (eds.), *Doing Good: The Limits of Benevolence.* New York: Pantheon Books.

Rubinstein, Jonathan. 1974. Gambling Enforcement and Police Corruption. In *Gambling in America: Final Report of the Commission on the Review of the National Policy toward Gambling,* Appendix 1. Washington, D.C.: GPO.

Rubinstein, Jonathan, and Peter Reuter. 1978. Fact, Fancy, and Organized Crime. *Public Interest,* 53 (Fall):45–67.

Sawyer, Grant (attorney, former governor of Nevada). 1976. Interview, August.

Schelling, Thomas C. 1971. What Is the Business of Organized Crime? *Emory University Law School Journal of Public Law,* 20/1:643–652.

Schreck, Frank. 1976. Interview with Nevada Gaming Commissioner, August, Las Vegas.

Schur, Edwin. 1965. *Crimes without Victims.* Englewood Cliffs, N.J.: Prentice-Hall.
———. 1980. *The Politics of Deviance: Stigma Contests and the Uses of Power.* Englewood Cliffs, N.J.: Prentice-Hall.
Schur, Edwin, and Hugo Adam Bedau. 1974. *Victimless Crimes: Two Sides of a Controversy.* Englewood Cliffs, N.J.: Prentice-Hall.
Scott, Marvin B. 1968. *The Racing Game.* Chicago: Aldine.
Selesner, Gary, and Michael P. Davis. 1982. "Greyhound Meeting: Florida Governor Attacks Casinos." *Gaming Business Magazine* (April):56–57.
Shawn, Robert, and Louise Root. 1980. Expansion of Casino Gaming in the East. *Public Gaming Magazine* (March):7.
Shoham, Shlomo. 1970. *The Mark of Cain: The Stigma Theory of Crime and Social Deviation.* Jerusalem: Israel Universities Press.
Sinclair, Andrew. 1962. *Prohibition: The Era of Excess.* Boston: Little, Brown.
Skolnick, Jerome H. 1968. Coercion to Virtue: The Enforcement of Morals. *Southern California Law Review,* 41:588.
———. 1978. *House of Cards: Legalization and Control of Casino Gambling.* Boston: Little, Brown.
———. 1979. The Social Risks of Casino Gambling. *Psychology Today* (July):22–27.
———. 1983. Gambling. In *Encyclopedia of Crime and Justice.* New York: Macmillan.
———. 1984. A Zoning Merit Model for Casino Gambling. *Annals,* 474 (July):48–60.
Skolnick, Jerome H., and John Dombrink. 1981. The Limits of Gaming Control. *Connecticut Law Review,* 12:762.
Smith, Dwight C., Jr. 1975. *The Mafia Mystique.* New York: Basic Books.
Smith, James F., and Vicki Abt. 1984. Gambling as Play. *Annals,* 474 (July):122–132.
Sosin, Milt. 1978. Meyer Lansky Says There Is No Mob Crime. *Miami News,* February 10.
Sosin, Milt, and Bill Douthat. 1978. Top Lawmen Say Casinos Here Will Increase Mob Crime. *Miami News,* February 10.
Starkey, Lycurgus M. 1964. *Money, Mania and Morals: The Churches and Gambling.* New York: Abingdon Press.
State of New York, Casino Gambling Study Panel. 1979a. Interim Report, New York City, April 16.
———. 1979b. Final Report, New York City, August.
Steinhoff, Patricia G., and Milton Diamond. 1977. *Abortion Politics: The Hawaii Experience.* Honolulu: University Press of Hawaii.
Sternlieb, George, and James W. Hughes. 1983. *The Atlantic City Gamble: A Twentieth Century Fund Report.* Cambridge, Mass.: Harvard University Press.
Suits, Daniel B. 1977. Gambling Taxes: Regressivity and Revenue Potential. *National Tax Journal,* 30/1:43–61.
Tec, Nechama. 1964. *Gambling in Sweden.* New York: Bedminster.
Thomas, William V. 1979. Gambling's New Respectability. *Editorial Research Reports,* 2/12 (September 28):707–724.
Thompson, Hunter S. 1971. *Fear and Loathing in Las Vegas.* New York: Random House.
Thompson, William N. 1984. Casino Drives in Colorado, Arkansas Likely to Die. *Gaming and Wagering Business* (formerly *Gaming Business Magazine*) (October):43–46.
Thompson, William N., and John Dombrink. 1985. Riding the Crest of the Third Wave: Legal and Illegal Gambling Policy. Consultant paper prepared for the President's Commission on Organized Crime, September.
Thompson, William N., Lee Gough, and John Wallace. 1976. Conflicts of Interest

and State Attorneys General. *Washburn University Law Journal,* 15 (Winter):15–39.

Tobin, Jim. 1978. Supporter and Foe Insist Happiness Hinges on Casinos. *Miami Herald,* June 8.

Turner, Wallace. 1965. *Gambler's Money.* Boston: Houghton Mifflin.

Twain, Mark. 1962. *Roughing It.* New York: New American Library.

Twentieth Century Fund. 1974. *Easy Money.* Report of the Task Force on Legalized Gambling Sponsored by the Fund for the City of New York and the Twentieth Century Fund, with a background paper by David Beale and Clifford Goldman. New York: Twentieth Century Fund.

Tyminski, Walter. 1978. The Impact of New Jersey and Other States. *Gaming Times* (April):19.

Udell, Jonathan. 1974. An Application of Durkheimian Integration Theory to Gambling Patterns in America and Sweden. Doctoral dissertation, Ohio State University.

United States Bureau of the Census. 1977. *Governmental Finances in 1975–76.* Washington, D.C.: GPO.

———. 1988. *Statistical Abstract of the United States, 1988.* Washington, D.C.: GPO.

United States Department of Commerce, Bureau of Economic Analysis. 1976. Survey of Current Business, August.

U.S. v. *Meyer Lansky et al.* 1974. U.S. District Court, Nevada, August 21.

Venturi, Robert, and Denise Scott Brown. 1968. A Significance for A & P Parking Lots or Learning from Las Vegas. *Architectural Forum,* 128/2 (March):36–43, 89–91.

Verna, John. 1984. Interview, September, Pueblo, Colo.

Vogel, Harold. 1978. Gaming Industry Commentary: Prospects and Perspectives. Institutional Report, Securities Research Division, Merrill Lynch Pierce Fenner and Smith, Inc., August 9.

Vogliotti, Gabriel. 1975. *The Girls of Nevada.* Secaucus, N.J.: Citadel Press.

Wall Street Journal. 1966. Charges of Tax Fraud, Mobster Ties Leveled at Casinos in Nevada, August 24.

Weiner, Sanford (political consultant to the Committee to Rebuild Atlantic City). 1978a. Interview, January.

———. (political consultant to the Let's Help Florida Committee). 1978b. Interview, April.

Weinstein, David, and Lillian Deitch. 1974. *The Impact of Legalized Gambling.* New York: Praeger Publishers.

Weld, William F. (United States attorney). 1982. Correspondence to Daniel M. O' Sullivan, director, Legislative Research Bureau. September 24.

White, Clay (Sheriff). 1985. Interview, June, Hot Springs.

Wiley, Peter, and Robert Gottlieb. 1982. *Empires in the Sun.* New York: G. P. Putnam's Sons.

Will, George F. 1976. Life Is a Gamble—Especially When a State Runs the Game. *Los Angeles Times,* October 16.

Wolfe, Tom. 1965. *The Candy Colored Tangerine-flake Streamline Baby.* New York: Farrar, Straus, and Giroux.

Yankelovich, Daniel. 1980. *San Francisco Sunday Examiner and Chronicle,* December 7.

Zola, Irving Kenneth. 1963. Observations on Gambling in a Lower Class Setting. *Social Problems* 10/4 (Spring):353–361.

Index